PHILOSOPHY AND MELANCHOLY

Cultural Memory
 in
 the
 Present

Hent de Vries, Editor

PHILOSOPHY AND MELANCHOLY
Benjamin's Early Reflections on Theater and Language

Ilit Ferber

STANFORD UNIVERSITY PRESS

STANFORD, CALIFORNIA

Stanford University Press
Stanford, California

© 2013 by the Board of Trustees of the Leland Stanford Junior University.
All rights reserved.

No part of this book may be reproduced or transmitted in any form or by any means, electronic or mechanical, including photocopying and recording, or in any information storage or retrieval system without the prior written permission of Stanford University Press.

Printed in the United States of America on acid-free, archival-quality paper

Library of Congress Cataloging-in-Publication Data

Ferber, Ilit, author.
   Philosophy and melancholy : Benjamin's early reflections on theater and language / Ilit Ferber.
      pages cm. — (Cultural memory in the present)
   Includes bibliographical references and index.
   ISBN 978-0-8047-8519-8 (cloth : alk. paper)
   ISBN 978-0-8047-8520-4 (pbk. : alk. paper)
     1. Benjamin, Walter, 1892–1940. 2. Melancholy (Philosophy) 3. Philosophy, German—20th century. I. Title. II. Series: Cultural memory in the present.
B3209.B584F465   2013
193—dc23

                                               2012041616

ISBN 978-0-8047-8664-5 (electronic)

Contents

Acknowledgments ix

Abbreviations xi

Introduction 1
The Idea of Melancholy, 1—Heidegger's Discussion of Moods, 5
—Melancholy in Benjamin, 8

1 Benjamin and Freud 16
At the Juncture of Melancholy, 16—Freud's Distinction
Between Mourning and Melancholia, 19—Loss, 21—
Commitment and Loyalty to the Lost Object, 32—
The Intentionless Nature of Truth, 41—Work and Play:
A View of Melancholic Productivity, 57

2 The *Trauer-Spiel* 67
Reflections on the Baroque, 67—Expressions of Pain
in the *Trauerspiel*, 74—The Bombastic Nature of Expression
in the *Trauerspiel*, 82—Pain and Spectacle: The Figure
of the Martyr, 96—Death and Meaning: The Figure
of the Ghost, 102

3 Melancholy and Language 118
Language and Loss: Benjamin's Concept of Expression, 118—
Creation and Loss: "On Language as Such," 127—Lament:
Language and Sadness, 141—The Ghosts of Language:
"The Task of the Translator," 152

4 Melancholy and Truth 163
The "Epistemo-Critical Prologue," 163—The "Monad": Leibniz and Benjamin, 169—The Monads' Configuration as a Hierarchy, 176—A Preestablished Harmony: Benjamin's Conception of Truth as Harmony, 183—*Stimmung*: Philosophy and Mood, 189

Notes 195
Bibliography 225
Index 233

Acknowledgments

This work was not written amid melancholy. It stems from great happiness and aspiration, made possible by many friends and colleagues whom I wish to thank. First and foremost, I am deeply indebted to Eli Friedlander for the special way he helped me discover my own voice and reminded me to always stay attuned to it. I thank him, as initially my teacher and now a colleague, for the inspiration of his example, his philosophical sensitivity, and his affectionate friendship. I would also like to thank Mike Jennings for welcoming me so warmly to the German department at Princeton University, where I was fortunate enough to spend two wonderful years while working on this manuscript. Mike was always generous and supportive toward my project yet continuously provided penetrating and stimulating criticism, and I thank him for his unwavering friendship. A special acknowledgment goes to Werner Hamacher, whose work served as a model of philosophical rigor for me; his intellectual friendship and generosity were a continual source of support and motivation.

I am indebted to Hagi Kenaan, who has been with this project from its very beginning, a presence supportive, as well as critical, in ways that have had a profound bearing on my philosophical thought in general and on the final manuscript in particular. I thank Ori Rotlevy, my good friend and attentive reader, for his insightful, thought-provoking comments and observations and for always being available for me with an eternal smile. I am also grateful to my friends and colleagues who read versions of the manuscript and provided me with their comments and insightful suggestions: Bettina Bergo, Rebecca Comay, Adam Lipszyc, Omer Michaelis, Ashraf Noor, Uri Pasovsky, and Eric Santner; and to my students at Tel-Aviv University, who asked me the most difficult and productive questions and whose interest in Benjamin and melancholy helped me improve and refine my research.

Several generous sources of funding have provided me with financial support during the years of writing this book. I would like especially to thank the Fulbright Foundation, the Colton Foundation, and the Rothschild Fellowship for helping me to devote myself to writing and assisting me in the travels necessitated by my research to Princeton University, the University of Chicago, and the Zentrum für Literatur- und Kulturforschung in Berlin.

I am deeply grateful to my extended family for being there for me in every respect and for serving as a constant source of love, concern, and strength; and to my beloved parents, who have always believed in me and been proud of me, regardless of anything I did or did not write. Finally, to my real inspiration in every imaginable respect: my husband and best friend, Roy, whose love, support, wisdom, and patience, together with his admirable strength and optimism, have guided me during the long years of writing. Our partnership is the source of happiness that underlies this work.

My three children were born and grew up alongside this work and were always there to remind me of what is really important in life. I thank Ori for being such a good listener, Adam for his inherent happiness, and Yotam for his hearty kindness. Then, as now, this work is dedicated to them.

Abbreviations

BT	Heidegger's *Being and Time*
GS	Benjamin's *Gesammelte Schriften*
LAN	Benjamin's "On Language as Such and on the Language of Man"
PPL	Leibniz's *Philosophical Papers and Letters* (see Chapter 4n7 for breakdown of individual essays)
RL	Benjamin's "The Role of Language in *Trauerspiel* and Tragedy"
SE	*The Standard Edition of the Complete Psychological Works of Sigmund Freud*
SW 1	Benjamin's *Selected Writings*, vol. 1, *1913–1926*
SW 2	Benjamin's *Selected Writings*, vol. 2, *1927–1934*
SW 3	Benjamin's *Selected Writings*, vol. 3, *1935–1938*
SW 4	Benjamin's *Selected Writings*, vol. 4, *1938–1940*
TS	Benjamin's *The Origin of German Tragic Drama* (the *Trauerspiel* book)
TT	Benjamin's "The Task of the Translator"

PHILOSOPHY AND MELANCHOLY

Introduction

The Idea of Melancholy

In the prologue to his book on the German sorrow-plays, the *Trauerspiel*, Walter Benjamin argues for the inherent relation between truth and language. One interesting example of his claim appears when he describes the vocation of philosophy as a struggle for the presentation of words: "Philosophy is—and rightly so—a struggle for the presentation [*Darstellung*] of a limited number of words which always remain the same—a struggle for the presentation of ideas" (*TS*, 37).[1]

Ignoring the history of accepted philosophical terminologies for the purpose of their refinement inherently implies disregard of the burden of memory and the load of meaning they have so far carried. Yet what does Benjamin intend by the use of the word *struggle* in this quest? In what way is Benjamin aiming toward a practice different from that of Nietzsche's antiquarian, who, while knowledgeable of the art of preserving the past, fails to master the generation of new life? Benjamin's suggestion here is not permeated with the antiquarian's passion for nostalgia or with any type of conservativeness; its perception of the past is not meaningful for its own sake, nor does it originate in any kind of romantic homesickness. His suggestion is, rather, directed at our grasping the past's "afterlife" together with the present's experience of that past.

Following Benjamin's description of the vocation of philosophy, I take "philosophy's struggle" to be a linguistic undertaking involving the re-presentation of the inner life of those few terms that continue to serve as philosophy's cornerstones: truth, justice, and reason, among others. This inner life has a dynamic of its own, and it is precisely this dynamic that prevents the struggle for words from being strictly nostalgic and turns it into a philosophically meaningful practice: the transformation of mere words into ideas.

One pristine example of the philosophical struggle for presentation is *melancholy*, a word whose presence can be traced to the inauguration of thought. Melancholy's meanings extend from the personal to the collective, from body to soul, and from pathology to inclination.[2] Melancholy has always been marked by acute contradictions in its depiction, invoking an expansive array of meanings: it encompasses positive, creative facets—such as depth, creativity, and bursts of genius—as well as negative qualities—including gloominess, despondency, and isolation. The history of the term is saturated with different and at times conflicting articulations that, paradoxically, seem to consistently point to more or less the same set of features. Notions of closure, contemplation, loss, passivity, sloth, and genius have always been linked to melancholy in one version or another,[3] referring to body or soul and vice versa.[4]

In the fluctuating movement of its internal history melancholy has been described as a somatic condition (a humeral imbalance resulting in the excess of black bile) brought on by the melancholic's sins (sloth or *acedia*, in the religious context of the Middle Ages); an inclination or mood (in the Renaissance); the consequence of demonic undertakings or witchcraft (in the seventeenth century); a desirable state inducing productivity and genius; and, finally, a pathology (in the nineteenth century). This plethora of interpretations invites queries as to their tentative complementarity rather than to their overt opposition, opening up the possibility to enrich our understanding of the idea of melancholy.

This complementary structure of melancholy's meanings invokes another famous image conjured up by Benjamin when he discusses his conception of history: the image of the whirlpool, which supplants the developmental understanding of history as a riverbed (*Flußbett*). Here, as in many other instances, the image of the whirlpool cuts through his philosophical convictions. That is, thinking of the history of melancholy as resembling the movement of a whirlpool unfetters that history from any evolutionary concept of its development. Melancholy's conceptualization as a whirlpool, as a repetitive historical movement in which "the prehistory and posthistory of an event, or, better, of a status, swirl around it" (*SW*, 2:502), transforms melancholy into a field of gravity, quite different from a teleologically structured narrative. Understood in this way, melancholy's somatic sense is not replaced by an alternative theological or psychological denotation but is, rather, supplemented by them. This internal anatomy enables Benjamin to turn melancholy from a mere word into a philosophical "idea."

Melancholy, weighted down with the intricacies of its historical burden, can likewise be thought of as what Benjamin calls "a worn-out word" (*SW*, 2:503), a word that has become a ragbag for endless states and implications (what Robert Burton called a "Babylonian tower of symptoms"),[5] a word that has been so repeatedly reproduced that it has become worn-out. Such a word, writes Benjamin, "can evoke an entire period" (*SW*, 2:503). His phrase implies the stress that Benjamin places on the historical contextualization of language in its entirety, with melancholy serving as the major case in point. That is, according to Benjamin, exploration of the term's diverse, rich history and the internal motion of its historical "load" is, surprisingly, precisely what provides it with stability.

Dürer's famous engraving *Melancholia I*, which so accurately captures the manifold nature of melancholy, especially its affinity for scholars, is sensitively described by Klibansky, Panofsky, and Saxl as overcoming the diverse peculiarities within this complex state of mind to unite "in a single whole, full of emotional life, the phenomena which the set notions of temperament and disease had robbed of their vitality." They add that Dürer "conceived the melancholy of intellectual men as an indivisible destiny in which the differences of melancholy temperament, disease and mood fade into nothing, and brooding sorrow no less than creative enthusiasm are but the extremes of one and the same disposition."[6] The acuity of this depiction lies in its revelation of melancholy's transcendence beyond all internal discords and conflicting currents; it points to melancholy's fascinating inner stability, which lies beyond any comparison between health and disease, creativity and paralysis.

Despite the remarkable nature of the term's internal history, all these interpretations center on the subjective, psychological, and somatic nature of the individual overcome by melancholy. This tendency runs through the history of melancholy, be it in the medical descriptions of its source in excessive bile, its association with a punishment for sins committed, or the more recent psychoanalytic designation of melancholy as pathology. The strength of the psychoanalytic bent has transformed melancholy into a privileged private state, overshadowing the more far-reaching meanings the term encompasses. However, even in the psychoanalytic framework, we can still detect the traces of the historical association between melancholy and genius. One striking example is Freud's provocative admission that the melancholic patient has a "keener eye for the truth" (*SE*, 14:246).

Even when dealt with in philosophical contexts, where one could expect to find a more structural, systematic, and analytic point of view, melancholy has also been frequently explicated as the philosophical state of mind, the gloomy mood accompanied by deep abstract thought and dismal temperament believed to mark philosophers as men of genius. In all these cases melancholy is conceptualized as inherent in the nature of the "true" philosopher, a prerequisite for his distinctive status, as well as his most profound flaw; seldom, however, has it been attributed to philosophy. Even Hume, well known for the correspondence he imputed between his philosophical work and melancholy, treats melancholy as a subjective, psychological state rather than a structural, philosophical one. His intriguing account of the deep divide between his "philosophical melancholy and delirium" and his mundane and social engagements is always poignant: "I dine, I play a game of backgammon, I converse, and am merry with my friends; and when after three or four hours' amusement, I would return to these [philosophical] speculations, they appear so cold, and strained, and ridiculous, that I cannot find [it] in my heart to enter into them any farther."[7]

From this perspective the history of melancholy can be viewed as parallel to, albeit not directly associated with, the history of philosophy. Philosophers' affinity for melancholy has become a cliché, that of the glum, pensive thinker, struggling with the bottomless depths of his desolation. Yet the more decisive question regarding the prima facie connection of melancholy to philosophy—but not to the philosopher—is rarely tackled. Such a question requires an almost counterintuitive detachment from the allure of psychological, pathological, anthropological, and other versions of the subjective forms of melancholy and a rethinking of the term from a philosophical and structural perspective.

The struggle for the presentation of melancholy sometimes takes the form of a struggle aimed at challenging its invisibility within the structure of philosophical systems. Prospects for revealing this important presence lie, first and foremost, in releasing melancholy from the grip of its subjective, psychological, and pathological thrust and, second, in reestablishing its correspondence with mood.

Heidegger's Discussion of Moods

One of the most compelling accounts of moods in philosophy no doubt belongs to Heidegger. Although Heidegger does not dwell on melancholy (for him, anxiety and boredom are the dominant states of mind), he does teach us how to think of moods philosophically. Considered more radically, Heidegger's work demonstrates that any scrutiny of the history of philosophy and the structure of philosophical thought requires consideration of the pivotal role moods play in it. In *The Fundamental Concepts of Metaphysics* Heidegger writes that his aim is to awaken mood (*Stimmung*) and attunement so as to make their presence felt in the act of philosophizing itself while reconsidering their presence in the history of philosophy: "Thus we shall not speak at all of 'ascertaining' [*Fest Stellen*] a fundamental attunement . . . but of awakening it. Awakening means making something wakeful, letting whatever is sleeping become wakeful."[8] Heidegger's idea of "awakening" indicates that his objective is not to bring mood back into philosophical activity but to disclose its presence as what is always already there.

Mood, for Heidegger, offers an opening toward conceiving an alternative to the predominance of the subject-object divide in the history of philosophy. Heidegger proffers mood not only as a substitute for the reign of epistemology that has come to prevail in philosophy but also as what undermines the preeminence of the thinking subject, exemplified in modern philosophy in Cartesian or Kantian thought. Mood makes its first appearance in Heidegger's 1925 lecture course at the University of Marburg and remains central to his understanding of philosophy and Being up until his 1966 Zollikon Seminars.[9]

Heidegger's discussion of mood is important, first, in his provision of a philosophical methodology for the examination of moods. This model considers moods not as possessing subjective, psychological, or personal attributes but, alternatively, as evincing an ontological structure. This crucial shift emerges from the structure of *Dasein*, in which the subject-object antithesis is challenged: mood, therefore, does not belong to the subject nor to the world but stands exactly at their intersection. With this structure Heidegger undermines the epistemological constitution of modern philosophy. In fact, not only does it undermine the predominance of the thinking subject, but it is also presented as what conditions epistemology in the first place. His understanding of Being as always already a "Being-in-the-world" proffers mood as what is constitutive to the ontological structure of Being and not merely one of its contingent attributes.

Second, Heidegger points to the disclosive nature of moods; he writes that "mood is a primordial kind of Being for Dasein, in which Dasein is disclosed to itself prior to all cognition and volition, and beyond their range of disclosure" (*BT*, 175 [136]).[10] Elsewhere he states, "The possibilities of disclosure that belong to cognition reach far too short a way compared with the primordial disclosure belonging to moods, in which Dasein is brought before its Being as 'there'" (*BT*, 173 [134]). With these claims Heidegger departs from the traditional conception of affect and sensuous states that are secondary to the "higher" cognitive faculties of reason and will.[11] He perceives mood as revealing the fundamental qualities of our Being-in-the-world, preceding and thus conditioning any "cognitive" disclosure undertaken with the faculty of reason.[12]

Put differently, and in non-Heideggerian terms, mood or attunement is the way the world discloses and unfolds itself—how we find ourselves in it and how it matters to us. "The fact that this sort of thing can 'matter' to it [Being-in as such] is grounded in one's state-of-mind; and as a state-of-mind it has already disclosed the world" (*BT*, 176 [137]). Mood discloses the world as meaningful. Yet this meaningfulness does not have a structure resembling that of desire, in which a certain object passionately grabs our attention. Mood is configured as an all-encompassing mode, as totality. In that sense mood is necessary for the disclosure and appearance of the world in its entirety as hopeful, boring, or anxious. The world, in other words, is not "colored" or veiled by a certain mood; on the contrary, the world is constituted of, and made intelligible by, mood.

Mood, however, does not disclose separate objects in the world but the totality of the world itself, in an act of absorption that could not be farther away from the intentionality of cognitive comprehension or emotive passion. Heidegger adds that no thought exists without mood's providing the initial conditions of its possibility; hence, "understanding always has its mood" (*BT*, 182 [143]). What Heidegger offers here is a novel perspective from which to account for the relationship between mood and philosophy or, more precisely, the *only* possible structure in which, according to his perspective, the relationship of philosophy to the world can be conceived.[13]

As a constituent of Being-in-the-world, mood does not determine our experience of a specific object or situation within the world; rather, it provides the conditions permitting the very experience itself. In this sense mood does not reveal a specific object but the totality of the world itself. In anxiety, to take Heidegger's exemplary mood, it is precisely the fundamental lack of an object or occurrence in the world that anxiety discloses. Being bereft of any possibility of responding to this missing object generates anxiety, a mood that transmits what Being-in-the-world as such is about. Through his elaboration of the structure of anxiety, Heidegger fleshes out the precise way in which mood provides a point of entry into the world's totality, rather than grounding the intentional grasping of a specific object in that world.

In consolidating Benjamin with Heidegger, I do not mean to suggest that the former is by any means "Heideggerian," although some of the two philosophers' thoughts on history can be fruitfully aligned. Rather, I take Heidegger's claims as a conceptual structure that finds an interesting realization in Benjamin's writings. Considered from this perspective, Heidegger will provide the structural imperative of this book's conceptual framework. I find Heidegger's claims regarding mood's crucial role for philosophic work—how it discloses rather than conceals the world—to be decisive to the understanding of melancholy's place in Benjamin's thought. There, too, the melancholic mood rests at the foundation of the philosophical structure and determines its constitution.

As I have shown more extensively elsewhere, both thinkers are preoccupied with the possibility of offering an alternative to the dominance of the subjective element of knowledge and experience as expressed in modern philosophy. The aim to dismantle this underlying structure built on subjectivity, therefore, constitutes a mutual philosophical determination of their writings and lies at the crux of their shared (albeit separately explicated) interests. Mood is one of the important notions with which each of them approaches this problem, and each, having a distinct point of view and emphases, offers a different way in which mood can overturn the prevailing subjective/objective relationships between human beings and the world.[14] This reciprocity also reveals what in the last few years has been proven beyond doubt: Benjamin's oeuvre is more philosophically articulate, and bears deeper, more rigorous philosophical markings, than some would admit.

Melancholy in Benjamin

This book adopts Heidegger's framework and proposes to establish melancholy as a fundamental mood of philosophical disclosure. In setting aside the attraction to the more subjective nature of melancholy, it scrutinizes the hidden traces of the melancholic mood in the structure of metaphysics and ontology. It attempts to unpack the concept of melancholy outside its customary usage and to think of it as a philosophical, structural edifice—as one of the states of mind governing philosophy itself. Despite the far-reaching span of these concerns, the book restricts itself to one particular case: that of Walter Benjamin. In tackling the relationship between melancholy and philosophy in Benjamin's early writings, the book confronts some of the aforementioned major challenges of philosophical inquiry.

First, there is the natural, almost instinctive, attraction to Benjamin's own melancholic disposition (to date, most of the scholarly work exploring this "melancholic connection" has been preoccupied with this aspect). Scholem wrote that Benjamin was marked by a "profound sadness," while Adorno dwelt on his denial of any form of devotion to happiness, which is, in turn, "won only through regretful sorrow . . . which is as rare in the history of philosophy as the utopia of cloudless days."[15] In her thoughtful article for the *New York Review of Books* Susan Sontag wrote that Benjamin was what the French call *un triste* and cites him as having said that "solitude appears to me as the only fit state of man." Even

Benjamin himself testified that he "was born under the sign of Saturn," a remark having endless historical connotations in reference to gloominess, despondency, and genius. This interpretive stance has also, and perhaps understandably, dealt with the unhappy circumstances of Benjamin's own fate: the rejection of his habilitation work, his constant struggle for funding, the grave political situation in Europe of the 1930s, and, inevitably, the tragic circumstances of his suicide.

Second, the search for a connection between Benjamin's subject matter and his own melancholy is unavoidable. His writings on the sorrow-plays, Baudelaire and modernity, Kafka, Proust, and, above all, history, all point to their deep bearing on the role of melancholy and its reverberations in Benjamin's writings. The "angel of history," perhaps his most famous image, encompasses all that melancholy is about: loss, memory, helplessness to the point of paralysis, together with deep sadness and despondency. However, most discussions of the angel of history specifically allude to the *figure* of the angel—they, again, concentrate on the subjective nature of melancholy. It is through the angel's own eyes and wings, by way of his subjective glance on the mounting debris, that history becomes melancholic.

These tendencies are all legitimate. Benjamin was indeed gloomy, and the circumstances of his life closely correlate with his disposition. It would also be accurate to say that his choice of subjects has always echoed this relationship. Were we to delve into these associations, we might arrive at a portrait of the close affinity between the conduct of Benjamin's life and the idea of melancholy. The question remains, however: Is it possible to approach the notion of melancholy within the context of Benjamin's writings differently? Can we plausibly set aside established ideas of melancholy as related to Benjamin's pathological mental state, or as emblematic of thinking about photography and history, and examine this mood from a philosophical perspective?

My aim in this book is to show that melancholy has a far deeper affinity for Benjamin's philosophy than has yet been articulated—that beyond being a personal trait or choice of subject, melancholy represents a cornerstone of his epistemological and metaphysical claims. In this sense we deem the power of melancholy over Benjamin to go beyond his personal mood to permeate the deepest underpinnings of his thought.

Instead of following melancholy's historical narrative, I offer an analysis into the depth of melancholy in order to reveal the diversity of its internal configuration. This means, in effect, that this work is not another link in the chain of the evolution of thinking about melancholy but, rather, an attempt to expose the structure of its innermost form. The history of melancholy thus opens before us a vertical rather than horizontal direction of investigation, from which alone an exposure of its inner- and afterlife can be made possible. Because of the term's complex and diverse history, pulling in all possible directions, I find it necessary to construct a rigorous and exhaustive conceptual scheme of this concept.

This structural view of melancholy and its history concentrates on the different ways in which the melancholic state of mind determines the relationship between a subject and the world, demonstrates the forceful transgression of the boundaries between the internal and external, and challenges the stark demarcation separating life from death. I introduce this configuration through the following categories: loss, commitment, absence of intentionality, work, and the transgression between inside and outside, between life and death. These concepts can be found in the various accounts of melancholy throughout its history. They are also found, in a very distinctive form, at the foundations of Benjamin's early philosophy.

Accordingly, philosophy's aforementioned struggle for the presentation of a limited number of words entails yet another endeavor: that of understanding philosophy's own affinity for a reduced set of words. Following Benjamin, we can claim that a philosophical inquiry should strive to understand the special way in which philosophy itself is saturated with melancholy. Melancholy is thus more than a word or idea crucial to Benjamin the person; it is intimately and eminently connected to the foundations of what philosophy itself means to him.

In this book I focus on Benjamin's early writings, specifically those written between the years 1916 and 1925. This time frame appears in the dedication to Benjamin's *The Origin of the German Trauerspiel*,[16] which he notes as having been "conceived" in 1916 and written in 1925. Benjamin's study of the *Trauerspiel* bears heavily on several other unpublished fragments written during 1916, most notably, "*Trauerspiel* and Tragedy," "The Role of Language in *Trauerspiel* and Tragedy," and "On Language as Such and on the Language of Man."[17] The *Trauerspiel* study, together with these fragments, forms the corpus of my exploration. Through these works I establish a philosophical portrait of the melancholic mood and then examine melancholy's role for Benjamin's metaphysical and epistemological contentions.

Benjamin probably wrote the *Trauerspiel* book between May 1924 and April 1925.[18] The book's importance for substantiating my argument regarding the kinship between melancholy and Benjamin's early thought is grounded in two of its features. First, the book centers on the baroque *Trauerspiel*, the sorrow-plays, and is thus directly concerned with the mournful and melancholic features of these plays, while connecting them to the baroque's melancholic state of mind. Second, and more crucially, even when Benjamin does not directly discuss the melancholic nature of the plays, melancholy is evident and all the more present in his own philosophical methodology in the book. The book is, therefore, saturated with Benjamin's understanding of melancholy; furthermore, it clearly demonstrates how this conception of melancholy had found its way into his philosophical undertaking.

The *Trauerspiel* book was written as his *Habilitationsschrift* (habilitation work), a required qualification when applying for a professorial position in the German academic system. In a long and arduous process the manuscript was rejected from the Department of Literary History at the University of Frankfurt and transferred to the Department of General Aesthetics. At this point Benjamin's friends (including Gershom Scholem) advised him to withdraw his habilitation work in order to avoid the humiliation involved in its public rejection.[19] It is commonly known that this repudiation left an indelible mark on Benjamin's scholarly life, dooming him to eternal exile within his own practice of writing. More important, however, is the intimate connection between Benjamin's treatment of his book's subject matter—the German baroque *Trauerspiel*—and the handling of his own work in academia. One of Benjamin's most pronounced motivations for entering into this work was the *Trauerspiel*'s historical neglect, misinterpretation, and lack of appreciation as a genre in theater and literary criticism. In fact, it is precisely the term *genre* that preoccupies Benjamin so extensively in the book's prologue, where he proposes that the *Trauerspiel*'s underestimation rests on its being virtually unable to fit into any given genre.

Drawing on Konrad Burdach and Benedetto Croce, Benjamin criticizes art history's recurring attempts to assemble series of works of art according to their common features, what he calls "the average." Such a methodology, so fundamental to art history, can only present works of art as a collection of historical or stylistic genres instead of critically establishing each work's essential qualities. According to Benjamin the main reason for the *Trauerspiel*'s underestimation lies in the application of Aristotelian criteria of the tragic to its text. The *Trauerspiel* is consequently thought of as a caricature of tragedy, a play taking on "the appearance of an incompetent renaissance of tragedy" (*TS*, 50). Notwithstanding his fierce critique of what he considers erroneous, even detrimental, criteria, Benjamin argues that it is "inconceivable that the philosophy of art will ever divest itself of some of its most fruitful ideas, such as the tragic or the comic" (*TS*, 44).

Benjamin's alternative, fully explicated in his book, is located in a compelling yet at times impenetrable position, in which the "tragic" and "comic" function in a highly divergent way. These are not genres but what Benjamin calls "ideas": "In the sense in which it is treated in the philosophy of art, the *Trauerspiel* is an idea" (*TS*, 38). Benjamin's project, realized in the book, is to present the idea of the *Trauerspiel*; that is, he commits himself to identifying the exemplary features, "even if this exemplary character can be admitted only in respect of the merest fragment," and to viewing his own work of criticism as what is shaped immanently, that is, in the inner development of the language of the work itself, bringing out "its content at the expense of its effect" (*TS*, 44). The affinity to Benjamin's own habilitation, and the smothered call to a chimerical reader, is evident. To unfold these ideas and their fruitful intersection, we must draw out their inner anatomy.

This book's first chapter is devoted to unfastening the almost intuitive connection between melancholy and psychoanalysis—specifically, Freud's account of melancholic pathology. By interlacing Freud with Benjamin, I demonstrate the ways in which Benjamin's conception of melancholy diverges from that of Freud's, a differentiation emerging, among other things, from Benjamin's challenge to Freud's clear distinction between melancholy and mourning and between the pathological and the normative. By avoiding any such clear-cut divergence, Benjamin is able to develop a much more complex examination of the melancholic state, which he invokes in his accounts of the seventeenth-century baroque *Trauerspiel*. By understanding melancholy as socially normative and not as psychologically pathological, Benjamin opens before us the prospect of scrutinizing melancholy as a philosophical mood. This chapter thus invokes the basic structural categories through which I read melancholy within Freud's psychological framework, as well as Benjamin's account of the baroque. The first three categories I use—loss, commitment, and non-intentionality—refer to the special relationship the melancholic maintains with the lost object. These categories offer an analysis of the reaction to loss, the endless commitment to loss, and finally, the specific structure of melancholia, in which loss is undetermined by being deprived of an intentional structure. The last structural category, that of work, alludes to the way in which Benjamin opens up the possibility of viewing melancholy as a productive rather than a passive and paralyzing mood.

The psychoanalytic terminology governing the first chapter will show that one of the prominent causes for the understanding of melancholy as pathological has to do with its inability to differentiate between the internal and the external or between life and death. Chapter 2 focuses on these two categories within the framework of the *Trauerspiel*'s content and examines a similar blurring of boundaries in relation to the plays' figures and figurations. The fundamental adumbrating of the boundary between the internal and the external is introduced in relation to the notion of pain, referred to in both its mental and physical framework. In the *Trauerspiel* the figure of the martyr embodies this specific transgression. The martyr epitomizes the state of extreme physical pain, on the one hand, while obscuring the boundary between the internal feeling of pain and its external manifestations, on the other. The second category of adumbrated borders, that between life and death, is represented through the recurring figure of the ghost in the *Trauerspiel* plays, a figure likewise marked by the repeating acts of transgression between life and death that are so fundamental to its nature, together with the ethical implications associated with such acts.

According to Benjamin language is the cornerstone of philosophical truth, yet it is always permeated by melancholy and loss. The essential relationship constructed here, that between language and melancholy, rests at the heart of the third chapter. In presenting this connection, I claim that Benjamin's theory of language is thoroughly imbued with a sense of language's own inherent loss. The problems discussed in Chapter 2 reenter the scene through Benjamin's early essays on language, albeit in a different context. The relationship between subtle, inner pain and its bombastic, superfluous expression is all the more present in Benjamin's early texts on language, although in a much more theoretical form. The relationship between loss (of the ability to express) and proliferation (that which would compensate for such loss) is found here not so much in the theatrical context but in the more general framework of expression; the categorical structure of the analysis, however, remains fundamentally the same. This chapter thus deals with the role and structure of lament, commitment, and history in the context of Benjamin's philosophy of language.

Chapter 4 introduces a more explicitly philosophical model of melancholy through the reconstruction of the conceptual encounter between Benjamin and Leibniz. In the prologue to the *Trauerspiel* book Benjamin briefly refers to Leibniz's monad and presents it as a model for his own thinking about "the idea." I argue here that irrespective of the limited number of paragraphs in which Leibniz is directly addressed, his presence can be felt throughout Benjamin's book, especially in relation to melancholy. The essentially enclosed, solipsistic structure of the monad corresponds, as I show, to the structural categories I establish in the earlier chapters. The special form of the monad's encounter—or disencounter— with the world calls for concretization of the relationship between melancholy and philosophy in Benjamin's work.

Stimmung, German for "harmony," is a term that can be variously conceived. Not only is it related to musical harmony; it also alludes to attunement and mood. The turn to mood allows me to position the discussion of melancholy in a sphere that is not merely psychological or subjective but also objective. This structure is central for establishing the connection between melancholy and philosophy and, following Heidegger, the way in which mood determines philosophy's encounter with the world.[20] In this configuration mood serves as a (Heideggerian) opening and passage to the encounter with and expression of the world rather than, as sometimes conceived, as a contribution to the paralyzing closure from that world.[21] This book, therefore, claims to present Benjamin's work as exemplifying this relationship between closure and melancholy, on the one hand, and between philosophy and expression, on the other. Benjamin writes that it is in the constant return to the same set of words that historical and philosophical objectivity is established. This is the objectivity I hope to imbue with melancholy.

1

Benjamin and Freud

At the Juncture of Melancholy

Given the manifold nature of its history, the concept of melancholy has remained curiously stable despite the dynamic transformation of the meanings it has acquired.[1] Yet in spite of its remarkable steadfastness, a distinct moment of rupture can nevertheless be identified during the closing days of the nineteenth century—a moment when the struggle to "present . . . a limited number of words which always remain the same" had ceased and *melancholy* was transfigured into *melancholia*. This moment was the emergence of psychoanalysis.[2] My discussion begins, therefore, at this juncture, when Freud wrote his account of melancholia (1915), a moment almost concurrent with Benjamin's preliminary work on his habilitation, *The Origin of the German Trauerspiel*, the main text in which he examines the concept of melancholy.[3]

At this crucial moment, the discourse on melancholy is relocated within the psychoanalytic discourse of depression. As Jennifer Radden shows, the end of the nineteenth century marks a borderline in our traditional understanding of the concept; it is the point where "melancholy" parts from "melancholia" and its clinical categories of depression. The psychoanalytic turn shifts our focus from the apprehension of melancholy as a mood or normal inclination of the mind that only occasionally takes on morbid colorations to an entirely pathological understanding in which melancholia comes to describe an exclusively abnormal reaction to loss. More particularly, Freud considers melancholia a state that is accompanied by self-loathing and self-reproach, and he thereby assigns it a particularly negative character.[4] The implications of this rupture in the term's genealogy not only bring about a radical change in its apprehension; they also obscure the vast expanse of connotations once attributed to the concept, rendering melancholy into something almost synonymous—at least intuitively to the contemporary mind—with Freudian pathology.

Moreover, Freud's account effaces the powerful dialectic formerly believed to be inherent to melancholy and indicative of the intricacy and convolutedness of the term, which could contain both negative and positive, normal and pathological traits. In replacing this dialectical, one might say "flexible," nature of melancholy with a far narrower definition, Freud extends the rigid boundary he establishes between health and pathology.[5] Both the motivating force and analytic strategy of Freud's psychoanalytic project can accordingly be traced to his insistence on distinguishing the normal or healthy from within the adjacent state of pathology; in other words he is keen on using human nature's pathologies to shed light on its normality.

Freud's commitment to the idea of a perimeter separating the healthy from the pathological makes it difficult for him to fit melancholy's diverse and at times conflicted history into the psychoanalytic scheme. The history of melancholy is distinguished precisely by the fact of an inherent unwillingness of this phenomenon to surrender to any pregiven category (be it health or illness, the psychological or the somatic). Freud's transformation of melancholy into melancholia can be seen, from this perspective, as an attempt to "tame" or at least bend melancholy to make it comply to his system's trajectories. Given the strength and rigor of Freud's psychoanalytic theory, it is clear why his confrontation with melancholy marks an essential change and a deep rupture in the signification of the term.

The relationship between Benjamin and Freud has been extensively explored in recent years. It has been described in terms of a "constellation," a "long-distance love affair," a mutual dependence, and a relation of "intertextuality"; all interpretations have stressed the indirect character of their correspondence while nonetheless demanding a careful reconstruction of its genealogy.[6] Nägele argues that any serious reader of Benjamin should question the latter's relationship to Freud, while maintaining that Benjamin's resistance to Freud actually discloses a close affinity between them. He proposes that resistance is at work in this relationship, a resistance pointing precisely to where Benjamin's own thinking becomes rigorous.[7] Ley

Roff, who reads this relationship as one of "intertextuality," claims that it is possible to examine significant areas of contact between Benjamin and Freud under this rubric despite the apparent lack of direct mutual influence. Application of such an approach may indicate that the structure of Benjamin's attitude to psychoanalysis is that of deferral, that Benjamin read psychoanalytic texts long before he actually responded to them.[8] Rickels maintains that the question of influence cannot be measured, at least in this case, by criteria of sameness. He claims that "only what has been mutated, digested in part—part object, part objection—resisted, disavowed, and displaced can count as influence on the sliding scale from transference to telepathy."[9] These incisive accounts all posit, in one way or another, that direct influence should not be considered the precondition for examining the relationship between Benjamin and Freud, a claim that I substantiate here.

In *Constructions in Analysis* Freud describes his work as that of liberating a fragment of historical truth from its distorted form of appearance in the present and leading it back "to the point in the past to which it belongs" (*SE*, 23:268). The task of psychoanalytic investigation is, therefore, to reveal the intimate connection between the material of present disavowal and its original repression. The effectiveness of the psychoanalytic method, as Freud describes it here, lies in its recovery of fragments of lost experience; the crux of the pathology of delusion is, then, its "convincing power to the element of historical truth, which it inserts in the place of the rejected reality" (ibid.).[10]

Essential here is the lingo of liberation and freedom used to describe the attachment of the past to the present, as is Freud's insinuation that the present should be relieved of the past's sovereignty. The reason is that any relationship of this sort inherently entails the risk of what Freud would identify as a pathological inhibition. This structure implies that despite the great authority exercised by the past over the present, this authority cannot be sustained simultaneously with a healthy psyche. This structure can shed light on the transformation initiated by psychoanalysis—melancholy's complete departure from melancholia and depression. For the *melancholy* of the past to make room for the *melancholia* of the present, a new route has to be taken. This break from the past (the term's history and those of its historical features that invade the present) will henceforth be understood as the conditions enabling the establishment of *melancholia*'s new meanings and dominance.[11]

Freud's Distinction Between Mourning and Melancholia

In "Mourning and Melancholia" (1917) Freud defines two possible and opposing responses to loss—mourning (*Trauer*) and melancholia (*Melancholie*). These responses represent two distinct types of object-relations, both of which arise in response to bereavement. The almost keen difference between the two phenomena has long since become virtually synonymous with the understanding of loss as inviting either a normal or pathological response. It should be noted, however, that Freud's definitions are not stable throughout his writings. In his early "Draft G [Melancholia]," from 1895, he writes of a much closer relationship between mourning and melancholia: both stand on the same axis of a "longing for something lost." The element of work, so present in mourning, is not yet fundamentally present here (see "Draft G [Melancholia]," *SE* 1:200–206). In his later writings, especially in "Beyond the Pleasure Principle" and "The Ego and the Id," Freud complicates the distinction between mourning and melancholia, making it much vaguer. My analysis of Freud's view of melancholia is therefore largely based on his 1915 "Mourning and Melancholia."

In the beginning of his essay Freud discusses loss solely in terms of these two categories, while stating his intention to introduce mourning into his argument for the purpose of shedding light on melancholia by means of their contrast.[12] Freud thus draws a deep dividing line between the two responses, a line placing the two on opposing sides of the demarcation separating normality from pathology. This dissociation, he continues, is based first and foremost on the feature of self-reproach. To Freud, mourning is a normal, natural response to loss and, despite the difficulties and great pain it engenders, still part of a healthy process. Comparing mourning to melancholia he writes:

> The distinguishing mental features of melancholia are a profoundly painful dejection, cessation of interest in the outside world, loss of the capacity to love, inhibition of all activity, and a lowering of the self-regarding feeling to a degree that finds utterances in self-reproach and self-reviling, and culminates in a delusional expectation of punishment. This picture becomes a little more intelligible when we consider that, with one exception, the same traits are met with in mourning . . . It is easy to see that this inhibition and circumscription of the ego is the expression of an exclusive devotion to mourning which leaves nothing over for other purposes or other interests. It is really only because we know so well how to explain it [i.e., mourning] that this attitude does not seem to us pathological. (*SE*, 14:244)

This statement is curious because it positions our understanding of mourning as congruent with normality, suggesting that Freud deems the familiar and easily understood as nonpathological. Yet melancholia, also according to this passage, although intimately related to mourning is transformed by self-loathing into a pathological counteraction. The picture is far more complex, however, since the melancholic's self-reproach carries far deeper implications than ate initially apparent. What clearly differentiates the two responses—and what gives birth to self-reproach—depends on whether the loss has been accepted and acknowledged.

Freud's mourner and melancholic begin with a corresponding basic denial of their loss and an unwillingness to recognize it. But soon, the mourner, who is reacting in a nonpathological manner, recognizes and responds to the call of reality to let go of his lost love-object and to free his libidinal desire. The mourner's recognition of the loss makes it possible for him to perform the work of mourning, whereas the unabridged, and therefore unidentifiable, nature of the melancholic loss makes it almost impossible to detach oneself from the loss, since for the melancholic there seems to be nothing from which a detachment is at all possible. The melancholic, therefore, remains immersed in loss (with "an excessive devotion"), unable to acknowledge and accept the need to cleave to a substitute object of attachment. In self-destructive loyalty to his lost object, he internalizes that object and makes it part of his ego, thus circumscribing still further the conflict aroused by the initial loss. The lost object continues to exist, now as part of the dejected subject, who can no longer clearly demarcate his own subjectivity from the lost object he has embraced. Freud regards the structure of this response as antithetical to the ego's basic well-being, the survival of which melancholia puts at risk.[13]

Such a distinction does not exist in Benjamin's texts. In fact, in the *Trauerspiel* book he uses *mourning* and *melancholy* interchangeably.[14] This identical use of the two terms appears often in the book, mainly at the end of the first part (entitled "*Trauerspiel* and Tragedy"), which centers on an explanation and explication of the nature and structure of the *Trauerspiel* plays.[15] In this part of the book Benjamin concentrates on the different figures prominent in the plays (such as the sovereign, tyrant, martyr, and creature), compares *Trauerspiel* to tragedy (a comparison essential to the understanding of Benjamin's interpretative enterprise), and, finally, discusses the history of melancholy and its various emblematic and historical expressions. Benjamin summons melancholy to reinforce and enrich his discussion of the special type of sorrow and mourning expressed in the plays. He therefore employs melancholy to better understand mourning rather than to distinguish between two phenomena. Moreover, Benjamin frequently attributes a "mournful" state of mind to the melancholic individual and describes the mournful as those suffering from melancholia. It thus appears that his recourse to the term *melancholy* expresses rather considerably its historical accounts. Melancholy and mourning—or, one might say, the sorrow of the *Trauerspiel*—stand together here, with one underscoring the other.[16]

I suggest here that Benjamin challenges Freud's overly assertive distinction by rethinking the relationship between loss and affect, thus proposing an alternative view, which this chapter will elaborate. Rebecca Comay suggests that Freud's antithesis between mourning and melancholia echoes the bifurcated structure of melancholia itself, a division representing a systematic oscillation between denigration and overvaluation.[17] This structural rift is essential to the understanding of Freud's original, lacerated configuration of melancholia, in which the presence of divergence no longer indicates the initial, precise separation between the normal and the pathological but a further split, found in Freud's very account of the nature of loss itself. By not accepting the absolute demarcation between the two responses, Benjamin restructures Freud's ideas into an altogether different configuration, in which mourning and melancholia abide one with the other as an amalgamated mood.[18] In the following sections I analyze the four structural categories we can discern in Freud's essay as being pertinent to the understanding of Benjamin's position vis-à-vis Freud. For each category—loss, commitment, absence of intentionality, and work—I first scrutinize the role it plays in Freud's account of melancholia and then show how this account is transformed in Benjamin's book on the *Trauerspiel*.

Loss

Freud: The Internalization of Loss

Freud's "Mourning and Melancholia" is saturated with the question of loss and its implications. Loss for Freud is intimately tied to love, for it is always a loved object that is lost, be it a person, an ideal, or even a function an object fulfills *as* the subject's object of love (*SE*, 14:243, 245). Mourning and melancholia both emerge from loss, the first from an actual loss, the second (in its extreme cases) from an unidentifiable loss or, one might say, the complete absence in consciousness of any event of loss.

When opposed to the mourner's clear and locatable loss—which "reality shows" (*SE*, 14:244)—the melancholic's loss is blurred and impossible to situate; this indefiniteness provides the main reason why such a loss initiates pathological reactions. In some cases of melancholia one feels justified in maintaining that a loss of this ambiguous kind has occurred without being able to identify what has, in fact, been lost. Such events make it all the more reasonable to suppose that the patient, too, cannot consciously perceive what he has lost even if he is aware of the loss motivating his melancholia. More precisely, we may say that the patient knows *whom* he has lost but not *what* about him was lost. Correspondingly, Freud suggests that melancholia corresponds in some ways to an object-loss; however, this loss has been withdrawn from the patient's consciousness. During mourning, however, nothing about the loss is unconscious (*SE*, 14:245).

Circumstances of unidentifiable loss represent extreme cases of melancholia, in which the symptoms of a painful separation manifest themselves but without being directed toward any specific object or event. In addition the preponderance of the sense of loss lies not only in the event of separation but also in its implications. "In mourning it is the world which has become poor and empty; in melancholia it is the ego itself" (*SE*, 14:246), writes Freud, thereby locating loss in the midst of mourning and melancholia, albeit on entirely different levels. The mourner's loss renders the world surrounding him empty. The absence of the loved object seems to drain the world, as if the site of the loss is stretched to contain everything but the dejected subject.

Patients experiencing melancholia, in contrast, do not lose the world but their own selves. At the moment of separation they are not only deprived of the objects of their love; they also lose the very capacity to love (*SE*, 14:244). This occurs because the love for the lost object is so all-encompassing that it becomes impossible even to imagine loving another (in that sense a separation resembles the emptiness of the mourner's world). The consequential aftermath of this inability to mourn the loss or to let go of the object of attachment is the complete internalization of the lost object into the pain-stricken ego of the melancholic. The internalization of the loss turns the ego into a field of battle, a struggle that concludes with the ego's rending itself in two, from within. Freud describes the presence of this internalized loss within the melancholic's ego as an internal shadow that the object imposes on the ego, which transforms the object loss into an ego loss (*SE*, 14:249). Loss thus appears as a presence, an umbra, a memento of the lost object, as a ghost haunting a living psyche. This presence is ghostly insofar as it embodies the peculiar nature of the melancholic's lost object: a combination of an intangible object with a forceful ardent presence. The cleavage inflicted on the ego by loss transforms the relationship with the lost object into a pathological relationship with the self. This schizophrenic divide creates a space in which the ambivalence and hatred originally produced in response to the loss are now turned against the self, and the pathological identification with the lost object provides the grounds for the ego's assault on itself.

Despite Freud's engrossment in the pathological aspects of loss in "Mourning and Melancholia," his preoccupation with such questions can also be found in nonpathological contexts and appears to be fundamental to his psychoanalytic developmental theories. Freud defines melancholia as a pathology that acquires some of its traits from mourning and others from narcissism (*SE*, 14:250–51). The introduction of narcissism is important here not only as a source of some of the core features of melancholia but also because it is a classic example of a psychic structure that, while part of the individual's normal development, can turn pathological. In other words the place of loss—or, more accurately, the response to loss—rests on both sides of the boundary separating the normal from the pathological. The crux of narcissism lies in object-choice and identification, both of which are essential for understanding loss and separation, too. During the process of object choice that is part of healthy development, the subject selects an object and seeks to identify with it by means of internalization. In the melancholic response to loss, such an internalization becomes monstrously destructive (*SE*, 14:249). In the healthy course of events the ego is defined by its object-choices; in melancholia it is defined by its object losses. Once the ego's boundaries are redefined by the loss of an object, the melancholic's psyche comes to challenge its own sense of self.

Some of Freud's followers chose to interpret his account of loss in linguistic terms. Following Lacan's determination that the unconscious is linguistically structured, the importance of separation and symbol formation in the development of subjectivity became crucial. The turn to language is likewise important because it captures the structural element of loss while sterilizing this process of its personal-subjective components. That is, loss and separation can now be understood by means of the process of symbol formation, with language being a quintessential example of the process. This approach can be demonstrated as follows. Becoming an independent subject rests on one's ability to endure the experience of separation and loss. Acceptance of separation and understanding its crucial role in the process of individuation allows the subject to engage in relationships with others independently of their actual immediate presence. The ability to contain the loss of the other (whether temporary or permanent) thus exemplifies the transformation of this loss or separation into a symbol to which the subject has access. The moment that the other becomes an Other is the moment at which it can become a symbol, detached from its object. Loss is therefore a necessary condition for the constitution of language, as well as subjectivity. In contrast to mourning, the melancholic stance, which neither accepts nor acknowledges loss, is incapable of accomplishing such an act of symbolization. In melancholia the connection to the lost object's presence is so strong that it cannot be relinquished, even for the purpose of symbolization.[19]

In *The Ego and the Id* (1923) Freud discusses identification as a normal stage of development. He claims that the identification process linked to melancholia and the pathological failure to mourn is actually the "sole condition under which the Id can give up its objects" (*SE*, 19:29). In other words identification with the lost object, which had been linked to the destructive facet of melancholia, becomes the condition for the constitution of the self; it is only through the internalization of the lost other through the work of identification that one can become a subject in the first place. Within this process mourning provides us with a medium for preserving the lost object (rather than detaching from it, as Freud had stated in "Mourning and Melancholia") by way of turning it into the building blocks of our ego. Freud thus reconsiders the clear demarcation he noted in 1917 by collapsing the opposition between mourning and melancholia, turning melancholic identification into an integral element of mourning.[20]

Another aspect of loss as a stage of normal development is the way in which the split within the ego constitutes later object-relations. This separation, which is understood as pathological in melancholia, can be viewed as a precondition for having and for losing in the first place.[21] In other words primal loss is a necessary condition for being able to form object-relations (to have) but also for being able to tolerate the shattering of these relations (to lose). Separation as a normal condition is thus the basis of object-relations but also the point at which the fundamental loss of the first object is introduced.[22]

Benjamin: Loss as a Condition of Possibility

There are several portrayals of loss in the *Trauerspiel* book, which concentrates on *Trauer* and is, already at its outset, a discussion of loss and the response to it. More closely related to melancholy than to mourning, this loss is not, however, conspicuously accounted for in the book, or at least not clearly and precisely located. Allusions to loss are nevertheless scattered throughout, and its symptoms—the distaste for life, the detachment and distancing from the world, and the fundamental internal emptiness—are ever-present in the plays and their configurations, as well as in Benjamin's interpretations of them. As in Freud's account, loss functions both as the condition for the *Trauerspiel* and as the sphere in which its effects are felt. Although *loss* does not appear as a key term in the book, Benjamin's study carefully presents a vast structure of its symptoms. Not only is this implicit loss not attached to an individual character in the plays; it is not subjectively experienced at all. It is, instead, translated into a loss of the world itself, similar to the way in which Heidegger's Dasein encounters the world as such in mood and thus resembles the Freudian account of an unlocatable loss. In that sense the *Trauerspiel* book epitomizes the manifestations of melancholic loss since it does not address a specific event of loss but only its all-encompassing expressions.

Loss, however, is present not only in the content of the plays but, even more crucially, in the structure of the genre itself, as Benjamin conceives of it. He discusses the circumstances under which a work of art can be criticized and thereby presents loss as a condition of possibility for a work of art to become legible. With reference to the *Trauerspiel* he writes that

> from the very beginning . . . [the *Trauerspiel*] plays are set up for that erosion [*Zersetzung*] by criticism which befell them in the course of time . . . Its outer form [*Schein*] has died away because of its extreme crudity. What has survived is . . . an object of knowledge which has settled in the consciously constructed ruins [*Trümmerbauten*]. Criticism means the mortification of works. By their very essence these works confirm this more readily than others. Mortification of the works: not then—as the romantics have it—awakening of the consciousness in living works, but the settlement [*Ansiedlung*] of knowledge in dead ones. (*TS*, 181–82)

In this discussion death and loss become conditions for the legibility of works, in this case, the *Trauerspiel*. Terms like *erosion*, *death* of *Schein* (different from the English translation "outer form," it refers to an appearance, sometimes a false luster), and *ruin* allude to the extinction of the work's material aspect. In order to approach it critically, something in the work itself must be lost. This loss can be understood in abundant ways, with Benjamin's use of the term *mortification* a crucial feature common to them all.[23] Defining the activity of criticism as mortification places it first and foremost among the material aspects of a work. In states of erosion, ruin, or degradation something in the material becomes exposed; such a state thus opens the work up to the critical gaze. For Benjamin mortification reveals the material's truth; in dead material, material that has lost its vitality, mortification reveals that it has become *mere* material.

Benjamin illuminates the question of the loss of life by contrasting it to romantic criticism. The romantics, he claims, view criticism as what awakens the work or, rather, extends or prolongs its life. The constant asymptotic movement toward the absolute is understood by Benjamin as what initiates rather than what terminates life. Moreover, it prolongs the life of the completed work that, for the romantics, is impossible without its criticism. The relationship between the artwork and its critique is like that between different parts of the same living organism. In this sense, a work of art has an organic as well as an artificial aspect, both of which are at play in the criticism that must, by definition, become part of the work itself. For the romantics, according to this interpretation, the truth in criticism captures an everlasting flicker of life, thereby wishing to transcend itself and thus achieve the work's "afterlife."

The model that Benjamin proposes is diametrically opposed to the romantic model. Benjamin understands truth not as life but as death, not as iridescent warmth and movement toward the absolute—what he calls "dazzling brilliance"—but as the dead body's stillness.[24] "Mortification" is understood here as what befalls the work once the critical undertaking begins. In both cases the body of the work lies dead and mortified; only as such can the work offer itself to criticism. Accordingly, the "body" of the work should be understood literally: the work is a living body; when it dies, when life flows out of it, it remains as a corpse awaiting its autopsy. Benjamin then writes that "this transformation of material content into truth content, makes [for] the decrease in effectiveness, whereby the attraction of earlier charms diminishes decade by decade, into the basis for a rebirth, in which all ephemeral beauty is completely stripped off, and the work stands as a ruin" (*TS*, 182). Here, mortification paves the way for the work's reincarnation—although not in its original form or "dazzling brilliance"—but through the meticulous construction of a connection between its material and its truth contents, the pair of concepts Benjamin explored in detail in *Goethe's Elective Affinities*, written during the same period when he was working on the *Trauerspiel* book.[25]

Benjamin also directly alludes to the special stance taken by the *Trauerspiel*, which he describes as being a corpse from the very moment of its birth. What is so evocative about the *Trauerspiel* for Benjamin is its continuous state of death or, put differently, the way it makes constant reference to its own state of being the object of loss. From their very beginning these plays are in a state of decomposition and putrescence, as if the *Trauerspiel*, as a genre, is stillborn. This indicates that Benjamin's choice of the *Trauerspiel* as an object of study is not accidental; it exemplifies his interest in extreme cases of living-death, the quintessence of an object that is always already lost.

One specific type of loss, however, can be found when viewing the *Trauerspiel*'s structure and appears in the privation of the narrative and the linear, teleological nature of the baroque's conception of history. Judith Butler suggests that Benjamin explores the idea of the loss of narrative and its expression in the plays when he writes, "The developing formal language of the *Trauerspiel* can very well be seen as the emergence of the contemplative necessities which are implicit in the contemporary theological situation. One of these, and it is consequent upon the total disappearance of eschatology, is the attempt to find, in a reversion to a bare state of creation, consolation for the renunciation of a state of grace" (*TS*, 80–81). Here Benjamin delineates the structure of the plays as a response to the loss of an eschatological narrative. The *Trauerspiel*, in this reading, is structured on the disavowal of the collapse of the religious, redemptive narrative; it therefore constitutes an alternative in what seems to be a lost or shattered linearity. That is, the *Trauerspiel* responds to this temporal disintegration in its "transposition of the originally temporal data into a figurative spatial simultaneity": a spatial, simultaneous structure leaps down to restructure the plays and their narrative (*TS*, 81). This is relevant to Butler's suggestion that when established narratives begin to falter, it becomes apparent that the function of the disappearing narrative was to *contain* precisely what has been loss.[26]

The collapse of sequentiality and narrative leads to a spatial simultaneity that is, again, a response to their loss or, more accurately, to the loss of hope in linearity's capacity to contain salvation and, in essence, to promise any type of closure. Instead of a structure of temporal succession, everything in the broken continuum is placed side by side, spread out to cover the ground like seeds (*TS*, 92). The site where nature and history merge is the place where redemptive linearity is absent: this is where history is grasped as spatial and not temporal. This scattering of the continuum's elements, their dispersal in space—their spatialization—is the response to the loss of eschatology, a response that embraces loss as an internal and eternal trace of what can no longer be recuperated.[27]

The understanding of loss as a condition of possibility appears in the *Trauerspiel* book in yet another image: that of emptiness. Freud's claim that the mourner sees the world as empty after experiencing the loss of a love-object is echoed in Benjamin's discussion of the baroque religious backdrop, as well as in the *Trauerspiel* itself. Benjamin notes that the great baroque playwrights were Lutherans and thus possessed an antinomic attitude to the everyday—which reverberates in the plays they wrote: "The rigorous morality of . . . [Lutheran] teaching in respect of civic conduct stood in sharp contrast to its renunciation of 'good works'" (*TS*, 138). The Lutheran denial of "good works" rests on the application of their principles of faith and grace, specifically, that human actions no longer serve the believers as a source of salvation and are thus of no value. Hence, Lutherans depend on external grace, achieved only through faith, never deeds. This creed empties everyday life and its actions of their redemptive implications. According to Lukács's interpretation of Benjamin on this issue, the context of transcendence itself is lost because it no longer ascribes any religious substance to human deeds.[28] Transcendence itself is thus rendered empty. It follows that the Lutheran world is a world in which work no longer harbors any spiritual significance; only the *work of mourning* can fill this emptiness—dubiously, of course. Since nothing "substantial" is accomplished by mourning and no substantial change can be brought about by such work—being a continuous reproduction of its original conditions—this work becomes mere play.[29]

These two forms of loss—namely, the loss of the narrative and the devaluation of human actions—can be seen as operating on a similar plane, fathomed through the act of consolation. Having lost the embrace of eschatology and the redemptive value of human deeds, baroque men are left devoid of any form of consolation. The only wretched and yielding remainder is the sheer materiality of the world, manifesting an absolute absence of consolation. If Catholicism harbors the promise of redemption from its very beginning, found in confession and remorse, then Lutheranism stands clearly and starkly as a system of belief that leaves the world completely desolate. This understanding further illustrates the distance between Benjamin's understanding of melancholia and Freud's. For Benjamin, contrary to Freud, there is no redemptive, consoling outlook for suffering. Moreover, it is not the subject who bears the melancholic mood but the world itself, or, phrased as a Heideggerian gesture, mood is not a property of a subject but constitutes one's very being-in-the-world.

Conceiving the everyday as futile and trifling, as mere empty play, has produced melancholy in great men, writes Benjamin, while mentioning Luther himself as having suffered from melancholy and a "heaviness of soul." According to Benjamin, Hamlet, as the consummate Lutheran, also strongly protests this existential emptiness, expressed in his own melancholy. Benjamin cites Hamlet:

> What is a man,
> If his chief good and market of his time

> Be but to sleep and feed? A beast, no more.
> Sure, he that hath made us with such large discourse,
> Looking before and after, gave us not
> That capability and godlike reason
> To fust in us unused. (4.4)

Benjamin proposes that

> these words of Hamlet contain both the philosophy of Wittenberg and a protest against it. In that excessive reaction which ultimately denied good works as such, and not just their meritorious and penitential character, there was an element of German paganism and the grim belief in the subjection of man to fate. Human actions were deprived of all value. Something new arose: an empty world . . . For those who looked deeper saw the scene of their existence as a rubbish heap of partial, inauthentic actions. (*TS*, 138–39)

Godlike reason, Benjamin claims, seems to rot in the mind of the Lutheran since it lies there unused, depending on grace to descend from above. This gives rise to an empty world and to the melancholic reaction against it. Here Benjamin attaches to the melancholic state of mind the empty world that Freud ascribes to the mourner. The consequent meaninglessness of the emptied world causes baroque men and playwrights, like the paradigmatic Hamlet, to sink into themselves when in a state of melancholy.[30] In this combination of mourning and melancholy the internalization of the mourner's empty world into his psyche causes his ego to empty out still further.

Hamlet's melancholy is deeply rooted in emptiness because of the unlocatable nature of his loss. The foundations of his melancholy lie not in the loss of his father and his mourning for him but in altogether different grounds that are nowhere to be plainly found. These grounds can be discussed only in terms of emptiness, insofar as there is a basic absence of a site or an event. Ophelia and Laertes's loss of their father, Polonius, and Laertes's loss of Ophelia are clearly not the central losses presented in the play, and this is precisely because these bereavements are definable and thus not delineated as melancholic. Hamlet's case is altogether different: what seems to be a normal mournful response to his father's death at the play's beginning is soon revealed to be a melancholic reaction to what exceeds any concrete death or loss and refers rather to a much more fundamental state of disenchantment with what Hamlet sees as an empty, sterile, and barren world, which he describes as what "appears no other thing to me than a foul and pestilent congregation of vapours" (2.2).

This world made of only "vapours" is for Hamlet no more than a ruin of meaning, an empty cast of what was once meaningful to him and is now inhabited by nothing significant or redemptive. Grace comes only from the outside, if it arrives at all; hence, the melancholic's "distaste for life." Only in the play's last scene are meaning and redemption brought forth. This scene, however, is also the one in which most of the play's protagonists die. Meaning can thus be embodied only by the end of life, never within it.

Benjamin turns to the figure of the mask to speak of another aspect of the emptiness encountered in religious environments.[31] When describing mourning, Benjamin writes: "Mourning is the state of mind [*Gesinnung*] in which feeling revives the empty world [*entleerte Welt*] in the form of a[n empty] mask, and derives an enigmatic satisfaction in contemplating it" (*TS*, 139). Two facets of emptiness are implied here, that of the empty world and that of the mask into which this world is transferred or molded.[32] The world is "emptied" [*entleerte*] (not "empty," as the English translation has it), which means it stands as what once held meaning that is now lost. The meaningless world, lacking any potential for salvation, is echoed in the only way it can be approached—an empty mask. The mask is an image of loss, a death mask, a material sign of something that, once present, can be touched only through its skeletal remains. The mask duplicates the loss without replacing it with an alternative. The mask is also, of course, a theatrical mask—the empty mask of the *Trauerspiel* itself. It marks the contours of the loss to which it alludes; it embodies its traces. This description is closely related to the way Benjamin understands the allegorist's work throughout the book. For him the allegorist is someone who practices looking at the world as if it were a mask of the meaning—albeit in disintegrated and shattered form—that is waiting to be recovered.

Mourning is presented here not as a psychological quality but as a reference to the theater, perceived as the ultimate arena of its appearance. The mask is a theatrical element; as such, it completely changes the point of focus from the inner absorption of Freud's mourning to an ostentatious and theatrical response to mourning. The most profound emptiness is therefore manifested in utter externality, theatricality, spectacle. Loss becomes spectacle when the only things left are its traces, for spectacle conceals loss only insofar as it externalizes it. The mourner, in Benjamin's sense, attempts to revive the lost and emptied world in a manner different from that of Freud's mourner, who eventually accepts the loss and is willing to part from it. In Benjamin's alternative the mourner, when attempting to awaken life in what is lost, does so by contemplating a mask, the only material residue of the lost empty world, a basically theatrical gesture. Mourning of this sort can only revive life by summoning what is no longer there. This image of the mask in the context of loss can also be seen as closely related to Freud's conception of melancholia, however, in that it *contains* the emptiness rather than defying it.

Commitment and Loyalty to the Lost Object

Freud: The Persistence of Melancholic Commitment

The divergence between the mourner and the melancholic can also be understood in terms of loyalty and commitment to reality, to life and to the lost object. Freud describes the process of mourning as follows: reality establishes the event of loss and the absence of the object and then "proceeds to demand [*Aufforderung*] that all libido shall be withdrawn from its attachments [*Verknüpfungen*] to the object" (*SE*, 14:244). Because reality demands acknowledgment of the separation before the mourner is prepared to detach from the loss, this request initially appears implausible if not unbearable. The mourner, therefore, refuses to comply with these demands in favor of complete absorption in the lost object, accomplished by means of a hallucinatory, wishful psychosis, to use Freud's terms. With the passage of agonizing time, however, the mourner comes to understand and respect reality's importunities, even though its "orders cannot be obeyed at once. They are carried out bit by bit . . . and in the meantime the existence of the lost object is psychically prolonged" (*SE*, 14:245).

Freud describes this acceptance of reality as arduous but manageable. In his account the mourner makes a choice to be loyal to reality and to life rather than to what has been lost. Freud deems this choice a healthy one since opting for the presence rather than the absence of life allows the dejected subject to live and initiate new libidinal relations. "Just as mourning impels the ego to give up the object by declaring the object to be dead and offering the ego the inducement of continuing to live, so does each single struggle of ambivalence loosen the fixation of the libido to the object by disparaging it, denigrating it and even as it were killing it" (*SE*, 14:257). This formulation enlightens what Freud views to be the mourner's work, which is directed toward "killing" the lost object or, rather, killing it once more; to continue living, he must kill what is, for him, already dead. The mourner's eventual acknowledgment of reality thus serves as preconditions for the acceptance of loss. However tormented he remains from recent memories of his loss, he thereby demonstrates his utter commitment to life.

The case of melancholic commitment is entirely different. According to Freud the melancholic's libido is attached to an object for either a real or a projected reason; these are the object-relations that become shattered. Instead of answering reality's call to let go of the lost object and reattach his libido to a new object of love, the melancholic displaces the libido, now freed from the lost object, to his ego, which verily draws the object into itself and internalizes it.[33] The problem, then, lies not in freeing the libido, which occurs with the "disappearance" of the object, but in redirecting it. In redirecting his libido, the melancholic establishes an identification with the lost object. As Jean Laplanche writes: "Far from being my kernel, it is the other implanted in me, the metabolized product of the other in me: forever an 'internal foreign body.'"[34] This identification, in which the self becomes the surrogate for the lost other, as well as the carrier of the loss itself, splits the ego from within, denatures it, and subsequently allows it to be judged by some critical agency "as though it were an object, the forsaken object" (*SE*, 14:249). Loss of the object consequently evolves into loss of the ego. The conflict between the ego and the loved person results in a cleavage, that between the ego's inherent critical activity and its transformation into the lost object's receptacle. This melancholic bind can, according to Freud, be ruptured only by way of mourning.[35]

Nicolas Abraham and Maria Torok's analysis of "incorporation" is useful here. Incorporation is an essentially narcissistic response to a loss that restages itself within the borders of the psyche, thereby allowing the possession of the lost object by its metabolization:

So in order not to have to "swallow" a loss, we fantasize swallowing (or having swallowed) that which has been lost, as if it were some kind of thing ... When, in the form of imaginary or real nourishment, we ingest the love-object we miss, this means that *we refuse to mourn* and that we shun the consequences of mourning even though our psyche is fully bereaved. Incorporation is the refusal to reclaim as our own the part of ourselves that we placed in what we lost; incorporation is the refusal to acknowledge the full import of the loss, a loss that, if recognized as such, would effectively transform us.[36]

In this account that assumes a basic separation between subject and object, mourning and the work of separation must be essentially tied to the existence of an independent object in relation to which one can mourn or perform the work of mourning. The incorporated object does not lend itself to such a separation. Nourished by his own loss, the melancholic erects an internal tomb within his psyche, a tomb in which he can securely shelter his beloved lost object but from which it can never be rescued. The correlative of the lost object is now buried alive inside the melancholic's consciousness, thoroughly included within its internal topography. This is what Abraham and Torok call "cryptophoria."[37]

This destructive internalization embodies the endless commitment and responsibility felt by the melancholic toward the lost object. When in this state, the melancholic does more than refuse to respond to reality and to the continuation of life; he "permits" his very refusal to be penetrated by a persistent commitment to the lost object. Freud thus writes that by being suppressed and internalized, the object triumphs over the ego in melancholia. This curious victory points to the fact that the melancholic gesture of abolishing the object actually demonstrates his extreme fidelity to that object.[38] From a different perspective one could say that by refusing to acknowledge his loss, the melancholic affirms that loss all the more strongly.

The subject's life and libidinal health are thereby exchanged for a strong inclination to protect and keep the lost object. By devouring the object into the self, the subject tries to keep it from being fully lost. The loved object thus takes sanctuary in the ego to avoid extinction. No mourning is possible here because the work of parting is blocked. As Freud continues, an undercurrent of ambivalence appears, reflecting the melancholic's simultaneous wish to hold on to the object yet let it go. Freud advocates killing off the traces of the other in the self as a method for reestablishing mental health and returning to life,[39] advice indicating that a subject can repudiate attachments to lost others and still exist. Benjamin would deem such an admission problematic, since for him the essence of work undertaken in mourning is the deepest articulation of the undying traces of loss and not its overcoming.

The conflict between the retention of the object and its loss hinders the possibility of a healthy detachment from it, since precedence is given to commitment to the lost object (*SE*, 14:257). Comay notes that acknowledging a loss always entails a surreptitious disavowal of that same loss, which touches on the persistent ambivalence inherent to the melancholic stance. "Buried alive within the vault of a self fractured by the persistence of what cannot be metabolized, the lost object would seem to assert its continued claim on those still alive. Melancholia would articulate this claim. Its tenacity would be the measure of the incommensurability of a loss whose persistence points both to the infinite need for and to the final impossibility of all restitution."[40]

Melancholic stubbornness is fundamentally ethical in nature because it manifests a pristine responsibility to the lost object. For the melancholic, loss functions not as a starting point for recovery, directing one to a horizon of a new reality, with new love-objects and attachments; instead, it clings to lost objects out of a stubborn responsibility. Freud describes cases in which melancholia arose from a feeling of guilt or responsibility for the loss itself. Melancholia thus does not embody responsibility for a specific case of loss or guilt for what could have been done. The commitment here is of a more profound nature; it is a commitment to loss itself and an obligation to contain that loss, even at the price of self-destruction. In consequence, mourning renounces the lost object through a process of symbolic mediation that, from the melancholic's perspective, is considered an immoral act.[41]

Reexamining the two responses to loss—mourning and melancholia—in terms of responsibility opens up another realm from which these positions can be viewed: the ethical realm. When examined from an ethical perspective, the work of mourning can be seen as an egotistic rather than a healthy response. The selfish aspect in mourning introduces a narcissistic tendency, here linked to Freud's "reality principle," which the mourner obeys when detaching himself from the lost object. Yet this same narcissism can also be interpreted as precisely the element shattered during loss, the moment at which the love-object ceases to be a living reference for the ego.

Opposite mourning stands melancholia, with its overwhelming commitment to loss, which overtakes the psyche at the price of a relinquished self and ego. The economy of the self becomes marginal in relation to the ego's commitment to that which was lost. Within this constricted space nothing can replace the absent object; no symbolic mediation, not even memory, ever suffices. The melancholic thus gives up the external world as a resource for the self's construction, to remain satisfied (albeit destructively) with his split, tormented interiority. Sacrifice of the self is, however, only one part of the process—all-consuming melancholia also deprives the lost object of its own otherness by incorporating it into the melancholic's self. Unremitting commitment thereby shows its alternative face, one of destruction and betrayal.

Benjamin: Melancholic Betrayal and Commitment

Benjamin paints the ethical responsibility of the melancholic toward loss in somewhat different tones in his description of the courtier (also called the intriguer or plotter) in the *Trauerspiel*. He presents this figure in the plays as deeply fissured: it has the double-face of an intriguer or conspirator and a faithful servant. The movement of the courtier between these two poles, and the inability to hold them together in unity, is what situates him in an extreme melancholic position, his ego defined by its utter internal breach. Embodying the evil genius of the ruler, together with the innocent suffering of the saint (*TS*, 98), the courtier experiences an all-encompassing loss that leads him to loyalty and devotion coupled with habitual betrayal: "treachery is his element," writes Benjamin (*TS*, 156). As Samuel Weber has convincingly shown, the courtier's amoral calculatedness exploits the shaky mechanism of human actions in a way that turns his actions into a game or exhibition of virtuosity rather than a strategy. The fluctuating dynamics of the plotter's schemes render him closer to the court's fool than to the sovereign prince. The intriguer thus heeds the rules of the game without the expectation of resolution.[42]

The tormented split ego is not, however, the only connection to Freudian melancholia; what distinguishes this peculiar configuration of the courtier is the mélange of devotion and betrayal that is directed not toward humans but toward the world of things. The courtier's anticipated melancholic devotion to people, especially to the prince he serves, is replaced by his deep loyalty to the material world. In this sense his position has an interesting relationship with Freud's lost "object"—in both cases there is a strong commitment to the world of the dead object instead of toward the human world of the living. Although Freud's "object" is usually instituted by a living person, he or she soon becomes a mere object for the psyche. Benjamin describes the logic of the figure of the courtier as follows:

> Crown, royal purple, scepter, are indeed ultimately properties, in the sense of the drama of fate, and they are endowed with a fate to which the courtier, as the augur of this fate, is the first to submit. His unfaithfulness to man is matched by a loyalty to these things to the point of being absorbed in contemplative devotion to them. Only in this hopeless loyalty to the creaturely, and to the law of its life, does the concept behind this behavior attain its adequate fulfillment. In other words, all essential decisions in relation to men can offend against loyalty; they are subject to higher laws. Loyalty is completely appropriate only to the relationship of man to the world of things. The latter knows no higher law, and loyalty knows no object to which it might belong more exclusively than the world of things. And indeed this world is constantly calling upon it; and every loyal vow or memory surrounds itself with the fragments of the world of things as its very own not-too-demanding objects. (*TS*, 156–57)

In this apparently paradoxical shift—loyalty is directed only to that which has no power over him—the courtier betrays his prince for the sake of material objects, and he does so at a moment of crisis, when "the parasites abandon the ruler, without any pause for reflection, and go over to the other side," namely, to the world of material things. The almost inconceivable unscrupulousness revealed in the figure of the courtier indicates a dismal, melancholic submission to the antithesis of human values (*TS*, 156). By designating the object of loyalty as material object rather than the living prince, the courtier both questions the ethical import of his actions, as well as the implications of his choice.

The example of the courtier functions here to illuminate the distinctive relationship maintained between loyalty and ethics. According to Benjamin's understanding of loyalty, this relationship cannot function as the highest law in the realm of human relationships given that it cannot embrace any ethical relation. Only in the world of inanimate things can human devotion function as the highest possible law; only then does responsibility lose its ethical nature and turn into blind fidelity.

Simultaneously, the choice to invest himself in nonliving things immerses the courtier in the earthly and material, thereby completely detaching himself from the human world. These two polarities, the material and the human, thus present the courtier's faithlessness to the prince as the obverse of his faithfulness to things. And, although the latter occupies a dead realm, one of despair and immobility, it is the only realm that contains meaning (even if that meaning is subjective and arbitrary) for the melancholic.

The courtier's nature, writes Sontag, reflects an "inconsolable, despondent surrender to an impenetrable conjunction of baleful constellations [that] seem to have taken on a massive, almost thing-like case." She goes on to explain that those who understand the motivation for this state of mind, for the courtier's sense of historical catastrophe and innate despondency, will never despise him. His faithlessness to the human realm, specified in the figure of the prince in the *Trauerspiel*, is always matched by a deep, contemplative faith in the world of things.[43]

Yet devotion to things can persist only insofar as they can contain meaning—something made possible through the courtier's subversive plunge into the world's material fragments that are presented for his contemplation.[44] The feasibility of persistent loyalty lies, for Benjamin, in the distinct character of what he conceives as the melancholic tenacity of intention (*TS*, 139–40), a state in which the melancholic contemplator is fixed on material objects—the only things whose existence is secure, in opposition to meaning which is fleeting and elusive.

The flip side of this deep tenacity is, as mentioned, a state where loyalty becomes entangled with betrayal of the material world:

> Clumsily, indeed unjustifiably, loyalty expresses, in its own way, a truth for the sake of which it does, of course, betray the world. Melancholy betrays the world for the sake of knowledge. But in its tenacious self-absorption [*Versunkenheit*] it embraces dead objects in its contemplation, in order to redeem [*retten*] them... The persistence which is expressed in the intention of mourning, is born of its loyalty [*Treue*] to the world of things... Faithfulness is the rhythm of emanatively descending levels of intention which reflect the appropriately transformed ascending ones of neo-Platonic theosophy. (*TS*, 157)

A dialectic is, then, inherent in loyalty. Deep devotion is always saturated with a secret desire to "take over" the object of devotion, to appropriate its meaning. In that sense devotion is very similar to the destructive loyalty of Freud's melancholic who, filled with commitment and fervor, internalizes the object, thereby destroying it within the confines of his consciousness. Devotion thus conceals a forceful power relationship. Understood in this way, the melancholic's motivation regarding the lost object, although originally one of responsibility and commitment, becomes destructive once the commitment is utilized by means of internalization. The melancholic internalization is prompted, therefore, by a commitment to resist the loss and ends with a complete destruction of the object of love.

The dialectics of loyalty to and betrayal of things is, then, closely connected to the loss of meaning and consolation, as noted in the aforementioned context of religion. After the loss of faith, expressed in the absence of linear-redemptive historical narratives, one is left solely with objects on which to focus one's devotion. These objects become eternal reminders of the emptiness remaining after all meaning and hope for salvation have disappeared, like the mask discussed earlier. Nevertheless, the power of this emptiness lies in its capacity to be recharged, to acquire new signification. The mask of the material world, of things, is, therefore, the image of a loss having an inherent (albeit partial) potential for a dubious recovery.

Benjamin illuminates the role of material objects within the melancholic stance through his opposition to the Neoplatonic view, which he describes as maintaining the view that we should take leave of the material, objective world as a prelude to reaching truth (*TS*, 157). The Neoplatonists appear to be in kinship with Freud here in that both advocate detachment from the object in order to progress to higher levels, to an uninhibited life of the mind or the psyche. In both cases the actualization of separation from the lost object provides the conditions necessary for both versions of progression.

In the description of the melancholic courtier and his peculiar attachment to things, Benjamin thus offers a contrary description of philosophy's task and the distinct object-relations it appropriates. Philosophy, he implies, should not detach itself from the material but, rather, immerse itself within it through deep contemplation. In Benjamin's model truth is achieved through immersion in the object, not through detachment from it. To him, truth resides *in*—and not *beyond*—the material. Benjamin connects this idea to what he calls "the descending levels of intention" (*TS*, 157), one of the methods with which philosophy approaches its object. The correspondence between the devotional absorption in the material and the idea of intention is crucial for Benjamin and bears immensely on his criticism of Husserl's concept of intentionality, on which I elaborate in the next section.

It is important to bear in mind that the world of things is insentient. Declaring faith in the inanimate means, in effect, declaring faith in oneself; herein lies the subjective core of the courtier's truth. Despite the first impression of the courtier's loyalty to the object, it is, in fact, completely detached from the object's identity and bears only on himself. This structure is very close to the mourner's relation to his lost object, which only fulfills a function but bears no autonomous value. The dialectics of loyalty and betrayal pertains, furthermore, to the indispensable nature of the object, on the one hand, and the proliferation of objects, on the other. It seems impossible to grasp the notion of loyalty in this context without envisioning a singular or exclusive object toward which that loyalty is directed. Once the object of devotion is revealed to be replaceable (owing to the multiple objects available for use), the essence of loyalty necessarily evaporates or becomes neutralized. The unyielding sense of necessity and indispensability that accompany any tenacious attachment to an object, if endlessly replicated, eventually dissipates completely.

For Benjamin betrayal, the obverse of loyalty to objects, can also be considered a form of sadism, behavior involving the humiliation and devaluation of objects: "The voluptuousness with which significance rules, like a stern sultan in the harem of objects, is without equal . . . The function of baroque iconography is not so much to unveil material objects as to strip them naked" (*TS*, 184–85). Power enters here, too, in the description of the almost violent relation to the object. A sultan who rules over his objects, who humiliates and controls them to the point of pouring arbitrary meanings into them, represents a direct allusion to the allegorical practice of power. Benjamin's introduction of sadism into the discussion relocates the melancholic's relationship to objects from the psychic to the bodily realm. Meaning is metaphorized as the object's humiliation and devaluation while occurring in a lexicon containing associations with sexual exploitation. These metaphors sound surprisingly similar to Freud's description of the melancholic's ambivalence, expressed in his aggressive treatment of the lost object: "Hate comes into operation on this substitutive object, abusing it, debasing it, making it suffer and deriving sadistic satisfaction from its suffering" (*SE*, 14:251).

The dead object thus stands bare and breathless, like a corpse exposed to the unimpeded cruelty of the sadist. Yet Benjamin writes elsewhere that "in the midst of the conscious degradation [*wissentlichen Entwürdigung*] of the object, the melancholic intention keeps faith with its own quality as a thing in an incomparable way" (*TS*, 225). In other words while sadistic degradation remains faithful to the object's "thingness," this faithfulness is directed mainly at the sadist himself and at the external meaning he imposes on the object. The latter's own inherent meaning inspires no such dedication. Moreover, the structure of the attitude toward objects and that relationship's oscillation, which swings between fidelity to the object and indifference to its specificity, is extremely important here. This fidelity to the unspecified is, in many senses, a form of fidelity to oneself, a structure having great affinity to the melancholic's ownership and destruction of his object.[45]

So the melancholic's involvement in the thingly world is always given within the context of the imposition of meaning. It is from this perspective that the courtier can be taken to be a political version of the allegorist. The melancholic's reading of the material world is similar to the courtier's reading of the theatrical world in which he finds a home (the only home he has, Benjamin adds). The material world of things yields to the melancholic gaze in a way nothing else would, remarks Sontag. The more lifeless things are, the more ingeniously can the mind contemplate them and assign meaning to them.[46]

The Intentionless Nature of Truth

Freud: A Missing Loss

In his analysis of loss Freud raises an important distinction located in the types of loss experienced by the mourner and the melancholic rather than in the structure of their responses. The mourner, he writes, knows exactly what has been lost; the process of acceptance and the work of separation from the lost object is therefore locatable and identifiable. This fact renders mourning, beyond its painful and sometimes unbearable elements, to be one of the foundations of separation and cure. The loss felt in melancholia is divergent and has a more abstract nature:

> The object has not perhaps actually died, but has been lost as an object of love . . . In yet other cases one feels justified in maintaining the belief that a loss of this kind has occurred, but one cannot see clearly what it is that has been lost, and it is all the more reasonable to suppose that the patient cannot consciously perceive what he has lost either. This, indeed, might be so even if the patient is aware of the loss which has given rise to his melancholia, but only in the sense that he knows *whom* he has lost but not *what* he has lost in him. This would suggest that melancholia is in some way related to an object-loss which is withdrawn from consciousness, in contradiction to mourning, in which there is nothing about the loss that is unconscious. (*SE*, 14:245)

In the case of mourning, the loss is evident, given to recognition; we are left only to perform the work of mourning. In melancholia, however, the loss has a diametric structure: it is completely absent. This special unidentifiability of loss makes it difficult, almost impossible, for the melancholic to detach himself from the lost object since there is, in fact, nothing from which to be detached.

Freud invokes one of the more intriguing traits of melancholia: loss's unlocatable or unidentifiable nature is a quality that, instead of averting the pain and dejection involving the loss, rather deepens them. The mourner has an available object to which he can attach his sorrow; moreover, his "work" of mourning can be accomplished only insofar as he can locate and identify the object from which he is required to detach himself. The tangible nature of the lost object is, in essence, what provides the work of mourning its focus and enables it to be executed, thereby establishing the probability of its finalization.

Melancholia, defined as reflecting a more abstract and in some cases an unidentifiable loss, inherently yields a more complicated picture. When Freud describes the melancholic loss as unlocatable and, furthermore, when he characterizes the melancholic's incapacity to identify his state as a state of loss, he is describing a situation in which it is not only the object but loss itself that has disappeared. The difficulty in overcoming such a state stems from its complete absence of locus, from the inability to concretely direct the "work" of separation. The melancholic is incapable of directing feelings of dejection at anything specific, and it is this internal structure that renders melancholia virtually incurable.

Giorgio Agamben offers an interesting albeit questionable exegesis of Freud's idea of missing loss. In *Stanzas* he pushes the elusive nature of melancholic loss still further by claiming that the melancholic has actually lost what was never his to possess; a relationship with the imaginary ensues. Agamben explains that in melancholia the libido acts as if a loss has occurred although nothing concrete has, in fact, been lost. Accordingly, the libido stages a simulation in which that which cannot be lost (since it was never possessed) appears to be lost; insofar as it is successful, the staging enables appropriation of the object in the only way left possible—as lost. This staging responds to one of the deepest ambiguities of the melancholic undertaking: the will to transform an object of contemplation into an object of love. According to Agamben, in so doing, melancholia opens up a space for the existence of the unreal and allows the ego to enter into a relationship with this unreal object, thus appropriating a possession that no loss can ever threaten.[47]

The melancholic therefore mourns what he has not yet lost but also what was never his to lose. The simulation staged by the libido contemplates the very possibility of loss as proof of some possible relation to the object. The unfulfilled desire for the unattainable object—its possibility—impels simulation of its loss, thereby appropriating the object *as if* it were lost—the only option available for owning it or even of being in a relationship with it. In other words melancholia functions here not as a regressive response to loss but, rather, as the force of imagination, driven to transform an unattainable object into something lost.

This simulation creates a space in which nothing can threaten the melancholic's relationship to the object: because it does not exist, nothing else can possess it, and because it does not really belong to the melancholic, it cannot be lost. This protected space, as created by the melancholic, appropriates the lost object only to the extent that it affirms its own loss. The importance of Agamben's interpretation lies in its ability to conceptualize the possibility of containing and maintaining a relationship with an absent lost object (and not with loss as such, Freud emphasizes). Freud reconciles the battle of love and hate surrounding the object—one attempting to achieve separation and the other attempting to achieve attachment—through his description of the configuration and inner laws of the unconscious, what constitutes one of the most fruitful ideas in the realm of psychoanalysis. Agamben understands this duality as rooted in the structure of fetishism, specifically, in the conflict between desire and perception of reality. The fetishist chooses neither side of the duality, in a way similar to the melancholic, in that "the object is neither appropriated nor lost, but both possessed and lost at the same time. And as the fetish is at once the sign of something and its absence, and owes to this contradiction its own phantomatic status, so the object of the melancholic project is at once real and unreal, incorporated and lost, affirmed and denied."[48] However, Agamben's emphasis on the imaginary and its importance in understanding the melancholic stance distances his discussion from the unintentional nature of the loss and diminishes this characteristic in favor of a merely psychological interpretation.

The nonintentional structure of the melancholic loss demonstrates two facets. First, the loss itself cannot be located and is therefore unidentifiable. It is an absent loss, or the loss of a loss, and the melancholic therefore displays an essential inability to be directed at, or to lean toward, the lost object. Second, according to Freud the lost object is not, in fact, absent but is, instead, unavailable to the work of mourning since it is internalized by the melancholic into his ego. In other words the inability to accept and account for the loss causes the melancholic to assimilate it and make it part of his own psyche. These two facets, the loss or absence of the object, together with its assimilation into the ego, are clearly interconnected in the Freudian structure and cannot, in effect, exist independently of one another. Structurally speaking, however, they should be kept distinct since each yields an entirely different form of object relations.

Benjamin: "Truth Is the Death of Intention"

Inasmuch as I am outlining here a critical—rather than pathological (or therapeutic)—concept of melancholy, I want to clarify the philosophical context of the phenomenon's structure, which should be conceptually separated from that of the *Trauerspiel*. If we are to fathom Benjamin's idea of the "death of intention," and its significance in the unfolding of the role of melancholy in the *Trauerspiel* book, an understanding of this structural context is particularly important. Although I devote the fourth chapter to an elaboration and development of the philosophical facets of Benjamin's structure of melancholy, I introduce this structure here to lay a foundation for my later exposition.

Benjamin's reference to the notion of intention implies a strong philosophical framework that can be viewed as a direct response to Duns Scotus's scholastic discussion of intention, as well as to the philosophical dominance that Husserl attributed to intentionality.[49] Responding to Brentano's use of the term, Husserl employs intentionality to delineate what he takes to be the phenomenological structure of experience. Intentionality, as distinguished from mere intention, refers to the structure of the human awareness of the world, which is characterized as directional, as an internal movement always pointing toward an object of consciousness. With the intentional structure in which consciousness is always underway beyond itself, Husserl emphasizes the inherent role of the external world to our acts of consciousness, which are no longer independent, thereby rendering subsidiary the egocentric, sometimes solipsistic, accounts of human consciousness.

Intentionality provides the conceptual structure that Husserl applies to explain the awareness of the world as inherently object-oriented. Nonetheless, the intentional structure is not a property of objects and is therefore not an ontological quality; rather, it distinguishes the structure of consciousness itself. For Husserl the notion of intentionality functioned to strengthen his account of another key phenomenological term: *epoché* (or methodical "bracketing"). Focusing on the intentional structure of consciousness enabled Husserl to "bracket" the ontological state of reality, thereby inhibiting reality's acceptance in favor of a focus on the process of consciousness itself, viewed as independent from its objects of intention.

Benjamin's negative allusion to the term *intentionality* conveys his criticism of two main presuppositions inherent in Husserl's intentional structure: first, the separation between the subject and the object of consciousness and, second, the separation between the object and the intentional act of the subject taking awareness of it. The crux of both of these presuppositions is the fundamental chasm in the structure of Husserl's phenomenological method—that between the subject and the object. Benjamin's criticism of this stance concurs with the special form of subjectivity he promotes, that which is not determined by subjective confrontation with an object but, rather, by immersion in it.

This idea is already pronounced in Benjamin's appraisal of the Kantian system, specifically, of what he calls its meager and inadequate conception of experience. I find a common nucleus in Benjamin's criticism of Kant's concept of experience and his rebuke of Husserl's structure of intentionality, namely, the emphasis that both thinkers (despite their polar positions) put on the subject. In his rigid outline of the borders of experience Kant invokes a radical subjectivism that rests solely on the epistemological sovereignty of the subject. In Benjamin's reading of Kant, the latter can only proffer a concept of a hollow experience, "virtually reduced to a nadir"; that is, Kant denies the metaphysical dimension from his epistemology (*SW*, 1:100, 102). Kantian categories, Benjamin argues, constitute experience but also diminish it to its rudiments. The subject confronts the object, but from a very distinct and limited perspective, one unreceptive to the conception of experience Benjamin wants to promote, his so-called higher experience (*SW*, 1:102). According to Benjamin the heart of the problem lies in Kant's conception of knowledge, which amounts to the "relation between some sort of subjects and objects or subject and object—a conception that he was unable, ultimately, to overcome, despite all his attempts to do so" (*SW*, 1:103).

Benjamin's proposed "program of the coming philosophy" aims precisely at overcoming this internal disparity: "The task of future epistemology is to find for knowledge the sphere of total neutrality in regard to the concepts of both subject and object; in other words, it is to discover the autonomous, innate sphere of knowledge in which the concept in no way continues to designate the relation between two metaphysical entities" (*SW*, 1:104). With "neutrality" Benjamin offers here a hint for the alternative he seeks in his critique of the Kantian conception of experience. Looking for a neutral sphere, Benjamin is after a structure in which the relationship between subject and object is overturned and is no longer configured by the principle of intentionality, as what figures the problematic relation between an independent subject intentionally confronting external objects.

This proposal takes a somewhat different form in Benjamin's criticism of Husserl. Focusing on intentionality, Benjamin discusses a philosophical scheme that does not avoid the division between the thinking subject and the objects of his consciousness but challenges the intentional structure such a division begets. This is most clearly demonstrated in the prologue to the *Trauerspiel* book, in which Benjamin aphoristically writes that "truth is the death of intention." Apart from the negative allusion to Husserl, this obscure statement intimates Benjamin's distinction between truth and knowledge—a distinction that can be apprehended as reflecting the conundrum of intentionality.

By defining truth as the death of intention, Benjamin wishes to establish an alternative model that will challenge the Husserlian structure of intentionality by allowing the subject to immerse himself in the object rather than inhibiting him from doing so. If the epistemological model in both Kant and Husserl (albeit in very different ways) is based on the subject's primacy, then Benjamin suggests an alternate model in which the object and the subject's immersion in it are dominant. When abiding by an intentional structure, knowledge is possessed by the knowing subject, and "its every object is determined by the fact that it must be taken possession of—even if in a transcendental sense—in the consciousness. The quality of possession remains" (*TS*, 29). Understanding its task as that of acquiring knowledge and establishing a coherent system on those foundations, philosophy treats its objects as if they "came flying in from outside," into the spider's web woven for the purpose of taking hold of it. The unity of truth, Benjamin continues, does not lie in its coherence but in its inner law of essences, which can never be possessed or approached intentionally. The form of existence peculiar to truth, Benjamin explains, is

> devoid of all intention, and certainly does not itself appear as intention. Truth does not enter into relationships, particularly not intentional ones. The object of knowledge, determined as it is by the intention inherent in the concept, is not the truth. Truth is an intentionless state of being, made up of ideas. The proper approach to it is not therefore one of intention and knowledge, but rather a total immersion and absorption in it. Truth is the death of intention . . . The structure of truth, then, demands a mode of being which in its lack of intentionality resembles the simple existence of things, but which is superior in its permanence. (*TS*, 35–36)

This passage presents the fundamental distinction between knowledge (pertaining to concepts) and truth (pertaining to ideas) and reinforces this distinction by utilizing the notion of intentionality. Knowledge is always about a relationship between the subject and the object of his consciousness; it is thus fundamentally a relationship structured on intentionality. The intentional, perspectival, and purposeful nature of conceptual analysis bears too strongly on the subject's deliberative undertaking of the acts of knowing and judging. In consequence, for Benjamin, knowledge always exists on a judgmental plane and is thus always predisposed toward a fundamental binarism. Truth, on the contrary, as totality, can never encompass the binaries of true and false, right and wrong. Renouncing the judgmental structure of knowledge thus entails repudiation of any form of intentional relations. Ideas replace concepts, and totality substitutes judgment. Instead of the intentional structure of subjective awareness that Benjamin assigns to knowledge, truth operates within an entirely different order, where immersion and absorption provide the conditions of possibility for truth's presentation [*Darstellung*]. By forgoing an intentional configuration of the relations of consciousness, Benjamin conjures up an alternative structure that is not based on object-relations in a way comparable to that associated with knowledge.

Benjamin's argument regarding the separation of the structure of truth from that of knowledge advocates that a nonintentional object-relation is to be maintained with the object of truth. This distinctive disposition bears deep affinities to the melancholic, fathomless attachment to an object that is not in fact there; or, put differently, it suggests a bond to an object with which it is impossible to maintain an intentional relationship. This structure echoes the two distinct facets of the nonintentional structure of the melancholic loss as Freud presents it—namely, first, a missing or absent lost object, and second, a loss that has been internalized into the melancholic ego. The unique philosophical object-relations characterized by Benjamin in the *Trauerspiel* book stand precisely at the perimeter of these two facets, as I will show in detail. What we can discern here is an endeavor to think of melancholy as a truth-relation. This statement requires a careful consideration and explication.

The nonintentional nature of melancholic loss positions that stance within a relationship to the world rather than to an individual context (as in mourning), a feature crucial to Benjamin's application of nonintentionality to truth. Being "the death of intention," truth—Benjamin proclaims—precludes the possibility of intention and desire. Weber describes this as the disconnection between a pointing-at (the movement of mind or language) and that at which one points, or an opposition to the unity between form and content that Benjamin associates with poetic work.[50] Moreover, the structure of an intentionless relationship undermines the classic subject-object relationship, placing the discussion of truth and ideas outside the subjective and psychological realm and the emotional relationship to objects.

Benjamin's discussion of the functioning of feeling and emotions in the baroque plays and their special connection with objects provides a constructive basis from which to explore the nature of this intentionless object relation. I quote from the prologue at length:

> For feelings, however vague they may seem when perceived by the self, respond like a motorial reaction to a concretely structured world. If the laws which govern the *Trauerspiel* are to be found, partly explicit, partly implicit, at the heart of mourning, the representation of these laws does not concern itself with the emotional condition of the poet or his public, but with a feeling which is released from any empirical subject and is intimately bound to the fullness of an object [*empirischen Subjekt gelöstes und innig an die Fülle eines Gegenstands gebundenes Fühlen*]. This is a motorial attitude which has its appointed place in the hierarchy of intentions and is only called a feeling because it does not occupy the highest place. It is determined by an astounding tenacity [*Beharrlichkeit*] of intention, which among the feelings is matched perhaps only by love—and that not playfully. For whereas in the realm of the emotions it is not unusual for the relation between an intention and its object to alternate between attraction and repulsion, mourning is capable of a special intensification [*Steigerung*], a progressive deepening of its intention. Pensiveness [*Tiefsinn*] is characteristic above all of the mournful [*Trauerigen*]. On the road to the object—no: within the object itself [*auf der Straße zum Gegenstande—nein: auf der Bahn im Gegenstande selbst*]— this intention progresses as slowly and solemnly as the processions of the rulers advance. (*TS*, 139–40)

The constitution of the *Trauerspiel* inheres in mourning: not in mourning's subjective, personal meaning (that of the poet or the poet's public) but in its very structure. That is, the connection between subject and object is determined by what Benjamin describes as a "motorial" or automatic reaction—or attitude—to a "concretely structured world." This world itself functions as the object of intention rather than merely some specific "thing" located within it, a "target" toward which the act of consciousness is directed. Such an attitude, because it operates in a world of objects, sterilizes the desire felt in the attachment to a single object. This motorial attitude begets the immediacy inherent in intention but without being causally related to any specific object. The intending subject is, therefore, situated *within* a world, not simply positioned opposite the object of desire. The sterilization of desire consequently revokes the inherent distinction—and ensuing relationships—between subject and object.

What Benjamin offers here is therefore a structure of intention that is immediate without being directed toward a specific object. This structure uncovers the complexity of the relationship between Benjamin and Husserl in that also for the latter, as much as for the former, the immediacy of intentionality does not necessarily take the form of a thematic awareness of an object. Benjamin's configuration of intentionality is another manifestation of directedness toward the world as a whole rather than the attachment of desire to a specified object. It thereby demonstrates what Benjamin takes to be a melancholic structure of relations: relations that are intensive as much as they are nonintentionally structured. Benjamin continues to describe the feeling (*Gefühl*) that guides the subject to the object as intimately bound to the object's fullness (*Fülle*). In elaborating his approach, he points to an interesting relation that obtains between feeling and fullness (or even plenitude or completeness). Benjamin explains this fullness toward the end of the book: baroque lyricism is characterized by its special quality, which has "'no forward movement, but . . . swell[s] up from within'" (*TS*, 183). This quality of swelling up reflects the completeness of the object toward which the subject directs his feeling.

In his rigorous interpretation of this special form of melancholic subjectivity, Pensky argues that the relation between subject and object encompasses what Benjamin views as the essential polarity inherent in *Trauer*: its enclosure of subjective as well as objective moments. The objective, real state of affairs thus resonates with feelings that remain locked within the subject. Pensky characterizes this object of feeling as the empty world, a world devoid of meaning, which stands as an empirical object, continually taking upon itself a multiplicity of historically contingent forms. This abundance of meaning constitutes the "real insight into the ontological status of the world of human experience."[51]

Benjamin discusses this specific type of feeling and the subsequent attachment in terms of love. His use of the term *love*, I argue, is close to Freud's formulation of object-choice and the attachment to objects, as linked to libidinal desire. These two relationships share a persistent clinging to the object of choice, almost irrespective of the actual nature of the connection, something that conveys a "blind," narcissistic quality. Such a form of tenacious love raises the question of the object's significance: does it matter in and of itself, or is it an empty mask concealing something completely different from itself (be it meaningful or meaningless)? This is another occasion to reconsider Benjamin's treatment of intentionality in comparison to Husserl. On the one hand, Benjamin offers the tenacious absorption of what is clearly avoided by Husserl: the ontological quality of the object (from which Husserl wishes to disconnect the phenomenological account of consciousness); on the other hand, like Husserl, Benjamin seems to discuss a form of detachment from the object, manifested in his emptying out and divesting the object of its inherent qualities in favor of the melancholic's empty, instinct-like attachment to it. It is important to note, however, that Benjamin describes a state in which consciousness can in fact free itself from an object-oriented structure in which intentionality always has a final mark, a structure contrary to Husserl's.

What Benjamin offers here bears an allegorical hallmark: clinging to the object is intrinsically homologous with indifference and disregard since the object's hollowness can be filled with almost anything, a structure resembling that of allegory. The tenacity of the mourner's hold has a reflexive quality, an instinctual clutching incapable of freeing itself from the object of intention.[52] Adorno, alluding to Benjamin's passage as cited above, notes that within this type of relationship the object takes on a state of transparency, which endows intention with its tenacious strength while nevertheless leaving it empty.[53]

In Benjamin's differentiation between intention and emotion the latter constantly oscillates between attraction and repulsion (in a structure having a close affinity to Freud's description of ambivalence in the melancholic).[54] Mourning is the intentional, grappling feeling that does not know ambivalence and remains fixed on its object. The totality of its fixation joins together a manifold of contradictory feelings present in the *Trauerspiel* but not necessarily in an individual figure; it is scattered among various effigies.

Benjamin clearly declares that the state he is describing involves immersion bereft of interest, desire, or intention. This path, winding *within* the object, can be mistaken for empathy, a stance enabling entry into a separate entity. In cases of empathy the subject projects his or her own person onto the interiority of the other, the object; the difference and distance between the two personalities then diffuse to the point of almost disappearing as the self becomes the other. The structure of empathy is therefore inconsistent with that of internalization. During internalization, the subject deprives the object of its individual identity and otherness by eradicating the distance between self and object. This cancellation also detaches the object from its original context by relocating it within the subject. Internalization, like empathy, entails a merger with the object but in opposing directions: in the first, the object is incorporated into the subject; in the second, the subject relocates himself within the object.

Benjamin attacks empathy as a bourgeois category on various occasions. In *The Life of Students* he writes that "empathy [*Einfühlung*] appears as a refusal to acknowledge otherness and the stakes of conflict."[55] He claims that empathy rests on *understanding*, alluding to an insight into the other and its place. He considers empathy to be a pathology, one where the historian insinuates himself into the place of the creator through the principle of substitution, "as if the creator were, just because he created it, also the best interpreter of his work—this has been called 'empathy', in an attempt to provide a disguise under which idle curiosity masquerades as method" (*TS*, 53–54).[56] However, the immersion (*Versenkung*) with which Benjamin is occupied in the *Trauerspiel* book functions as an antonym to empathy since it does not involve judgment regarding the object and its state but absorption *into* that object.

This tenacity characteristic of immersion seems to be the opposite of the nonintentionality required by truth, mentioned in the preface to his book. In one of the finer discussions of Benjamin's *Trauerspiel* book Nägele contrasts the passage on the tenacity of intention to the section about the unintentional nature of truth in the book's preface. He writes that Benjamin describes melancholy, like knowledge, in terms of intention; truth, in contrast, is described as an intention-free entity, and "melancholy, as an intention that ranks rather low in the hierarchy of intentions, appears in a highly dubious light."[57] Here Nägele presents what seems to be an equitable explanation of the clear opposition between intention and the intention-free state (referring to the difference between truth and the object of knowledge according to Benjamin's presentation of these terms in the preface [*TS*, 32]).

My claim suggests, however, that the place of melancholy in the structure of truth can also be viewed differently. Melancholy neither equals truth nor is the mood uncovering truth. Instead, it shares some extremely important elements with truth. Hence, the road's relocation from an approach *to* the object to an approach *into* the object indicates Benjamin's interest in the idea of intention and its complexity, as well as his clear cognizance of the difference between the two processes. The kind of intention negated with respect to truth in his preface is therefore the straightforward intention that relates a subject and the object of its interest. From the perspective of the object's interiority, however, this intention appears quite differently; it resembles the aforementioned immersion in the material. Truth's persistence and alienation from the world does not, therefore, contradict its nature.

But in what sense is this aforementioned intensification and deepening of intention equivalent to the lack of intention? The lines following the passage cited (*TS*, 140) explain the specific kind of lack of intention that Benjamin attributes to the melancholic. On the one hand, Freud's melancholic is full of intention, a fullness expressed in the loyalty, commitment, and responsibility felt for the object. On the other hand, the melancholic cannot focus this intention on anything since the specific loss is absent or unidentifiable; the consequent reaction is internalization. Freud's melancholic thus incorporates this absence—in the form of an absent lost object—and directs his or her destructive loyalty toward the self. This structure is echoed in Benjamin's citation. When describing the state of utmost tenacity and persistence, Benjamin locates it not "on the road to the object" but, rather, on the path found *within* the object itself.

The English translation misses an important point in this quote, namely, the difference that Benjamin constructs between the road *to* the object and the road *within* the object, not only in terms of location and direction but also in terms of what characterizes the road itself. Going toward the object we find a *Straße*, but in the object—a *Bahn*. Namely, *Straße*, the street that leads only to another street, in which you can turn back and forth, walk around, is contrasted to a *Bahn*, a far more intentional orbit. A *Bahn* possesses more of the character of intention or goals; it is a path to be followed on its own, in one direction and impossible to leave. This investment in the *Bahn* inside the object means that the subject taking that *Bahn* has completely permeated the object; it is no longer on its way to it but has "arrived." The difference between the two paths is that the *Straße* to the object is so saturated with intention regarding the object that it almost suffuses it. Alternatively, the *Bahn* within the object is not intentional, in the simple sense of a subject being directed at an object of interest, but duplicates the structure of intention within the object's interior; hence, the subject no longer has any interest or desire for it. The tenacity with which the *Bahn* is taken is demonstrated by the said inability to turn around or change course.

This formulation of intention, which is internal to the object, sterilizes desire and nullifies love's quality of attachment (or object-choice in Freud). No subject stands opposite the object; the intention-containing object stands alone. This intention "progresses as slowly and solemnly as the processions of the rulers advance" (*TS*, 140), writes Benjamin in his opaque conclusion to his sentence. This "procession" raises an important question regarding the relationship between the inner and the outer, internalization and externalization. The slowness of the rulers' torpidity stems from their presentation of themselves, devoid of any open claims; simply being present, advancing, seems sufficient. In such a context Benjamin's road to the object and discussion of intention rest precisely on the difference between internalization and externalization, a difference crucial to the structure of melancholy in general. The rulers' ostentation as they march in the procession therefore alludes to the question of role of intention within the object.

In a short piece on Calderon and Hebbel, Benjamin expounds on the relationship between sadness and intention. He writes that "sadness . . . would be boundless, were it not for the presence of that intentionality . . . which manifests itself with an assertiveness that fends off mourning. A mourning-game [*Trauer-Spiel*], in short" (*SW*, 2:373). Benjamin positions sadness and mourning here as antithetical to intention, thereby assigning to intention the power to defend itself against the two states. Intentionality thus has the power to encapsulate sorrow, to set it within the threshold of the intended object and prevent it from expanding endlessly and curelessly. This explication parallels the characterization of the melancholic, whose loss is undefined and therefore boundless. Since there is no tangible object at which the melancholic can direct his sorrow, his gaze can only turn inward, in a Nietzschean gesture, toward a place where it can find only the boundlessness of his own loss. Benjamin's distinction between truth and knowledge, as it appeared in the preface to the *Trauerspiel* book, can now be reread in light of the distinction between intention and absence of intention toward the object.

The characterization of truth as totality, reinforced by truth's nonintentional nature, is demonstrated by the tenacity of its attachment, which knows neither conflict nor inner struggle. Hence, totality proves to be the only appropriate approach for achieving complete immersion in the idea. The quality of scission distinctive to knowledge parallels the aforementioned emotions—attraction and repulsion—which are unstable and hesitant in their connection to the object at hand. Their stammering is as far from truth as can be, and the alternation in emotions between attraction and repulsion resembles the flatness of knowledge, which is rendered superficial by its intrinsic lack of totality. Truth, being complete and inclusive, echoes the melancholic's tenacious grappling, which is attached to the object's fullness (namely, its opposition to the polarity and flatness of emotions and knowledge, respectively). The difference between truth and knowledge is also related to the distinction between possession and immersion—or to the external and the internal attitude, respectively. The presentation (*Darstellung*)[58] of truth also alludes to its quality of fullness. Furthermore, because the idea expresses truth, it abstains from judging knowledge, which thus remains doomed to suffering the duality between the true and the false.

The relevance of Heidegger's discussion of moods' relation to philosophy reemerges here. Heidegger takes the Husserlian phenomenological project, with its basis in intentionality, and transforms it into an underlying structure already couching intention. In this sense Heidegger's reflections on moods are not object-oriented, as Husserl suggests, but, instead, are objectless and intentionless (*BT*, 186–87 [230–31]). Heidegger most lucidly explains the difference between intention and lack of intention when he compares fear and anxiety: Fear is a state of mind constituted by the threat posed by a specific and identifiable object; in other words we are afraid of those objects or situations that threaten us. Fear thus evinces an intentional structure; it is always directed toward something specific. Heidegger approaches anxiety from the opposite direction, however. Anxiety is primordial precisely because nothing specific performs as its cause. In states of anxiety it is nothingness itself that is disclosed, a structure epitomizing Heidegger's "being-in-the-world." Unlike our response to fear, we are overtaken by anxiety in a way that is, first, unintentional and, second, undirected. No subject-object relation emerges; one's being-in-the-world is itself conditioned by mood.[59] This structure is pertinent to the discussion of Benjamin's definition of the nonintention since truth or authenticity is at stake in both cases. In Benjamin truth is intentionless in opposition to knowledge; in Heidegger primordial mood is opposed to simple emotion.

Benjamin's discussion of the need to seek neutrality with regard to subject and object in his critique of the Kantian account of experience can thus be read against the background of his preoccupation with the structure of mood, primarily melancholy. Mood, according to Heidegger, is precisely what can be understood to be neutral with regard to subject and object. To recall, mood is neither internal nor external and thereby belongs neither to the subject nor to the objects he confronts. Mood is rather what conditions the possibility of being-in-the-world in the first place. In undermining the structure of intentionality as the primary foundation of experience (as Husserl has it), mood offers a neutral position inasmuch as it demonstrates the impossibility of the very structure that establishes intentionality: the separation between subjects and the objects they perceive. This interpretation of neutrality is of prime importance for the underscoring of mood's role in Benjamin's early writings: it establishes Benjamin's critique of Kant and Husserl as the background of his attraction to mood and, at the same time, utilizes mood as having profound ontological implications that reach far beyond any psychological or subjective attribute.[60]

Work and Play: A View of Melancholic Productivity

Freud: The Work of Mourning

Freud defines the work of mourning (*Trauerarbeit*) as a service performed by the mourner during the long, intense process of detachment from the lost object after accepting the reality of loss. This work, writes Freud, is "carried out bit by bit, at great expense of time and cathectic energy, and in the meantime, the existence of the lost object is psychically prolonged" (*SE*, 14:245). The arduous work of mourning maintains the lost object within the psyche, throughout the gradual acceptance of its loss and the subject's toil directed toward untangling the attachment. This work is composed of a slow, painful movement through each of the strands attaching the object to the dejected subject, what Freud depicts as a thousand links (*SE*, 14:256). Detachment is thus finally achieved through the meticulous work of untangling the initial attachment, which is composed largely of memories. Freud is unconcerned about whether the memories "worked upon" are worked through simultaneously or in a certain sequence, yet he notes that "in analyses it often becomes evident that first one and then another memory is activated, and that the laments which always sound the same and are wearisome in their monotony nevertheless take their rise each time in some different unconscious source" (*SE*, 14:256).

Laplanche addresses similar aspects of Freud's work of memory and mourning in his discussion of the myth of Penelope. Weaving and unweaving her father-in-law's burial shroud so as to defer choosing a suitor in the absence of her husband, Ulysses, Penelope unravels the shroud so that her "work" will never end. Laplanche asks whether Penelope's work is that of weaving (only to unweave and thus stall for time until her husband returns) or of unweaving (only in order to weave anew). But Penelope does not cut the threads as in Freud's account of mourning; instead, she unravels them. There is a *Lösung* of threads—a problem, a loss—in her work of mourning.[61] The distinction between cutting threads and unraveling them is essential in this evocation of work. In Freud's account the mourner eventually succumbs to reality and detaches himself from the lost object. However difficult and even unbearable this work may be, it ends with the complete loosening of all attachments and releases the subject from entanglement with his loss: "The ego becomes free and uninhibited again" (*SE*, 14:245). The reality principle and the passion for life take over and direct the mourner to focus on the important work of detachment, all for the sake of continuing a healthy, libidinal life.

The aim of detachment has, therefore, little to do with the object but everything to do with the subject, who has to be freed. The object exists merely as a drawback, a predicament to be pushed aside in order for reality to prevail. As Freud writes: "Mourning impels the ego to give up the object by declaring the object to be dead and offering the ego the inducement of continuing to live" (*SE*, 14:257). In that sense the subject's interest lies not in untangling the threads but in cutting them. The work of mourning is therefore meant to kill death (*SE*, 14:256).

Hamacher offers an intriguing account of the notion of work, which he claims must always comply with two mutually exclusive demands. First, work must recognize its closest imaginable affinity to death, which is what it is meant to guard us from. Simultaneously, work must assert that it is more powerful than death: it is immortal and indestructible.[62] I read Hamacher's conditions as touching on some essential elements of Freud's argument: the work of mourning similarly oscillates between a close kinship with death and a struggle against it. This fluctuation allows the work of mourning to defer the fulfillment of its aim and replaces it with a basic inactivity that evidences what Hamacher identifies as "resistance to itself." Despite this internal equivocation, however, the work of mourning does end with complete detachment from loss.

In contrast, the melancholic stance does not endorse work.[63] Not only does the vehemence of internalization prevent the melancholic from performing the work of mourning; it is the act itself that forestalls the possibility of detachment in the first place. When the object is made part of the pain-stricken ego, the work of mourning is rendered unfeasible. The lack of distance from the object and the blurring of its borders with the self allows the lost object to decompose within the melancholic ego without leaving any possibility for resolving its loss. Freud raises the possibility of work in melancholia but quickly sets it aside by claiming that melancholia "blocks" any opportunity for work owing to its fundamental ambivalence, swinging between holding on to the object (in the form of internalization) and letting it go (in the form of mourning). This congenital conflict, which in many ways marks the melancholic stance more than anything else, prevents, or at least hinders, detachment (*SE*, 14:257).

The destructive nature of the melancholic's response to loss is one of the crucial and most widely discussed features of melancholia. The melancholic devours his lost love-object in order to retain it; in demonstrating his endless loyalty, he destroys it. Therein lies the paradox: the only way to retain the object is to destroy it. By initiating its destruction, the melancholic's incorporation of his loss effectively transforms the object into something utterly different. What, it may be asked, does the melancholic devour if his object has lost its original integrity, or even its identity, the cause of its being loved and possessed in the first place? In response we turn to another sense of destructiveness, one often neglected (if acknowledged at all) in the context of mourning: the work of mourning can also be understood as a work of destruction since letting go of the object can come about only by taking it apart. The forlorn subject can be detached from the object only by destroying its relation to it bit by bit, done by detaching each individual strand in an almost surgical process. There is no way for the subject to detach itself from the object in its entirety; it must always be divested of its wholeness in order to be removed. Hence, the melancholic destroys in order to retain his loss, whereas the mourner, like Penelope, destroys in order to retain his own subjective integrity.

Benjamin: Trauerspiel, the Play of Mourning

One of the more compelling junctures where Freud and Benjamin meet during their individual journeys into melancholy can be found in Freud's disavowal of the possibility of work being performed by the melancholic. His distinction between mourning and melancholia yields a configuration in which the separation from a loss can only be a "work of mourning," never of melancholia. It is the feature of work, therefore, that marks the stark division between mourning and melancholia for Freud: the failure to mourn becomes the condition of possibility for the melancholic condition, and the unsuccessful execution of the work of mourning that determines the response to be melancholic. The melancholic's vehement commitment to holding on to the loss within him necessarily negates the possibility of working it through. This fundamental divorce of work from the melancholic stance can be taken to comply with the psychoanalytic undertaking, directed at separating the healthy psyche from its inhibiting losses. This divorce, however, is very much at odds with historical accounts of melancholy. Be it as a result of his disposition or, perhaps, an attempt to overcome it, the melancholic is deeply devoted to the dictum of work. As Sontag points out, the history of melancholy reveals a close connection between the Saturnine temperament and work. Convinced that his will is weak, the melancholic will make every effort to develop that will, sometimes by transforming it into a compulsion to work. This may explain why Baudelaire, who suffered from melancholia, ends many of his letters with impassioned pledges to work more, to work uninterruptedly, to do nothing but work.[64]

Benjamin is well aware of the history of melancholy and thus of the complex interconnection between melancholic passivity, or "heaviness of the soul" (*TS*, 132), and the injunction to work.[65] Benjamin, in his description of melancholy in the *Trauerspiel* book, turns to Ficino's account (among others) of the scholar's melancholy and his insistence on a fixed regimen of work, intended to reflect as well as counteract a melancholic disposition. The challenge to the Freudian distinction between mourning and melancholy he invokes is most clearly pronounced precisely by the constituent of work and its exclusion from the melancholic's psychological pathology. The correlation that Benjamin establishes between melancholy and work best demonstrates his alternative to the Freudian division.

In proposing this connection, he asserts his position regarding two essential postulates: first, the nonpathological nature of the melancholic state and, second, its deep relation to philosophical work. In other words Benjamin offers a structure in which melancholy is no longer defined and determined by its inability to complete the work of separation or by the failure of mourning; it is, instead, established in its own right, and not only negatively, as an arena of work. Therein lies the thrust of his argument: the coupling of melancholy and work, although of utmost importance to our understanding of the challenge Benjamin puts to Freud, is most germane to its ability to justify his move away from a physiological-pathological discussion of melancholy. Without the productivity of work and its capacity to operate within melancholy rather than being paralyzed by it, Benjamin could not have staked his claim for a melancholic view of philosophy.

Benjamin combines melancholy, with its deep acknowledgment and responsibility for loss and the mourner's work by turning the latter into *philosophical work*. He thereby blurs Freud's distinction between the melancholic and the mourner, a gesture that takes into account the intrinsic relations between commitment to loss and its working through, what Freud deems an impossible union. Benjamin, however, does not view work as labor directed toward detachment from the object, an act that will free the afflicted subject. For him, and this is a crucial difference, work aims at the complete opposite: the *presentation* of the object generated by philosophical work accompanied by the endowment of a voice to the object, thereby redeeming it.

It is evident that Freud's *Trauerarbeit* echoes the subject matter of Benjamin's book—the *Trauerspiel*. This reverberation marks, first of all, a firm opposition between the weight of work and play; however, the implications of the intricacy of the relationship between the two terms becomes even more consequential when put in the context of *Trauer*, mourning, and the choice to couple it in the first case with work and in the second with play. Here, again, Benjamin provides us with a formulation exceedingly close to Freud's, yet he completely undermines the latter's insistence on coupling mourning with the work intended to overcome it. In Freud's *Trauerarbeit* mourning is coupled with the work that is directed toward its own diminishing, whereas in Benjamin's use of the *Trauerspiel*, mourning or melancholy remains intact, played with, rather than being in the constant prospect of being untangled or undermined.

References to the *work*-of-mourning and the *play*-of-mourning, which seem to be opposed, can be located in Benjamin's preface to the book and in the body of the text, respectively. In the preface Benjamin describes his own philosophical agenda and methodology, his philosophical *work*, whereas in the body of the text he analyzes the *Trauer-Spiel*, the theatrical genre of the *play* of mourning.[66] Both cases contain elements related to both melancholy and mourning. This is demonstrated in the work of the allegorist, as well as in the preface to the book. The difficulty in discerning between Benjamin's stance and that of the allegorist, a complication to be faced by all the book's readers, can be located in this difference between *Trauerarbeit* and *Trauerspiel*.

The allegorist's seriousness is playful, and the "work" of heaping he performs is almost frivolous. Play marks the beginning and the end of life: child's play, puppet shows, theatrical play. For the allegorist play, or playfulness, is the only way to respond to death. Benjamin points out that the main concern of the baroque concept of "play" is its own product (this characteristic should be compared to classicism and romanticism, which are concerned with production, and with production together with product, respectively). For Benjamin it is not work or production but the product itself that occasions a fundamental playfulness in the face of such an intense and serious preoccupation with the absolute (*TS*, 82). Everything turns into a game: "So too with play and splendour will the victim's body be brought to burial," and "yea, after death time also plays with us, when maggot and worm burrow in our decaying bodies" (*TS*, 82–83). The melancholic response to the emptiness of life is thus the game, as "the only pleasure the melancholic permits itself, and it is a powerful one, is allegory" (*TS*, 185).

Allegory mediates this state of play; for the allegorist everything can become mere play. Melancholy and playfulness go hand in hand here, for the allegorist plays a grim game, bereft of the innocence of the child's playfulness. Nevertheless, the relationship's similarity to child's play lies elsewhere: in its self-absorption, in its detachment from the world around it, and in the complete immersion in the object at hand (in the *Trauerspiel* this attitude is not transformed into actual reflection as in Calderon, for instance [*TS*, 82]). This engagement is repetitively altered—into boredom, disappointment, and a "disconsolate everyday countenance" (*TS*, 185). Reiteration thus sinks the melancholic all the more into the self, while establishing and confirming the "bleak rule of a melancholic distaste for life" (*TS*, 140).

In the preface to the *Trauerspiel* book, however, Benjamin's description of the effect of mourning and melancholy does not yield play but work. The accuracy of Benjamin's account of the allegorist emerges from several affinities between the two conditions. Although Benjamin does not argue that allegory is philosophical, or vice versa, he nonetheless recognizes an element essential for his philosophical work in the playfulness of the allegorist, specifically, the latter's attachment to the material. It can be maintained that Benjamin's attraction to the *Trauerspiel* as a form is bound up with his detection that important features, such as the absence of a transcendent quality in allegory or the playfulness it harbors, proximate to his own philosophical work.

Freud directs his work of mourning toward terminating the relationship with the lost object, toward detachment from it and, in the end, its obliteration. Benjamin's conception of such work aims at the polar opposite: it manifests the object's presence. The major element in this account of work is the presented *object* and its independent, nonrelational character, not the freed and uninhibited *subject*, who no longer maintains a relationship with the lost object. In other words what matters to Benjamin is the release and redemption of the object and not the subject who is freed from its effects.

This shift is of utmost importance for understanding the absence of subjectivity in Benjamin's project, which revolves around ideas, "the objects of . . . [philosophical] investigation," and truth rather than the personal, subjective realm of expression (this, as I have already mentioned, relates to the nonsubjective and nonpsychological reading of melancholy that I apply here). It is, however, important to note that in the "work" of Freud and Benjamin, as presented here, a similar principle rules the work of mourning and the expression of the object by way of its presentation. In each of these cases the commitment to knowledge and its articulation, both of which are essential to fulfillment and resolution, is firmly underscored.[67]

"It is characteristic of philosophical writing that it must continually confront the question of presentation [*Darstellung*]" (*TS*, 27), writes Benjamin in the opening line of the prologue to the *Trauerspiel* book. Philosophical work is thus work entailing presentation and expression, the unfolding of the richness of the idea, its possibilities and potentialities—those actualized, as well as those yet unactualized: "the presentation of an idea can under no circumstances be considered successful unless the whole range of possible extremes it contains has been virtually explored" (*TS*, 47). Alluding to the concept of the "extreme" in the idea, Benjamin refers to one of the characteristics of truth—its exploration of the extreme rather than the mediate. Extremes demarcate yet enrich the idea's borders. Their presentation fully expresses and articulates the idea, "for by pursuing different levels of meaning in its examination of one single object it receives both the incentive to begin again and the justification for its irregular rhythm" (*TS*, 28). Benjamin's statement is another characterization of the rhythm and nature of philosophical work. It is work that reiterates the idea until it touches on the limits of its own exhaustiveness. Within this exhaustiveness another purpose of philosophical work is revealed: provision of an abbreviated outline of the image of the world (*TS*, 48). With this statement Benjamin alludes to the Leibnizian model of the monad (which I explore in detail in Chapter 4).

For the idea to present phenomena, the latter must undergo a process of destruction. Again, one of the stronger Freudian elements rears its head—the destructive nature of the melancholic is recast here. This is not the destruction resulting from a wounding and deleterious attachment but from the condition of the philosophical work of presentation: "Phenomena do not, however, enter into the realm of ideas whole, in their crude empirical state, adulterated by appearances, but only in their basic elements, redeemed. They are divested of their false unity so that, thus divided, they might partake of the genuine unity of truth" (*TS*, 33). Benjamin here conditions the expression of ideas with the work of divesting phenomena of their wholeness prior to entering the horizon of the idea—their organizing principle. Accordingly, as in Freud, a sense of destruction serves as a preliminary condition for presenting and expressing. This may seem counterintuitive since expression and fullness of meaning seem closer to retention of the whole than to its dismemberment, but this is exactly where Benjamin proposes his own view of the connection between melancholy and philosophical work. His understanding of the place of destruction and loss in the midst of philosophical expression is what renders melancholy and sorrow so prominent in his thought. Again, the destructive nature of Freud's melancholic is recast here.

This divestment of wholeness likewise relates to one aspect of dispossession, specifically, the detachment of phenomena from their natural surroundings. However, whereas Freud uses the concept of detachment in relation to the work of mourning, Benjamin does not ascribe detachment to the subject's well-being, assumed to be the outcome of mourning. For him detachment from original surroundings is requisite for entering the idea, a new context where divested and partial—even lost—phenomena are presented. Detachment thus enables phenomena to become the subjects of work. Hence, the work is not *of* detachment, as in Freud, but that which is made possible *by* detachment. Phenomena are removed not only from their natural surroundings but also from their sphere of life. They are deadened by this detachment, only to be redeemed through the presentation of their truth in the idea.

In contrast to Freud's concept of work, which effaces all traces of loss, Benjamin's concept clearly harbors such evocations. His concept of work, as described in the preface to the *Trauerspiel* book, is not concerned with the eradication of traces of loss and destruction—on the contrary, it stresses such traces all the more strongly. When referring to the mosaic, another figure Benjamin uses to illuminate the meaning of the philosophical idea, he writes:

> Just as mosaics preserve their majesty despite their fragmentation into capricious particles, so philosophical contemplation is not lacking in momentum.[68] Both are made up of the distinct and the disparate; and nothing could bear more powerful testimony to the transcendent force of the sacred image and the truth itself. The value of fragments of thought [*Denkbruchstücken*] is all the greater the less direct [*unmittelbar*] their relationship to the underlying idea [*Grundkonzeption*], and the brilliance of presentation depends as much on this value [*Wert*,[69] *Glanz*] as the brilliance of the mosaic does on the quality of the glass paste. (*TS*, 28–29)

The figure of the mosaic captures various important elements found in the idea, even more than does the image of the constellation, with which scholars are so preoccupied. The mosaic's particles are meaningless; they contain no image of any sort and are simply colorful pieces of materiality. Only when the pieces are placed side by side do they become charged with meaning, the picture emerging in its utmost beauty. Later, this image glows from within the ruins. Yet, however beautiful and full, this image remains eternally shattered, "ruined," for part of its splendor lies in how the mosaic's parts always remain separate, broken. The particles never entirely adhere to one another; the glue that binds them never overcomes this discreteness. In the preface Benjamin suggests that the mosaic's beauty, which parallels truth, is not sabotaged by its fragmentation. Rather, this fragmentation is what constitutes its beauty—just as truth is extracted and unfolded from the partial and the insignificant. The origin of the totality of truth is, therefore, partial and neglected; it is never complete and "undamaged." Yet materiality also has a strong presence in the image—in the particles and the glue that carry no autonomous content beyond their immediate function in the mosaic; this materiality is transformed into truth only when they are juxtaposed.[70]

"And the brilliance of presentation depends as much on . . . [the] value [of the fragments of thought] as the brilliance of the mosaic does on the quality of the glass paste" (*TS*, 29): not only is the power of the picture not affected by its fragmentation and ruination, but it is intensified by just those features. The glue, which seems at the outset in need of concealment or disguise, becomes a condition for the picture's force. This "imperfection" in the picture harbors its worth in its ability to represent traces of that which was lost. There is never complete closure or concealment of that loss, for philosophical work and its results perpetually contain it.

Like the image of the mosaic, the productivity of philosophical work, the work of presentation, can never completely conceal its destructive elements, or its inherent loss, as the conditions of its possibility. The idea, produced by work out of the condition of loss, will always bear its traces. This construction strengthens my claim regarding the importance of the work of presentation—rather than that of detachment—in Benjamin's oeuvre.

However, this presentation always carries with it what is no longer there and cannot be presented again. Its strength thus lies in what it lacks, in the loss it can only indicate without restoring. Benjamin does not reconstruct the destroyed material, nor does he rebuild that which was lost; he retains its quality of disintegration. He therefore neither overcomes loss nor mourns that loss. Instead, his manner of *working through* loss involves engagement with the loss itself, with the presentation *of* this loss. The glue's significance in the mosaic alludes to the importance of pointing out lacunae, the spaces missing and destined to be eternally unaccounted for.

The importance of this category of work lies in its ability to turn the Freudian melancholic's passive stance into that of activity and, more important, of productivity. It is only in this way that melancholy and philosophy can be joined to form a structure of fecund reciprocities. In his seminar on Benjamin's *Trauerspiel* book in 1932, Adorno notes that the deeper the melancholy, the more productive it is.[71] The working out of *Trauer*, together with the tenacity of intention, is what creates its plentitude and forcefulness. It is in this sense that meaning and melancholy stand together in the same context—the context of philosophical productivity.

2

The *Trauer-Spiel*

Reflections on the Baroque

Benjamin's preoccupation with baroque theater as caught in his study of the *Trauerspiel* inevitably entails an absorption in the baroque period itself and its *Zeitgeist* or *Weltanschauung*, its fundamental mood or ambience. This argument can be made in the opposite direction as well: any substantive account of the baroque period inherently involves an investigation into its theatrical history. Something about the baroque state of mind, or "reason" to borrow Christine Buci-Glucksmann's phrase, is essentially theatrical.[1] William Egginton recently claimed that "the baroque is theater and the theater is baroque."[2] Baroque theater embodies much more than a mere medium of stage representation; it offers an especially keen perspective into the historical, religious, psychological, and artistic setting of the period.

In this sense I take Benjamin's study of the *Trauerspiel* to be less a literary interpretation or theatrical history than a philosophical-historical undertaking into the abyss of the baroque state of mind—a state of mind or mood that is repeatedly and explicitly designated as melancholic, by Benjamin himself, as well as a long line of other historians and philosophers. The baroque is therefore clearly marked by its theatricality, on the one hand, its melancholy, on the other. This pairing demands detailed explication. How, given melancholy's essential self-absorption and closure, are we to join it with the openness, extravagance, and overacting inherent in the period's theatrical presentation? In what sense can these two opposing configurations operate with each other? The task of untangling these strands becomes even more complex when we recall that the term *baroque* is not merely a defined historical period. It refers to an artistic style but is also used as a descriptive adjective for what is especially extravagant and ornate, in addition to being a synonym for everything that is intricate and perplexing. I find the resolution to this conundrum in the specific way that Benjamin analyzes both the baroque theatrical structure and its melancholic mood. In this chapter I outline the connection while dwelling on the possible relationship between theater and melancholy as revealed in the *Trauerspiel*.

In *The Origin of the German Trauerspiel* Benjamin focuses on the seventeenth-century German theatrical plays referred to in literary history as the *Trauerspiel*. The *Trauerspiel*'s periodization situates it roughly between 1600 and 1700, the period of the Thirty Years' War, the fierce religious disputes between Catholics and Protestants, and the beginnings of "modern" philosophy with Descartes. The German baroque playwrights Benjamin is most concerned with in the book are Georg Philipp Harsdörffer (1607–58), Andreas Gryphius (1616–64), Daniel Casper von Lohenstein (1635–83), and Johann Christian Hallmann (1640–1716). The list is homogeneous; however, it is important to mention another prominent theatrical character that preoccupies Benjamin in the book: Hamlet. It is evident that Shakespeare as playwright does not stand at the heart of Benjamin's interest; it is rather Hamlet, the eponymous protagonist of Shakespeare's play, who intrigues Benjamin. He explains that only Hamlet, and not any character in the German baroque theater, was able to conjure a human figure corresponding to the dichotomy between the neoantique and medieval perspectives, in a way that corresponds to the baroque view of the melancholic. Only Shakespeare "was capable of striking Christian sparks from the baroque rigidity of the melancholic, un-stoic as it is un-Christian, pseudo-antique as it is pseudo-pietistic" (*TS*, 158). Benjamin devotes an independent section of the book to a discussion of *Hamlet*, something he does not do with any other play, figure, or playwright, and it appears that rather than being a mere example, the play serves him as an almost necessary exemplar of the *Trauerspiel*.[3]

One of the aims of Benjamin's project was to disentangle the historical and literary milieu of the Renaissance from that of the baroque period, specifically in the context of German theater.⁴ Generally speaking, baroque literature was enjoying a revival in the years that Benjamin was researching his book. As Jennings notes, however, Benjamin was the first to present the plays of the baroque not merely as aberrant or decadent dramas but as major creations, importantly responding to the period's historical experience.⁵ Benjamin, however, was not only interested in the relation between history and theatricality as reflected in the plays; he was also caught up with the history of the *Trauerspiel*'s reception in Germany at the time.

In fact, the second half of the book's prologue is concerned precisely with this question, an investigation that served as the primary motivation and chief objective behind Benjamin's undertaking. Benjamin directs his criticism against different theorists of art criticism whom, he believed, not only misunderstood the *Trauerspiel* and failed to identify it as an independent genre, but also acted according to a misleading hypothesis regarding the proper approach to the study of the history of art as such. The case of the *Trauerspiel* provided Benjamin with an occasion to criticize the very suppositions underlying the discipline of art history. The crux of Benjamin's thesis lies in the tendency of art historians to misconstrue works of art by searching for pregiven generic structures of artistic genres considered consonant with those works. According to Benjamin this problem was especially blatant in the contemporary treatment of the baroque *Trauerspiel*. The search for an "average" work of art, to use Benjamin's term, in order to fit it to a preconceived genre can, he continued, shed light merely on the common features of different works of art and obscure, even shroud, anything unique about a specific work:

> When facts are amassed in this way so that the less obvious original qualities are soon obscured by the chaos of more immediately appealing modern ones, the investigation in which this accumulation was undertaken—with a view to examining what these things have 'in common'—is left with nothing but some psychological data which, on the slender basis of an identity in the subjective reaction of the investigator or, at least, the ordinary contemporary citizen, are held to establish the similarity of things which are in fact quite different. (*TS*, 39)

The problem Benjamin points to here can also be formulated as a problem of gestalt, namely, the attempt to grasp the *Trauerspiel* according to preexisting genres and their structures, in this case, Greek tragedy. Benjamin's criticism here brings to the fore the weight that these theories add to the subjective investigator's stance and, in some cases, that of the viewer—a subjective stance emphasizing the patterns of their own perception of the plays rather than the internal structure of the observed works of art.

It is important to stress here that Benjamin is not searching for the author's original intent, nor is he approaching works of art in order to reconstruct how they "really were" (a historicist point of view, what Benjamin sometimes defines as empathy, and which he fiercely opposes). Rather, he is in search of the essence of the plays themselves, independently of any external and artificial requirements to uncover correspondences. He formulates his task as an endeavor to present the *idea* of the *Trauerspiel* rather than its *concept*.[6] He defines the difference as follows:

> In the sense in which it is treated in the philosophy of art the *Trauerspiel* is an idea. Such treatment differs most significantly from a literary-historical treatment in its assumption of unity, whereas the latter [literary-historical treatment] is concerned to demonstrate variety . . . Conversely the idea is the extreme example of a form or genre, and as such does not enter into the history of literature. *Trauerspiel*, as a concept, could, without the slightest problem, be added to the list of aesthetic classifications. But not as an idea, for it [the *Trauerspiel*] defines no class and does not contain the generality on which the respective conceptual levels in the system of classification depend: the average. (*TS*, 38)

The *Trauerspiel* is therefore an extreme form of art, demonstrating its own uniqueness and variety. To touch an extreme form requires an exploration of its essence, the idea of the plays, a diametric stance from that taken by art history, which seeks the average expression of a given genre. Benjamin invokes Burdach's 1918 research to emphasize the importance of identifying differences rather than similarities between works of art, an act manifesting a need rooted in principles of human perception and cognition, which are in constant need of systemization (*TS*, 40). Such unity and systemization correspond to the internal structure of human cognition rather than to the inner structure—one could even say, essence—of the artworks themselves. Despite his clear confidence in these claims, Benjamin is careful not to throw the baby out with the bathwater: he refuses to give up important art historical categories such as "Renaissance" or "tragedy," yet he treats them as names rather than concepts. This means that as ideas, "such names perform a service they are not able to perform as concepts:

they do not make the similar identical, but they effect a synthesis between extremes" (*TS*, 41).

In supporting his claims, Benjamin makes a point of distinguishing between *Trauerspiel* and tragedy. This distinction has a dual significance for him. First, he uses their distinctiveness to explain his motivation for doing this project by outlining what he takes to be a misreading and misconception of the *Trauerspiel* as failed tragedy. By pointing at the essential difference between the two genres, Benjamin establishes his initial argument that the *Trauerspiel* plays cannot be justly evaluated according to the Aristotelian criteria of tragedy. He details (see his prologue) why the critics were all too ready to analyze the *Trauerspiel* as a distortion of "proper" tragic structure, a "caricature of classical tragedy" (*TS*, 50), and describes their flourishing as "an incomplete renaissance of tragedy" (*TS*, 50).

Second, Benjamin uses his critical comparison as a means to shed light on some of the important and unique characteristics of the *Trauerspiel*. Doing so enables him to characterize his own appraisal of the *Trauerspiel*. In this sense one can say that he replicates the methodology that he criticizes, being unable to completely relinquish the category of tragedy when attempting to define the *Trauerspiel* in isolation from tragedy's features. A similar methodology can be found in some other instances in the book, for example when he discusses truth by comparing it with knowledge or when he analyzes the literary structure of allegory by using the symbol as its background. Interestingly, this same structure can be found in Freud's discussion of the distinction between mourning and melancholy, where he writes that he will "try to throw some light on the nature of melancholia by comparing it with the normal affect of mourning" (*SE*, 14:243).

Taking into account Benjamin's commitment to the distinction between *Trauerspiel* and tragedy and, moreover, its vital importance in justifying his claims, it is worth noting one grave error in the English translation of the text's title. Osborne's translation of *Trauerspiel* as "tragic drama" ignores the efforts Benjamin makes to precisely distinguish the *Trauerspiel* from tragedy. "Mourning Play" or simply *Trauerspiel*, rather than "German Tragic Drama," would have been much more appropriate, and it does give the impression that the translator is at some odds with his own decision.[7] Benjamin outlines his distinction between *Trauerspiel* and tragedy in three main texts. The first two are fragments, written in 1916 and published posthumously: "*Trauerspiel* and Tragedy" (*SW*, 1:54–58) and "The Role of Language in *Trauerspiel* and Tragedy" (*SW*, 1:59–61). They served as Benjamin's preparatory notes to this third, most developed, text on the matter: the first part of the *Trauerspiel* book, entitled "*Trauerspiel* and Tragedy." Much has been written on Benjamin's distinction, notably by Weber and Friedlander, so I will refrain from elaborating on these accounts here.[8] However, some important features of the distinction that I find necessary for shedding light on the melancholic attributes of the *Trauerspiel* will nevertheless appear in different parts of this chapter.

Formulating his undertaking as an exploration and presentation of the "idea" of the *Trauerspiel*, Benjamin follows his own methodology in the prologue, where he thoroughly discusses the possibility of transforming given phenomena into ideas or, as he famously puts it in his essay on Goethe's *Elective Affinities* (*SW*, 1:297–360), the transformation of "material content" into "truth content." Benjamin searches for the idea of the *Trauerspiel* by examining its material content, namely, the plays themselves. In accordance with his methodological statement in the prologue, phenomena cannot enter the realm of the idea in their crude, raw existence but need to undergo a transformation, which in Benjamin's account entails taking them apart so as to touch their most basic elements (*TS*, 33). This strategy appears throughout the book and is most evident in Benjamin's painstaking reading of the plays, especially the role of their protagonists within the genre's structure, the descriptions of the stage properties, and the correspondence between the plays' narratives and contemporary political theories, in addition to the traces of the baroque melancholic mood on the period's stage. It is clear that Benjamin is occupied not so much with a literary or historical interpretation of each play separately but, rather, with laying bare the essence of the *Trauerspiel* itself. Such an endeavor can be achieved only by way of going beyond interpretations of the individual plays in an attempt to transcend the individual manifestations of the idea and to aim at presenting its own pure structure.

Accordingly, I follow Benjamin in attempting to comprehend the plays' inner structure, but I do so not to reveal the idea of the *Trauerspiel* per se but to unravel its innate correspondence with the melancholic mood. My aim, therefore, is not to offer an interpretation of the plays but to direct attention to the ways in which the structure of the melancholic mood operates within them and to demonstrate how melancholy functions in Benjamin's overall investigation of the *Trauerspiel*. This requires an elaboration on the essential relation between baroque and theatrical representation but even more so of theatricality and melancholy.

One of the main predicaments discernible in the psychoanalytic approach to melancholia that I have laid out is the problem of the melancholic's fundamental incapacity to detect the boundaries of his psyche. A marked example of this incapacity is the melancholic's inability to differentiate between the self's own ego and the existence or nonexistence of the external lost object—put differently, the distinction between the internal (ego) and the external (object). The crux of the pathology, resting as it does on this inability, results in the patient's inability to perform the work of mourning (which can be carried out only on an object differentiated from the self).

A second important case exemplifying this aspect of the melancholic condition in the Freudian account is that of the fundamental diffusion between life and death. The melancholic's lost object is either dead (in the case of human loss) or absent (in the case of a more abstract loss). In both cases the pathology lies in the subject's inability to recognize the loss and in the insistence on maintaining the dead object as "half-alive" within the melancholic consciousness, thus rendering the boundary between life and death indefinite and thus indistinct.

Taking these important psychoanalytic insights (or diagnoses) even further, the instability of boundaries in the case of the melancholic—that between the internal and the external, as well as between life and death—has implications beyond psychological pathology. In both instances the relationship between two antitheses is at stake, and, again in both, the border between them is rendered indistinct. In the context of psychoanalytic thought this blurring is considered pathological; in the *Trauerspiel*, however, it becomes the norm. The rigorous structure and internal logic of the psychoanalytic system allow only a limited, clearly defined account of the normal or healthy psyche while placing everything else—what is usually deemed "pathological"—outside it. This reasoning is invalid within the context of the baroque *Trauerspiel*, with its unique perception and convictions regarding mourning and melancholy and their unique way of constituting a relation to the world. It appears as if the internal logic of melancholia, with its lack of recognition of boundaries and differentiations, is absorbed into the content of the plays themselves; but more importantly, it also constitutes their literary and epistemological structures.

In what follows I focus my reading of the plays on two main points, both related to the problem of indefinite boundaries and their transgression. The first is the specific manifestation of pain and suffering (be it psychological or physical), specifically, the different ways in which pain is represented theatrically. When discussing the problem of the indefinite boundary between internal and external, I touch on questions of bodily pain, outward manifestations of mourning, the bombastic and exaggerated nature of baroque theatrical representations, and the fundamental connection between suffering and spectacle. These problems are illustrated by referring to one of the play's most prominent figures, repeatedly represented on the stages of the *Trauerspiel*: the martyr.

The second focus is on theatrical representations of the indeterminate boundary between life and death or, rather, between the living and the dead. I show how the plays are occupied by the question of the transition between life and death, the ways in which the loss of transcendence and redemption affect these representations, and what can be taken to be the moral stance underlying the baroque preoccupation with these issues. I demonstrate these themes through another figure repeatedly represented in the plays: the ghost. Through a close examination of the nature of this figure, its theatrical representations on the stage as well as what I take to be Benjamin's captivation by its implications for temporal and historical structures, I develop a theory of meaning that evolves precisely from within the indefinite ghostly structure, one where meaning emerges only from within an essential indeterminacy.

Expressions of Pain in the *Trauerspiel*

Throughout the *Trauerspiel* book Benjamin is utterly captivated by the scenes of exceptional cruelty and suffering so frequently depicted in the plays. He even asks at some point in his discussion of the martyr: "What is the significance of those scenes of cruelty and anguish in which the baroque drama revels?" (*TS*, 216). The *Trauerspiel*, indeed, presents an extraordinary number of scenes depicting physical cruelty, caught in explicit visual representations of violence on the stage (a typical example is the feast of cut-off heads that appear on Meurab's table in *Catharina von Georgien*), as well as in the unique poetic devices meant to literally tear language up from within so that it becomes analogous to the brutality of the period's historical events (*TS*, 53, 55). These plays abound with dismembered corpses, cries of pain, and clamorous lamentations, evident in the efforts made by the playwrights to detail the torture and suffering at the expense of furthering the play's narrative (Gryphius's *Papinianus* and Hallmann's *Sophia* provide illustrative examples).

This tendency is traditionally interpreted as corresponding to the historical events of the period, chiefly the Thirty Years' War, itself the subject of many baroque theatrical presentations. Benjamin refers to Louis Wysocki's book on Gryphius, in which he describes the plays of the *Trauerspiel* as "plays written by brutes for brutes." Wysocki stresses that extreme violence was demanded by audiences, who looked for something that could correspond to the bloody environment within which they conducted their lives. The scenes supplied by baroque plays appeared, therefore, quite natural: they were presented with a "picture of their own way of life," in which they "delighted naively and brutally in the pleasure offered them."[9]

The preoccupation of the baroque drama with pain and suffering is not, however, limited to bodily pain; it equally materializes in theatrical representations of lament, sadness, mourning, and melancholy. One of the central problems confronting the presentation of physical and psychological pain is their expression in the text and in the shaping of the protagonists onstage. The interrelation between feeling and expression is a dominant theme in Benjamin's discussion of the plays and converges with some of the important quandaries pertaining to melancholy and its theatrical articulation. I begin with the intricate relations linking pain and suffering, and the *Trauerspiel*'s unique forms of expression. There are two models to explore these relations: first, that of physical pain inducing physical, bestial forms of expression; second, that of mental pain and suffering and the various ways in which it is corporeally expressed.

In the first case, physical pain is paradigmatic precisely because it intrinsically connects the intense feeling of pain with its immediate, involuntary expression. Physical pain immediately directs itself outward, toward its physical expression in the form of a rudimentary cry or howl, reducing the human being to a creature whose bodily affliction brings about the mere corporal production of sound. Physical pain's nearly animal-like immediacy of expression is therefore essentially nonarticulate; instead of describing or communicating pain, it merely presents it. It is a pure cathartic exhalation, purging the pain in a purely physical sense. Such a voicing of pain embodies the most immediate and exhaustive sort of expression, in which there is almost no gap between the moment the feeling of pain emerges and its vocal dissemination.

This immediate cry of pain is thus not directed at anyone, nor does it function as any form of communication. Merely physical, it is the most spontaneous and primitive form of expression. But although its communicative aspect is absent, a quality of sharing is nevertheless involved. The cry of pain, while imparting no content, transforms pain into a public, communal utterance, touching and belonging to everyone and everything.[10] It is in that sense that the very act of expressing the pain is enough to allow it to transcend the confines of the individual subject and disperse. This dynamic is somewhat reversed in Benjamin's early essays on language, in which pain and melancholy are a result of the *inability* to express oneself (this is not necessarily the thwarting of pain's expression but a broader expressive paralysis, as I show in the next chapter).

The second case is that of pain that is not primarily physical, but mental: suffering, adversity, passionate anguish, or a response to loss. What happens when mental or "internal" pain actually crosses the body's boundaries and induces a physical form of expression? In psychoanalysis, especially in Freud, numerous cases can be found in which the symptoms of patients with grave psychical suffering actually manifest themselves on their bodies. In such cases, because it is usually impossible to identify a physiological cause for these symptoms, they are diagnosed as extensions of psychological adversity. For an interesting case in which the patient shows physical symptoms that result from psychical pain, see Freud's *Studies on Hysteria* (in *SE*, 2:135–81), in which he describes the analysis of the twenty-four-year-old Fräulein Elisabeth von R.

As J.-B. Pontalis has shown, Freud has a strong and persistent interest in the problem of pain and its bordering on the physical-psychic realms; however, this interest is problematic for him, and it is clearly evident that he finds it difficult to integrate a theory of pain into his writings. Following the movement between physical and psychic pain in Freud, we can trace an analogical structure in which there is a direct transfer between one register and the other, "as if, in the case of pain, the body transforms itself into psyche and the psyche into body." Pontalis adds that the functioning of pain in psychoanalytic theory demonstrates an essential coupling between several contradictory pairs (external and internal, reality and phantasy, past and present), and it is this tight embrace of such internal contradictions that is so difficult to undo in the case of pain.[11]

James Strachey, the editor of Freud's *Standard Edition*, defines *Trauer* as "both the affect of grief and its outward manifestation" (*SE*, 14:243), explaining that when one reads Freud in translation, the English word *mourning* should always be conceived as signifying both these denotations. Benjamin employs this interrelation between internal and external, which constitutes the basis of Freud's pathologic melancholia, along a much broader horizon. The border between the inner and outer, or (in Benjamin's thought) its internal and external manifestations, is located in the reciprocities maintained between feeling and expression.[12] One of the interesting questions that can be raised about *Trauer* in general and *Trauerspiel* specifically is, therefore, in what sense is sadness internal and in what external? Or, to extend the question, what is the critical point at which internal feeling is externalized? In what follows I show that in Benjamin's analysis of the *Trauerspiel*, the occurrence of such a transition is altogether undermined, or at least, becomes questionable.

Benjamin's suggestive remark on comedy's role in *Trauerspiel* can be helpful in unfolding the relation between internal and external. In an almost incidental observation he compares comedy and *Trauerspiel* to a dress and its lining: "Comedy—or more precisely: the pure joke—is the essential inner side of mourning which from time to time, like the lining of a dress at the hem or lapel, makes its presence felt" (*TS*, 125–26). This description is important in that it presents the lining as what constitutes the fleeting border between inside and outside, or what stands between the body and the publicly visible dress fabric. The inner layer is therefore always there, but its presence is only occasionally exposed. When hidden, it is felt by the bare flesh that it protects; when revealed, it disavows the skin, leaving it bare and abandoned.

This structure, which describes the relationship between mourning and comedy (in Benjamin's sartorial metaphor, its lining),[13] points to an essential component of melancholy—that of being constantly situated on the boundary between the inside and the outside. Comedy is not presented in the *Trauerspiel* as merely an episodic genre; it performs like the imperative lining—always there, the obverse of mourning, even if its presence is only occasionally revealed. This complex structure also raises the question of the place of the body, the flesh—which is what the joke is rubbed against, what is protected but also exposed.[14]

The *Trauerspiel* book is saturated with thoughts about disturbances in the flow of expression and the melancholy resulting from it. It is not only in melancholy that a hiatus is present, however—"laughter is shattered articulation," Benjamin writes elsewhere,[15] describing the affinity between laughter and sorrow as two forms of interruption to articulation in the *Trauerspiel*. The melancholic prince is commonly situated opposite the fool, serving as the lining of sorrow's dress, whose bad counsel awakens moments of laughter amid the most profound sorrow.[16] The stark immediacy found in the expression of physical pain aforementioned, is thus crucial, by way of opposition, to the clarification of expressions of pain that are disturbed, absent, or replaced by the disjointed expressions of either melancholy or mirth.

The two models of *Trauer*, that of the *Trauerspiel* and that of the Freudian melancholy, deserve comparison, in terms of the difference in their topographic organization of the psyche's relationship to the external world. The latter directs the focus of sadness inward, pointing to the way in which the melancholic patient positions himself in the pathologically inverted state of complete subjectivity and closure. According to Freud the melancholic loss and its effects are entirely situated within the confines of the subject, with Freud's array of terms (internalization, relation, a shadowing object, etc.) providing descriptions of such a subjective internal ambience. If an external object exists at all, it is the outcome of the internal split within the melancholic ego, meaning that the absorptive subjective apparatus is what has created this object in the first place. Freud thus uses the term *object* insofar as it functions as part of a relationship with the psyche (e.g., object-choice, object-relations, etc.).

In the *Trauerspiel*, however, sorrow occupies an altogether different position. Under the gaze of the baroque melancholic the site where sorrow takes place is the actual world and its realities and, ultimately, nothing beyond the physical body that resides in this world. Suffering and pain are deeply rooted in historical reality so that for Benjamin, questions of melancholy *are* in fact related to the world itself and not to the enclosed subjective apparatus. Benjamin's understanding of the baroque thus situates the suffering body within rather than opposite the world. The empty, fallen world, lacking any possibility of salvation or redemption, is not in any sense a projection or a way to describe how the world comes to affect the psyche—it is not a psychological state or a pathology but reality.

In a short essay entitled "Outline of the Psychophysical Problem" (*SW*, 1:393–401) Benjamin attempts to understand the metaphysical difference between the two sensations of pleasure and pain based on their physical manifestations; his model will serve me here. In this essay Benjamin posits a special relation between the body and self-consciousness (or a certain self-awareness) (*SW*, 1:394). One feels oneself through the body, particularly through feelings of pleasure and pain.[17] This self-discovery or self-feeling can be conceived of as the manner in which pain lets us feel anew and in some ways redefines our bodies. There Benjamin does not specifically address Freud but, interestingly, opens up two of Freud's major categories. In his "Inhibitions, Symptom, Anxiety" Freud refers to the use of the term *pain* for mental and physical conditions. He discusses the difference between the two states through their relation to loss: if mental pain, which results from loss, has to do with losing something that once belonged to you, then physical pain is its opposite, inasmuch as it has a quality of intensifying a feeling, or making us feel one of our organs (which is in pain) more acutely (*SE*, 20:171). In that sense we are "gaining" an organ, or a new feeling of such an organ, rather than losing it. This analysis positions these two types of "pain" as alternative and even contradictory.[18] Pain challenges, questions, the borders of our bodies—a body in pain becomes foreign and unfamiliar to itself. During extreme pain we suddenly seem to rediscover certain organs and feel our bodies' periphery anew. Something about pain thus reconnects us to ourselves; it unfolds our bodies before us.[19] According to Benjamin pleasure and pain not only mark a stark physical difference in experience, but first and foremost they manifest completely divergent metaphysical structures.

Approached this way, the view that pleasure and pain are forms of sensation positioned on opposite ends of one scale is undermined in favor of a conception that each of these types of sensation embodies a completely distinct metaphysical structure. In other words the difference is structural rather than quantitative.

In looking into the structure of pleasure and pain in conjunction with how the German language describes these two sensations, Benjamin claims that pain is more primary than pleasure because of the way in which language characterizes these sensations. That is to say, the metaphysical difference is here linguistically established. Whereas pleasure remains on the body's threshold ("sweetness" and "delight" relate pleasure to taste, the most peripheral and superficial of the senses), pain extends into the realm of the soul:

> With the words "pain," "hurt," "agony," "suffering" we see very clearly what is only hinted at in such a word as "delight" in the realm of pleasure—namely, that in pain, without any recourse to metaphor, the sensuous words directly implicate the soul. This may be explained by the fact that the feelings of pain are incomparably more capable of expressing genuine diversity than the feelings of pleasure, which differ mainly in degree. (*SW,* 1:397; emphasis added)

Although the pain described here is physical (in contrast to mental pain or adversity such as responses to loss, mourning, or sadness—which are all emotional pangs), it nonetheless has a privileged—rather than metaphoric, as Benjamin stresses—access to the soul. Thus, when looking into the psychophysical problem alluded to in the essay's title, we find pain occupying a crucial role.

At this point Benjamin turns to what seems to be of utmost importance to his earlier essays on language: the problem of expression. Pain not only has a special relation to our souls; it is also something we, as humans, share with nature. Furthermore, something about pain seeks, as well as yields, a unique way of expression in humans:

> Undoubtedly there is a connection between the fact that the feeling of pain applies more consistently to the whole nature of man and its ability to endure. This endurance, in turn, leads directly to the metaphysical differences between the two feelings . . . Only the feeling of pain, both on the physical and metaphysical planes, is capable of such an uninterrupted flow—what might be termed a "thematic treatment." Man is the most consummate instrument of pain: only in human suffering

does pain find its adequate expression; only in human life does it flow to its destination, of all the corporeal feelings, pain alone is like a navigable river which never dries up and which leads man down to the sea. Pleasure, in contrast, turns out to be a dead end wherever man tried to follow its lead. (*SW*, 1:397)

Here the expression of pain is described as a "flow," a "river," reaching a destination, and so on. Such images strengthen the importance of the entanglement of pain with expression. Man is the most consummate instrument of pain since he carries pain via its expression "to its destination"; or, in other words, there is a teleological movement in human pain because it can be consummately expressed. In this, humans are unparalleled in nature (which includes plants as well as animals for Benjamin), which is incapable of actualizing its pain in the same way.

Although he concentrates on human expression here, Benjamin is not referring to expression that is merely physical. It is "physical and metaphysical," meaning an expressive structure that touches on a metaphysical structure that itself transcends the confines of the human body or psyche (this metaphysical direction is in greater evidence in Benjamin's 1916 essay on language).[20] This characterization of expression not only points to a certain quality of human expression; it also alludes to an important connection between pain and the principle behind expression. Standing between pain and pleasure, while placing pain as the primary condition, is the definition of expression as something flowing toward a destination. Pleasure leads to a dead end; this is the reason why its birth or origin is of primal importance. After its emergence pleasure simply dissipates. In that sense laughter in the *Trauerspiel* appears as bursts that erupt but soon subside.

In contrast, pain, for Benjamin, is a river that never dries up. The eternal quality of its flow is what makes it permanent, chronic, and uninterrupted (characteristics that define its flow *and* the quality of pain itself, with "chronic" understood here as an attribute of repetitive and continuous pain but also of expression [*SW*, 1:396–97]). The chronic nature of pain is significant here. This is not the product of a causal event resulting in immediate and severe pain that will shortly disappear (like the acute pain caused by being hit, for instance). In its chronic form pain is continually present in such a way that even if it once had an identifiable cause, this cause has disappeared. Pain's capacity to intensify links it to endurance (here in a religious sense as well) and to incessant upward movements. Such uninterruptedness increases and reinforces pain but also ensures that it reaches its destination—that is, publicly shared expression. There is a sudden transgression manifested in bursts of laughter signaling the intrusion of pain by mirth. In pain, however, its chronic flow prohibits such transgression and continuously issues forth from within a liminal position.

These questions of pain and its forms of expression are elaborated in Benjamin's reading of the *Trauerspiel*, specifically, its distinctive way of expressing *Trauer*, mourning, sadness, or melancholy. Benjamin's reading of the *Trauerspiel* gives the impression that no distinct differentiation separates the body from the soul so that the expression of sadness and suffering is actually manifested in the body, with no need to cross any border or leap out of itself. Employing the terms used in the essay on the psychophysical problem, we can say that there is no interruption. Expression flows effortlessly and uninterruptedly from soul to body and vice versa. Not only does the body become part of the apparatus expressing internal pain; it magnifies this expressive character to the point of excess. The body's presence in the *Trauerspiel*, its extreme materiality and the constant sensation of its boundaries—or, rather, of its borderlessness within the world—creates a curious realm whose radicalism captures Benjamin's interest.

The Bombastic Nature of Expression in the *Trauerspiel*

Positioned between the emotional and the physical, the materialization of expression is performed in the baroque *Trauerspiel* in an excessive, bombastic manner that is as far as can be from any natural form of expression. Baroque theater and in many senses the baroque state of mind tend to *overactualize* their pain and sadness. This overactualization differs significantly from the model of physical pain: it is neither immediate nor natural but contrived. The most dominant feature of physical pain is absent here. And whereas expression seems necessary, this necessity is voiced in a stylized, bombastic manner, eliminating its own possibility of being a natural or immediate response.[21]

Relocating the question of expression in the realm of feeling and mental states suggests a different model in which the expressive structure can be described as "self-sufficient" or self-contained. But how is feeling, if defined as internal and self-contained, to be enclosed within the confines of the subject, and which expressive model should it use? Sadness and melancholy appear to be, at least intuitively, a stifling of internal pain, an experience drawing us in rather than compelling us toward excessive external expressiveness. This dual structure once more calls forth a comparison between physical and mental pain, together with the varying forms of expression.

Consider the expression of sadness. It seems that the *Trauerspiel*'s playwrights treat sadness almost as *bodily affliction*. They thus render it as an adversity that demands creaturely, corporeal expression. This shift from the internalized and "quiet," cultivated sadness to one of extreme externalization—almost to the point where what is externalized becomes detached from the suffering subject—is characteristic of the structure of *Trauer*. *Trauer*, then, is located on the fold between the inner and the outer, between extreme closure and radical, ineluctable expression(ism). The use of artificial and exaggerated bodily gestures in the *Trauerspiel* bears witness to the absence of self-sufficiency in baroque theater, which functions in a space inundated by expression or even expressionism (a tendency Benjamin mentions in the book's prologue). To use Michael Fried's terms, absorption becomes theatricality.[22]

Benjamin discusses the relationship between *Trauer* and ostentation as it is articulated in the case of the manifest artificiality of the *Trauerspiel*, the most overt form of expression and that which illustrates most distinctively the relation between interiority and exteriority. "A certain ostentation is characteristic of . . . [the baroque] people. Their images are displayed in order to be seen, arranged in the way they want them to be seen" (*TS*, 119). Here Benjamin interestingly relates the dialectics between the internal and the external that govern pensiveness and ostentation, demonstrating that these two traits appear in parallel in the baroque so that their disposition remains on the edge between the internal and external. Further along in the text he links pensiveness and the passionate interest in pomp, which he understands partly as an escape from the "restrictions of pious domesticity" and partly as a response to the "natural affinity of pensiveness and gravity." These connections provide, according to Benjamin, the basis for the relation between mourning and ostentation that is so brilliantly displayed in the language of the baroque (*TS*, 140).

Pensiveness and pomp go hand in hand—the saddest, most private pain appears parallel to its most exaggerated externalization. The daily domesticity Benjamin describes is set against the pomp of the plays, the theatricality of which is as far from the mundane as can be imagined. That is, this attraction to the bombastic comes from the distanced and solipsistic melancholic disposition that Benjamin connects to pious domesticity. Crucially, there is no causal relationship between these two extremes—it is not that extreme inwardness leads to expression; they in fact appear in conjunction.[23] Moreover, there is no real point of transition between the two states. The necessity of expressing internal pain is thus structured differently from the instinctive reflex of bodily pain; instead, it acts on the borderline between the inner and the outer and is, in some sense, preoccupied with the threshold itself or with the question of whether such a threshold even exists. This act is not a "natural" response or reflex but, rather, a deep embedding within liminal dialectics themselves.

The said dialectics between inwardness and extensive externalization returns us to the relation between subject and world. Benjamin indicates in a note that "the word *Trauerspiel* was applied in the seventeenth century to dramas and to historical events alike" and uses Erdmannsdörffer's characterization of world events during the baroque to describe the way the *Trauerspiel* staged itself. In this analogy the "subject" and historical "objective" events dissolve into one another to become one, and the distinction between the "subjective" expression of social catastrophes and their historical manifestation is obliterated. What is customarily condemned as bombast in the plays from the baroque is the tendency of authors and playwrights to write texts that speak of war and its disasters in "an extravagant tone of plaintive lamentation," a tone that acquires the "character of a fixed mannerism; an incessant hand-wringing [*händeringende*] mode of expression." The writing of the time, continues Benjamin while citing Erdmannsdörffer, is completely lacking in nuance (*TS*, 64). This description speaks of the different ways in which the *Trauerspiel* chose to present itself. We immediately grasp that these traits all involve an extreme mode of excess and abundance, especially in light of Erdmannsdörffer's remarkable portrayal of this mode as "hand-wringing."

This specific account refers to the German term for expression, *Ausdruck*, whose literal meaning signifies precisely such pressing, wringing, or squeezing. The structure of expression thus has a tangible physical meaning—it is what is literally pressed and pushed out, *Aus-Druck*. In other words, in the baroque view, expression, in its general meaning, is contextualized within the *physical* realm. This goes hand in hand with the special physical quality of expression discussed earlier, in which mental dejection is physically placated. The plaintive lamentations and mannerisms also go together with an excessiveness of expression that "lack[s] nuance," a deficiency that is part of a play's bombastic quality. And because expression is always extreme and ineluctable, extravagance and ostentation are the *only* modes in which *Trauer* can be articulated. No restrained manifestation is possible. Since the existence of pain renders it immediately presentable, no internal pain exists in the *Trauerspiel*; every pain is immediately exteriorated.

Such a nuance-free mode of expression is indicated in Buci-Glucksmann's suggestion that what she calls "baroque reason" is in fact based on a stylistic and rhetorical form of reason in which "the baroque signifier proliferates beyond everything signified, placing language in excess of corporality."[24] She stresses the presence of the body in the baroque and the way in which the very display of the body (even if violated, or precisely because it is violated) evokes the infinite *jouissance* that defines the baroque's unique structure of meaning. Her account goes further by locating these characteristics specifically in the language of the baroque, following Benjamin's own main juncture with the *Trauerspiel*. The logic of the baroque, consequently, goes against the idea of a self-enclosed language; it appeals to allegory, oxymoron, and discordant details, whereas the real is emptied of its superabundance of reality.[25]

This proliferation of hyperbole constitutes the exact converse of what can be called an entirety or even of what can be called some form of consistency or self-sufficiency. In fact, the *Trauerspiel* is as far as can be from such self-containment, so easily found in what Benjamin invokes as the *Trauerspiel*'s mirror image: tragedy. The self-contained identity of the tragic hero is replaced in the *Trauerspiel* by an infinite number of figures, all approaching the single protagonist's glory but never quite able to realize it. We thus find that in the plays the only way to realize such fullness—if it can be realized at all—is through the communal presence of all the characters on the stage, a combined presence that is fundamentally excessive. According to Friedlander tragedy offers a concentration of fate in an individual protagonist, whereas in the *Trauerspiel* there is no identifiable single protagonist, and the polyphony of fate is therefore "scattered" among the different figures of the princely court.[26]

Expounding on the problem of the contrast between the two models of meaning—self-sufficient and self-contained meaning versus constantly oscillating meaning—itself suggests allegory. Allegory is not only the chief literary device used in these baroque plays; it is also what Benjamin locates at the crux of his interpretation. Writing in 1928, he declares that the *Trauerspiel* book is "devoted to exploring the philosophical significance of a vanished and misunderstood form of art: allegory" (*SW*, 2:77–78). One of the most important features of allegorical form, for Benjamin, is its unique structure of meaning, unstable and fluctuating, in a constant state of deferral—the complete opposite of self-sufficient meaning. Such unsteadiness similarly marks the allegorist's essentially melancholic state of mind, as he constantly searches for a way to stabilize meaning and control its turbulent, inconstant nature.

Benjamin's grasp of allegory is quite far from its traditional understanding. Instead of treating it as a form of literal narrative, he views it as a system of signifiers that does not maintain a stable, or codified, relation to what it signifies. As Jennings demonstrates, the production of meaning in allegory eventually breaks down as it resists the mimetic representation of meaningful objects. Instead of providing an integral relationship between signifier and signified, it treats meaning as arbitrary and chaotic.[27] In other words it resists meaning rather than constructs it. The correspondence between the object of allegory and its unstable meaning produces a literary construct in which meaning can only be secured subjectively. That is, since the object does not itself contain meaning, the signifying system in turn cannot provide it with meaning—we must remain satisfied, therefore, with the allegorist's own subjective interpretation.

A state in which "any person, any object, any relationship can mean absolutely anything else . . . is characterized as a world in which the detail is of no great importance" (*TS*, 175), and it leaves us with a world devoid of essential or natural meaning, a world open to any subjective and arbitrary point of view. Benjamin describes this condition through the antinomy of expression and convention—two diametric characteristics of

The Trauer-Spiel   87

allegorical practice. He thus writes that allegory is "convention of expression, and expression of convention"—and consequently engaged more with the authority of the interpreter than with any text's inherent, necessary meaning. The mirror image of allegory is symbol. Symbols contain intrinsic and comprehensive meaning. They are replete with meaning; they exhibit a stability totally contrary to that of allegory's structure. In Benjamin's analysis symbols thus show none of the indecisive, unstable movement identified with allegory's repeated attempts to hold on to meaning. The theatrical equivalents of these mirror images, symbol and allegory, are, of course, tragedy and *Trauerspiel*, respectively.

It follows that if tragedy is the keen manifestation of immaculate closure and the stability of meaning, the *Trauerspiel* is all about indeterminacy. This structure holds true for the discussion of expression and its limitations, too. Allegory's allegedly prolific and rich expressions are, in fact, revealed as empty masks, devoid of any inherent significance. Allegory does not, however, simply manifest the lack of natural meaning; it invests the world with new arbitrary meaning, in what Weber describes as a mere masquerade or spectacle. The world is, therefore, "no longer simply empty of meaning: it is, simultaneously, and hence inauthentically overflowing with meaning."[28] This is yet another version of the allegorical structure of an amalgam of emptiness and excessiveness.

After contemplating the structure of meaning in tragedy and *Trauerspiel*, Benjamin describes tragedy as, among other things, capable of presenting its own conditions of possibility. Alternatively, in the case of the *Trauerspiel* the plays neither express the conditions bringing about their grief, nor do they invoke grief in the audience. What they manifest most clearly is rather the depth of the current state of mourning and pain. In that sense these plays are intended for those *already in* mourning:

> The very name [of *Trauerspiel*] . . . already indicates that its content awakens mourning in the spectator. But it does not by any means follow that this content could be any better expressed in the categories of empirical psychology than could the content of tragedy—it might far rather mean that these plays could serve better to describe mourning than could the condition of grief. For these are not so much plays which cause mourning, as plays through which the mournfulness finds satisfaction: plays for the mournful [*Denn sie sind nicht so sehr das Spiel, das traurig macht, als jenes, über dem die Trauer ihr Genügen findet: Spiel vor Traurigen*]. (*TS*, 118–19)

Those who are already mournful within the baroque audience find satisfaction in the re-presentation of their own sadness on the stage. It is as if they see themselves presented on the stage in accurate mirror images that express the agony of their own lives: "Living as they did in an atmosphere of war and bloody conflict, they found such scenes quite natural; they were being presented with a picture of their own life. They delighted naively and brutally in the pleasure offered them" (*TS*, 53).[29] This, however, does not induce feelings of empathy or pity in response to the theatrical presentation, since such feelings are necessarily based on a fundamental distance from the drama, on an inherent lack of continuity between the audience and the characters onstage. When baroque spectators view the play, they see the actions and characters as resonating with their *own* pain—something that does not produce self-pity. In that sense the *Trauerspiel* is not so much concerned with a theatrical representation of the external world on the stage as with the presentation of their own reality. This structure is manifest in the close affinity between the subject matter of the plays and the contemporary historical events, the use of nonprofessional actors, and the barely discernible boundary between the stage and the audience (in stage structure, as well as in the audience's aforementioned responses)—all of which testify to the fundamental blurred borders between theater and reality, representation and presentation, artificial and natural.

The need to express their plight is here transformed into a need for the theatrical, the artificial—as if this were the only way for the people of the baroque to mollify their dejection. The ostentation that Benjamin describes is related to the only way such expression can come about in a theatrical, nuance-free manner: "The *Trauerspiel* is conceived as a pantomime," writes Benjamin, alluding to the exaggerated, overstated character of the form.[30] Lacking a linguistic component, pantomime is usually conceived of as a locus of particularly "ham" gestures. In the sense of its "pure," languageless appearance, pantomime seems to be clearer in its form of expressiveness than are other theatrical forms, yet its mute and exaggerated form nevertheless renders it excessively amplified and lavish. And, since more than one movement is occurring at the same time, those movements are choreographed; they "take the form of 'pantomime,' voiceless mimes that not only take the place of eschatological narrative

The Trauer-Spiel   89

but become the very means by which its loss is registered."³¹ Theatrical expression, given that the gestures on which pantomime is based lack a referent, therefore does not point at anything external to its own faltering expressive attempts.

Benjamin's discussion of "pantomimic" expression thus indirectly alludes to the *Trauerspiel*, which are *spoken* plays and not mute pantomime performances. The exaggerated manner suitable to silent plays is used in the *Trauerspiel* in more normative, nonsilent theatrical forms.³² The extreme artificiality of this mode of the externalization of sadness has to do with the inability of baroque theater to express feelings in a mild manner. Feelings are always extreme in their intensity, as well as in their expression, and the model of pantomime and excessive gestures does not necessarily contrast with the appearance of dialogues in the plays, but rather results from them. These dialogues, however, manifest language's deficiency in constantly supporting speech with excessive artificial gestures. The need for theatrical means to support the play and its text is a continual reminder that the play cannot support itself autonomously and is always doomed to depend on external measures.

Hamlet's odd behavior as the spectator at the theatrical representation of his father's murder, which he himself arranged, is an interesting demonstration of the relationship between such a linguistic deficiency and the theatrical representation. As we recall, Hamlet has arranged for the theater group to produce a play depicting his father's murder, as he understands it from the account given by his father's ghost. Hamlet plans to confront his uncle, Claudius, now King of Denmark, with a representation of Claudius's killing of the former king to bring the regicide to a point of crisis where Claudius will, so Hamlet believes, confess his crime. Throughout the performance Hamlet keeps interrupting by making vulgar outbursts, standing up and walking about, explaining all the events taking place on the stage, directly addressing the king and so forth. Instead of letting the play "speak for itself," his original intention, Hamlet acts as if he cannot rely on the staged self-presentation of truth. He behaves as if truth is in constant need of interpretation, reiteration, and support.³³

Such a stance with respect to truth as presented onstage is likewise embodied in the *Trauerspiel*'s tendency to repeatedly "announce" everything that is about to happen, considered to be the materialization of the baroque playwright's need to reinforce everything happening on the stage. This attitude makes it impossible for the play to independently "present itself" onstage and eliminates any opportunity for it to realize its dramatic power. The means and instruments meant to strengthen the play's effect ultimately undermine and diminish any self-sufficiency the play may inherently contain. The theatrical expression of this idea is thus rendered crude and coarse, lacking in nuance and focused on its being shown—or shown off—at any price, even that of unwarranted exaggeration. Such excess is also found in the allegorical structure that Benjamin describes as pompous, ornamental, and extravagant, so that the alleged richness of meaning in allegory is thus ultimately repetitive and vague. The ambiguity inherent in this literary form, expressed in its extravagance, sharply opposes the natural rules of economy, unity, and clarity applied to the presentation of meaning in tragedy.[34]

The stage accessories in the *Trauerspiel* provide further examples of the bombastic structure: their abundance emphasizes what the plays cannot, supposedly, present by themselves. The material objects scattered onstage take part in the expression of feelings, performing a role almost equal to that of the protagonists. In that sense the *Trauerspiel* differs immensely from tragedy—the latter is limited to the human sphere, whereas the former travels almost equally between the human and the material spheres. The fate of the protagonist in the *Trauerspiel* is therefore not only conditioned by the roles played by objects around him, but this fate is also shared by them. The tragic focus on dialogical form and a narrative structure that is fundamentally dependent on the hero's actions is transformed in the *Trauerspiel* into a preoccupation with mise-en-scène: the stage, spatial arrangement, stage accessories, and so forth. That is, the focus on the human is completely changed to an absorption in the protagonist's environment and the objects occupying it.

Benjamin refers to this characteristic as the rhetorical apostrophe that he dubs "look how . . . " (*TS*, 192): the positioning of artificiality's excessiveness in the explanatory realm. The constant explanatory interludes explaining and pointing-at ("look how") nearly empty the plays of their immanent ability to present meaning and surround the *Trauerspiel* with a dense ambience of elucidations and vindications that arrest the narrative at every possible turn. This ornateness soon makes clear why baroque plays have been so vigorously discounted by those who compare them to the epitome of self-sufficiency and immanence: Greek tragedy.

The implications of this interrupted structure on the protagonists of the *Trauerspiel* plays, but especially on their linguistic expressions onstage, are interestingly illustrated when Benjamin cites Ernst Wilken's comparison of the characters in these plays to the figures in old paintings who had scrolls extending from their mouths to designate what they are saying (*TS*, 197), a method similar to caricature or comics, another mode that uses exaggeration, outsized gestures, and so forth. R. M. Meyer is also cited as saying: "We find it almost horrifying that there was a time when every figure created by the hand of an artist had, so to speak, such a scroll in its mouth, which the observer was supposed to read like a letter, and then forget the bearer" (*TS*, 197).

This illustration of the scroll is powerful in two respects. First, it presents the question of externalization graphically, in a manner capturing the epitome of artificiality and exaggeration, while linking linguistic expression to the problem of the externalization of feeling. Second, it problematizes the question of subjectivity in that the figures coupled with the scrolls become virtually detached from what they are saying. A lacuna is formed between the figure and its text; the "content" becomes independent and unrelated to the figure uttering it, as if the externalization achieves a presence in isolation of who exteriorized it. The subjective agent becomes absent, with only his empty silhouette onstage, and the words become independent entities. A similar idea appears in the prologue when Benjamin characterizes the literary and philosophical form of the medieval treatise through a comparison of speech to the writing of the treatise: in speech the speaker uses both words and gestures to construct meaning, "as if producing a bold sketch in a single attempt" (*TS*, 29). The writer, however, "must stop and restart with every new sentence" (*TS*, 29). No support is ever sufficient for the form of writing the treatise demonstrates. Single strokes must do, and meaning can only be transmitted as partial.

One of the core questions in the context of the *Trauerspiel* is whether the externalization of feeling, specifically, sadness and melancholy, can be something other than bombastic and excessive in this form of theatrical expression. Would it be accurate to say that what the *Trauerspiel* in fact manifests is the idea that the only possibility to express feeling is by way of spectacle and extravagance? This view insists that quiet, cultivated expression implies feeling that is insufficiently deep, agonizing, and arduous; a calculated and preset manner of expression alludes to a processed feeling rather than to penetrating woe. Moreover, could it be claimed that such a type of expression like that manifested in the *Trauerspiel* has to do with the inability to contain and control feeling, specifically sadness?

This problem is manifested not only in the characters onstage but also when the chorus appears. The chorus, an integral part of Greek tragedy, serves Benjamin as an interesting point of comparison to expressions of *Trauer*, as well as to show, once again, the way the *Trauerspiel* was misjudged as not complying with tragedy's criteria owing to the critic's misconception of this form. The chorus in tragedy serves to curb, if not stifle, expressions of lament in response to pain: "Really the chorus of the tragedy does not lament. It remains detached in the presence of profound suffering" (*TS*, 121). It stands detached and impassive, not because of its indifference to the events but because of the role assigned to it. "Far from dissolving the tragic action into lamentations, the constant presence of the members of the chorus . . . actually sets a limit on the emotional outburst even in the dialogue" (*TS*, 121).

Hence, the chorus in tragedy does not collapse into lamentation and mourning but, on the contrary, occludes or forestalls such outbursts and sets bounds on the responses to what occurs onstage. The emotional extremes so typical of the *Trauerspiel* are here turned into their opposites. As Benjamin argues, the chorus might very well be the site where tragedy's restraints and inhibitions present themselves most clearly; that is, the chorus is a theatrical entity that demonstrates the way in which sorrow should be handled in "civilized society." No excessive moans or cries are allowed, no unnecessary outbursts. In holding everything together, it offers a model for a restrained, almost stoic, response to suffering.

In the case of the *Trauerspiel* the role of the chorus is completely different. It not only neglects to restrict sorrowful laments and moaning; it virtually serves as the vehicle of their intense, inflated expression. The baroque's reinterpretation (in Benjamin's terms) or failed imitation (in the hostile critic's terms) of the role of the chorus incited widespread criticism. Its modified role is described as follows:

The conception of the chorus as a *Trauerklage* [lamentation], in which 'the original pain of creation resounds', is a genuinely baroque reinterpretation of its essence... Its second function is less obvious. The choruses of the baroque drama are not so much interludes, like those of ancient drama, as frames enclosing the act, which bear the same relationship to it as the ornamental borders in Renaissance printing to the type area. They serve to emphasize the nature of the act as part of a mere spectacle. The chorus of the *Trauerspiel* is therefore usually more elaborate and less directly connected to the action than the chorus of the tragedy. (*TS*, 121–22)

Benjamin therefore understands the role of the chorus in the *Trauerspiel* as a theatrical device for restoring the primal cry of pain. It manifests the most profound and most "*Trauer*-ful" of all the figures onstage. In so doing, it opposes the tragic chorus in two respects: in voicing instead of stifling pain and in distancing itself from the actual scene to which it is linked. Any specific wretchedness and dejection is always decontextualized by the chorus so as to allude to a broader and more primal desolation. If the tragic chorus serves as an interlude and uses its arresting character to smother the expression of pain, the chorus in the *Trauerspiel* chooses not to interfere in the action so that expressions of pain and woe can be deepened rather than obstructed.[35]

This framing and decontextualization (rather than interruption) of the act is related to the ornamental character of the chorus in the *Trauerspiel*. Its being on the play's outskirts, a mere illustration, points to a certain quality of flatness. Lament is thus not intensified but flattened through empty repetition. These "frames" are transformed into spectacle, preventing the audience from classic-Aristotelian identification with the play's characters while allowing only an external, detached gaze at those same characters. The pompous quality of the chorus thus echoes and duplicates the form of sadness found in the members of the audience themselves. The plays are thus "for the mournful," who find them to be a vehicle to achieve satisfaction in their grief.

This important problem can be illustrated through the figure of the ruler, to which Benjamin devotes some sections of the first part of his book. Benjamin emphasizes that this figure is defined and depicted chiefly in terms of its sovereign power and authority. The comparison of the ruling prince with the sun captures this characterization, stressing the exclusivity of sovereignty (*TS*, 67). The theatrical representation of such power is, however, usually presented negatively—namely, in the collapse of the ruler's consummate power. Benjamin presents this collapse by means of his critique of Carl Schmitt's theory of the "state of emergency," perhaps one of the most widely interpreted of the book's arguments.[36]

In a state of emergency the absoluteness of sovereign power is invoked in order to prevent catastrophe, albeit intensifying the acuteness of the situation. As Schmitt underscores, however, it is the sovereign himself who declares the state of emergency as a state of exception; moreover, it is the exception that validates the norm, or, in Benjamin's terms in the prologue, it is the extreme that sets the conditions of possibility of the average (*TS*, 35). This act of declaration of the exception is what, according to Schmitt, provides the sovereign with power. This conception redefines the realm of sovereign power: instead of power being an execution of the law of the state, it can only be executed in the extreme state of emergency. The sovereign is given unconditional and unlimited power, which in fact serves to protect the state from consequences resulting from the limitations of its lawful functioning in extreme states of emergency. Very soon, however, these extreme states become the norm and validate sovereign power only in the condition of exception.

Benjamin uses Schmitt's theory in his interpretation of a typical political practice during the Counter-Reformation: the assigning of dictatorial power to the ruler should war or revolt break out and instigate a state of emergency. The reasoning behind this practice was to ensure that the ruler have sufficient power to stabilize the community and ensure its continuity; however, this oft-considered and problematic political structure induces a constant state of emergency. Eventually, stricken by the outcomes of his excessive power, the ruler completely collapses into melancholy or insanity: "the seventeenth-century ruler, the summit of creation, erupting into madness like a volcano and destroying himself and his entire court" (*TS*, 70). As Weber has shown, however, despite his tone of admiration toward Schmitt, Benjamin in fact introduces the latter's terminology with some decisive modifications.

In opposition to Schmitt, Benjamin's analysis of sovereignty delineates the sovereign as he who excludes the state of exception and this not only with regard to the state in the political sense, but also to the state of exception as such, that which transcends the political state in general. Weber concludes that the importance of the notion of sovereignty for

Benjamin lies in its "transcending transcendence by making it immanent, an integral part of the state and of the world, of the state of the world... In this perspective, the function of the sovereign to exclude the state of exception conforms fully to the attempt of the German baroque to exclude transcendence *by incorporating it*."[37]

Agamben notes that sovereign power lies in its ability to legally and legitimately suspend the validity of the state's law. Accordingly, the paradox of sovereignty consists in that "the sovereign, having the legitimate power to suspend the law, finds himself at the same time outside and inside the juridical order... The sovereign *legally* places himself outside the law."[38] The state of exception is therefore always defined against the background of the legal order as what essentially stands outside of it; the legal order is, accordingly, maintained only in relation to the exception, and this in the very face of the rule's own suspension. This structure is demonstrated in Schmitt's claim that not only does the exception confirm the rule, but "the rule as such lives off the exception alone."[39]

Among the devices that Benjamin uses to delineate this paradoxical figure are his references to the sovereign's obsessive relations to the objects surrounding him, objects that symbolize his rule and power. The sovereign gathers them repeatedly about himself (in a way similar to the allegorical gathering of objects) in a utilitarian fashion, as if to secure (*TS*, 69), rather than merely symbolize, his sovereignty. In the process these symbols become much more important than the execution of ascendancy per se, to the point where they appear to actualize power itself. The sovereign comes to use the gestures of executive power even when unnecessary, a habit that culminates in imparting his passive submission to the plight of power to those same objects.

The turn to oversymbolization thus involves an element of cover-up, of veiling this impotency by focusing on objects.[40] In other words the symbols of such power effectively hide the ruler's lack of executive power. The exaggeration employed in pointing at objects such as the robe, scepter, or crown, items employed even when the ruler does not require them, empties the ruler of his capacity for active power. The problem of political sovereignty is translated into the world of the inanimate, of external yet empty expressions of power that cannot be exercised. This structure resembles that of the state of emergency, in which the definition of virtually every state as an emergency empties this term of its unique meaning. As Lutz Koepnick puts it, the very emptiness of the world is what provides the ruler with absolute power, yet that same emptiness invokes depression; it promises to turn its empty gaze back upon the ruler. It simultaneously generates and undermines the possibility of power's exercise.[41]

The crux of the ruler's paradox lies in his holding so immeasurable an amount of power that renders him incapable of exercising it; he is therefore caught between the mere possibility of exercising absolute power and a complete paralysis. As Friedlander shows, this internal contradiction between the sovereign's authority and his capacity to execute it is what causes him to become a tyrant. But not only that: it is the way the sovereign embodies divine or absolute power that is the reason for the internal conflicts that turn him into a mere creature. Understanding Benjamin's claim that the martyr and tyrant are two sides of the same coin (*TS*, 70) calls for a grasping of the underpinnings of the sovereign's position: that which requires the excessive use of power turns the sovereign into a tyrant on the one hand, but the essential incapacity to execute this power renders him a martyr on the other.[42]

Pain and Spectacle: The Figure of the Martyr

Benjamin's preoccupation with the figure of the martyr, especially in its intersections with sovereignty, is found most often in the "martyr-drama," a subgenre of the *Trauerspiel*. According to Benjamin there is a structural similarity in the struggles of both the sovereign and the martyr: the power and endurance of both is at (the) stake when they are struggling for the crown or grappling with torture and death in the religious context. The tyrant's central undertaking is the restoration of order in the state of emergency, whereas the aim of the stoic martyr is to incorporate, so to speak, the state of emergency into his very soul, where he is fortified by his endurance of the internal state of exception he now harbors (*TS*, 74). Benjamin thus links the suffering of the martyr in the Christian martyr-drama to the Passion of Christ: "Just as Christ, the King, suffered in the name of mankind, so, in the eyes of the writers of the baroque, does royalty in general" (*TS*, 73).

The exploration of the hyperbolic nature of the different forms of expression of physical and mental pain in the *Trauerspiel* leads us toward another important structural characterization of the plays. The extravagant nature of pain's expression not only marks an inherent deficiency in the play's inner configuration but also points at the essential interconnection and peculiar affinity between the configuration of pain and suffering in the *Trauerspiel* and their excessive, embellished form of expression. The martyr's suffering is consistently defined, within its religious context, as a suffering for all humankind, devoid of any subjective, individual pain, whether in reference to redemption or in the most material of senses. The martyr's tortured body becomes, in its suffering, everyone's body. Its lacerations revealed to all eyes, it provides a material equivalent to the terrible cries of "inner," private, sensations of extreme pain.

The Greek word *martyr*, the etymological source for the German *Märtyrer*, denotes a witness. The word's origin places the martyr's suffering in the context of the visible or witnessable in two possible senses. First, it is linked to the martyr's own witnessing of God's presence, marked by the very fact of suffering itself, which could not be feasible without such presence; second, it has to do with the fact that for the martyr to be so defined, his suffering and agony has to be *witnessed* by others, rendered publicly visible. The meaning of his suffering is thus defined by the communal nature of his pain: the public articulation, in cries and screams, as well as its public implications, as pain or suffering that brings universal salvation. This overt form of pain concerns the religious ordeal of suffering *for* others; hence, his tribulations must be witnessable even if not realized as a full-fledged spectacle. The martyr experiences his ordeal not only for himself but for his fellow human beings—he suffers so that others can sense God's presence through his own suffering, and thus be redeemed.

In this persistent correspondence between the ethical and the aesthetic, between pain and theater, martyrdom bears an extravagant quality: it is overdone in order to be seen. We therefore find a strong element of theatricality in the religious figure of the martyr. His pain is unremittingly on display. Furthermore, his "suffering" alludes not only to the pain itself but also to its endurance. One of the martyr's crucial qualities is his ability to bear pain. The Christian martyr is, by definition, a figure who suffers and publicly endures pain prior to his death. Body and soul are disjected: the body suffers affliction while the soul remains strong and rooted in its belief, a faith that, independent of the body, begets redemption.

Benjamin writes that the plays are "not so much concerned with the deeds of the hero as with his suffering, and frequently not so much with his spiritual torment as with the agony of the physical adversity which befalls him" (*TS*, 72). This is another striking difference between tragedy and *Trauerspiel*: instead of focusing on the deeds of the tragic hero, the martyr-drama revolves around the suffering of its characters, concentrating on their extreme physical torments. This remark stresses two important components of the martyr's suffering. First, there is a physical aspect of pain which outweighs its spiritual dimension; the body of the martyr is emphatically material, and it submits itself to be molded by pain. Internal conflicts, sadness, or woe are not part of the specific type of torment suffered by the martyr, whose body becomes the battlefield but whose soul remains aloft.

Second, this pain, in Benjamin's words, "befalls" the martyr at the expense of "deeds." There is a strong element of *passivity* characterizing the martyr's pain: the body surrenders to the inevitability of pain rather than bringing it about. For the martyr, in fact, and this has very strong Christian overtones, the only activity is endurance: "The hero . . . shows magnanimity in all circumstances and courageously overcomes the pain which causes sighing, loud cries, and much lamentation."[43] Yet this passivity is more than matched by the form in which endurance is enacted: unrestrained, in clamorous moans and cries in which the body's stamina finds voice in loud and inescapable sounds. Such wailing presents, once more, a picture of externalized anguish, loudly signifying the overflowing of the body's boundaries, in a transgression also found in accounts of physical torture.

All cases of physical torments of the martyr (as opposed to the sovereign who turns into a martyr when madness strikes him) are presented as acts of tyranny, the results of a despot's arbitrary decision. Since it is clear from the start that the protagonist is a martyr and not a villain, there is no space for contemplation regarding the cause of torture, which usually befalls the protagonists because of their faith (usually Christian). In most cases the plays progress rather quickly to the punishment scene and focus on graphic depictions of physical torture and unjust punishment rather than on the purported causes for these woes, and the plasticity of the protagonist's agonies come to occupy center stage.

This is evident, for example, with the eponymous heroine of Gryphius's *Catharina von Georgien* (Benjamin takes special note of the female martyrs of the dramas [*TS*, 73–74]).[44] Catharina embodies an exemplary figure of the martyr, and the play is filled with allusions to the similarities between the protagonist and Jesus Christ. These allusions are suggested by Catharina in several occasions in the text, especially when she describes a dream she had in which the roses her damsel gives her turn into a crown of thorns in her hand (act 4, lines 339–70). Catharina's only crime is her fidelity to her religion and the unwillingness to save herself by converting to Islam.[45] By not accepting the Chach Abas's proposal of marriage, which requires her conversion to Islam, Catharina chooses a horrible death: her torturers beat her, cut her flesh, place steaming iron pliers on her skin, and finally burn her at the stake. The grotesquely graphic accounts of her brutal torment (mainly in acts 4 and 5) remain stirring even to the postmodern ear. In act 5 of the play Serena, one of the maids, describes Catharina's torture in a disturbing account: Catharina's body is completely torn open and the marks of the violent beating are fiercely engraved into her tortured skin. When the steaming iron forceps touch her body "with a scalding sound," her flesh disappears, almost vaporizes and melts like "snow touch[ed] with a flame." Her blood shoots out of her veins and over her scorched skin, and pieces of flesh hang down from her thighs and expose the material interiority of her body. Her lungs are literally opened up and exposed, so that her soul can be seen as it begins to leave her disfigured body.[46] It is as if Catharina's anguish literally leaves the interior of her body and is scattered in the (at least theatrical) world. This graphic description is a startling manifestation of the previously discussed theatrical modes of expression in the *Trauerspiel*.

The extreme corporeal, somatic aspects of the martyr's pain raise the question of materiality and its importance for the structure of meaning in Benjamin's interpretation of the *Trauerspiel*. Benjamin's interest in the figure of the martyr lies not only in its being a dominant theatrical figure in the baroque *Trauerspiel* but, perhaps foremost, since the martyr represents for Benjamin a figure having meaning, in its emphasizing the dominance of materiality in his account of the appearance of meaning in the *Trauerspiel*, indicating that its importance also lies in its extreme materiality: "The human body could be no exception to the commandment which ordered the destruction of the organic so that the true meaning, as it was written and ordained, might be picked up from its fragments. Where indeed, could this law be more triumphantly displayed than in the man who abandoned his conventional, conscious physis in order to scatter it to the manifold regions of meaning?" (*TS*, 216–17). Here Benjamin moves from a theatrical interpretation to an account of the structure of meaning, where the tortured human body is found on the same plane as other material sources of meaning. Choosing to cast the human body as "organic," Benjamin immediately positions it in a realm that is no longer solely human, and the question of whether this body is alive or on the verge of death has no consequences for its being mere material.

There is a consequential echo here between the role of materiality in the theatrical figure of the martyr, on the one hand, and the structure of allegory, on the other. The lacerated body of the martyr comes to resonate with the allegorical work of extracting meaning from material fragments. This resonance appears, in the most literal sense, in *Ars heraldica*: "'Hair signifies many and varied thoughts,' while 'die Herolden' cut the lion right in two: 'The head, the breast, and the whole front part signify magnanimity and courage, but the hind part signifies the strength, rage, and anger, which follow the roar'" (*TS*, 217). The violence performed on the figure of the lion, violence that includes the actual slitting of its body, becomes the condition of possibility for the extraction of meaning. The allegorist is compelled to violate his material so that meaning can emerge, and the allegorical scene thus obtains the character of almost sexual violence.[47]

Bringing the body of the martyr together with the body of allegorical material allows Benjamin to amalgamate the material aspects of the body together with their linguistic implication. "The language of the baroque is constantly convulsed by a rebellion on the part of the elements which make it up . . . Even in their isolation the words reveal themselves as fateful . . . In this way language is broken up so as to acquire a changed and intensified meaning in its fragments" (*TS*, 207–8). Such a linguistic convulsion is echoed in the martyr's dismembered corpse, a figure to be understood in its most literal sense: fragments of text, interruptions, and gaps accord with cuts and bruises as sites of meaning. The physis is abandoned and supplanted by meaning that can only be accessed from the living body's debris.

The martyr's cadaver also signals another core theme in the *Trauerspiel*—the state of being between life and death. The body, in its excruciation, is no longer alive but not yet dead—a living corpse standing on the verge of these two extreme opposites while maintaining its grip on both. The martyr, hovering between life and death, literally embodies this diffusion in his enduring suffering. His relevance for our inquiry into *Trauer* lies exactly in this elemental loss of vitality, a state crucial in the Benjaminian structure of meaning:

And if it is in death that the spirit becomes free, in the manner of spirits, it is not until then that the body too comes properly into its own. For this much is self-evident: the allegorization of the physis can only be carried through in all its vigour in respect of the corpse. And the characters of the *Trauerspiel* die, because it is only thus, as corpses, that they can enter into the homeland of allegory. It is not for the sake of immortality that they meet their end, but for the sake of the corpse. (*TS*, 217–18)

The body's "coming into its own" points to a state of legibility, of meaning. The description of the martyr in these last pages and of the corpse in the above citation should be relocated into the realm of meaning. Meaning "comes to its own" when life is spent, when its last shred disappears into the material. Truth manifests itself only when physis remains, when the material character of the body takes over.

In this process of the emergence of meaning, the importance of the martyr's extreme physical pain does not lie in a Cartesian dualism but in the baroque doctrine of psychophysical determination, namely, in the way in which baroque philosophy and science provide an account of the spirit's encounter with the world (*TS*, 217). This is quite apparent, for instance, in Descartes's treatise "The Passions of the Soul" (1649), in which he gives a detailed account of the ways in which soul and body unite and work conjointly.[48] This occurs in the realm of the physical, specifically, in the pineal gland, which is where Descartes locates the point of interaction between perceptions, sensation, emotions, and reasoning. The interconnection between body and soul accordingly implies interdependence. It is not only the spirit or soul that becomes free but also the body, which then "comes into its own," to use Benjamin's words. Meaning is revealed in the body no less than in the soul.

The difference between *Trauerspiel* and tragedy can now be better understood since the tragic hero's immortality can find no place where meaning emerges from the loss of life. Immortality, in that sense, buries rather than exposes truth. Hence, the cadaver—not the immortal hero—is the site of meaning. The figure of the martyr brings new meaning to Benjamin's famous phrase "Criticism means the mortification of works." Mortification should be understood here in its utmost material form, in which the torn body of the martyr becomes the site of work, and work is performed on mere material. It recalls Freud's definition of melancholia as that which "behaves like an open wound" and "must act like a painful wound" (*SE*, 14:253, 258).

Death and Meaning: The Figure of the Ghost

In materializing its excessive and lethal pain, the figure of the martyr reveals the border between life and death to be torn open. The living body, in its capacity to contain the pain that will ultimately lead to its death, can be seen as a typical *Trauerspiel* site in that it tolerates the inability to differentiate between life and death. Freud's overtly parallel account of the melancholic's lost object as what is not yet dead but no longer alive pertains to this theme since it marks the crucial difference between psychoanalytic thought and Benjamin's understanding of the *Trauerspiel*.

Freud deciphers the relation of the melancholic to the lost object as pathological because the patient does not recognize the loss as a consummate one. The pathology lies in the fact that the border between death and life, or the recognition that death is completely separate from life, is blurred to the melancholic, or at least not definitively accounted for. Unable to surrender to mourning, the melancholic carves out an internal tomb for his lost object, engendering an internal topography in which the living ego and the dead object coexist. However, the spectral nature of Freud's definition of the melancholic reaction is not limited to the blurred border between life and death—it also harbors another crucial quality of the ghost: the lost object, now buried alive, haunts the melancholic. Nicolas Abraham insists that his own conceptualization of what he calls the "phantom" is not applicable to Freud's theory of melancholy (he explains that in the case of melancholy, what haunts is the tomb the melancholic carves within his own ego, whereas what the phantoms come back to haunt are the tombs of others [171–72]), but his insightful remarks about this figure are very useful. Abraham describes the phantom as a metapsychological construal in which it is not the dead that haunts the psyche but rather the internal gaps and breaches that are left within us by their secrets. In his interpretation of Freud, Abraham distinguishes the phantom as what can vanish from the psyche only when the radically heterogeneous nature of its relation to the subject is recognized and revealed.[49]

What is haunting and pathological in Freud turns out to be an inherent, almost essential, violation of borders in the structure of the melancholy baroque, where what seems to the psychoanalytic eye to be a pathological deviation from a norm is viewed as a customary epistemological structure applied and manifested in the baroque's theatrical presentations. Ghostly apparitions, or the "virtual space of spectrality," as Derrida puts it,[50] are usually considered (at least in Western culture) to be fictional constructs or, at times, images indicating a pathological-irrational point of view. These apparitions rupture the "reasonable," unambiguous divisions between life and death, or real and unreal, healthy and pathological, and suddenly expose them. Spectral images appear before the living usually when there is an essential conflict inherent in the event of their death or in their unresolved relationship with those before whom they appear. These circumstances render the spectral apparition with a very specific context of an "unfinished business" or a persistent demand to settle something that has been left unresolved.

Benjamin finds similar characteristics in the seventeenth-century *Trauerspiel*, which tolerates the inability to differentiate between the two sides of the ultimate border separating life and death, while at the same time emphasizes the essential connection between this blurred border and the idea of an unresolved predicament. Benjamin sees the modern determination of the ghostly as pathological to be irrelevant to the *Trauerspiel* and therefore finds its pertinence to the spectral alluring. The *Trauerspiel* presents an astounding number of ghost figures, indeed, which appear in the majority of the period's plays, sometimes as the ghosts of the dead returning to haunt the living and, sometimes, as specters of the living people appearing onstage.[51]

Pertinent among the characteristics of the *Trauerspiel* to consider here when uncovering the role of ghosts in them are the plays' relation to and presentation of death. Death does not mark the end of life, and life is, in fact, not so far removed from death: the two states exist concomitantly, a condition exemplified by the figure of the ghost. In the *Trauerspiel*, death, the epitome of finitude, is revealed as finite and contingent. In the plays death no longer provides either resolution or closure; instead, it challenges the alleged conclusiveness of death with utter indeterminacy. When comparing the status of death in the *Trauerspiel* and in Greek tragedy, Benjamin writes:

> A tragic death is an ironic immortality, ironic from an excess of determinacy. The tragic death is over-determined . . . Death in the *Trauerspiel* . . . is no conclusive finality . . . The *Trauerspiel* is mathematically comparable to one branch of a hyperbola whose other branch lies in infinity. The law governing a higher life prevails in the restricted space of an earthly existence, and all play, until death puts an end to the game, so as to repeat the same game, albeit on a grander scale, in another world. It is this repetition on which the law of the *Trauerspiel* is founded. Its events are allegorical schemata, symbolic mirror-images of a different game. We are transported into that game by death. (*SW*, 1:56–57; translation altered)

If tragic death marks an excess of determinacy, a finalized and conclusive ending, then death in the *Trauerspiel* heralds the opposite. It is incessant and indefatigable. Benjamin describes death's repetitive character here as hyperbolic, alluding to its incessant movement, which never comes to completion.[52] The branches of the hyperbola, both of which extend to infinity, are capable only of being asymptotic, thus moving closer to one another but never actually touching or reaching the end of their movement. The literary term *hyperbole*, or the Greek ὑπερβολή, means a state of excess, and it suits Benjamin perfectly here in describing the status of death in the *Trauerspiel*. Like the hyperbola, death in the *Trauerspiel* is infinite, never at rest. In the baroque vision, death, which is regularly thought of as a complete stop, becomes repetitive and excessive.[53] The gravity and conclusiveness of tragic death is replaced by the nonunified character of the *Trauerspiel*, in which no resolution is possible within the realm of the drama itself (*SW*, 1:57). Accordingly, the *Trauerspiel* presents ever-recurring mirror games in which the approaching end is continually reflected. Death plays the game and is itself a game since it does not lead to any sort of closure or resolution.

For this reason, Benjamin points out, the *Trauerspiel* usually has an even number of acts (as opposed to the odd number customary of tragedy) (*TS*, 137), a structure that allows an ending to have no upper hand; it is a game without a winner and without a determination. The introduction of terms such as *hyperbola* and *mirror* into his account points to the fact that repetition and unremitting movement replace the fixed, single-course movement of tragic, determinate death.[54] For this reason "the dead become ghosts" (*SW*, 1:57), revenant and repeatedly returning. One suggestive example is *Hamlet*, which concludes at what seems to be the farthest possible distance from the tragic drama's determinate action, evoking the question of whether the play has reached its termination at all, let alone its resolution. In Abraham's psychoanalytic interpretation the play inaugurates an unconscious process and keeps it alive, failing to put it to rest.[55] In this sense death, in its finalized state, has no dwelling space in the *Trauerspiel*: it can only transform the dead into ghosts or, rather, refuse to allow them to "become dead" in the first place. In such circumstances the deceased are no longer alive, but they have not yet entered the nether reaches.[56]

A sense of failure inheres in these repetitions of death, in the *attempts* to die rather than in the successful conclusion of a death. Repetition in this context serves the same purpose as bombast does. Both appear when subtle and accurate expression fails. Death thus repeats itself in what seems to be an almost paradoxical gesture, after prior failed attempts. The need to replicate death points, in effect, to the basic failure to execute it, which constitutes a defeat of the most fundamental sort, one that demonstrates the invalidation of life's greatest certainty, the most general and concrete of tasks. The failure to die, to arrive at complete closure and stable meaning, can be said to mark the essential failure separating the *Trauerspiel* from tragedy.

The inability to reach a conclusive resolution in death, together with the frustrated attempts to do so, are accompanied by another level of replication and repetition—that of death itself. Benjamin refers to the staging of Hallmann's *Sophia*, in which it is not ghosts that appear but multiple renditions of demise itself: two figures of death dance together in a cruel and uncanny whirl signaling a liminal relationship, somewhere between alliance and struggle (*TS*, 194). Not only does the character, Sophia, not reach the end of her life, but more than one death is at hand—the number of deaths exceeds and replaces the repeated failure to realize it. Benjamin interprets the simultaneous appearance of the two deaths as the two options that await Sophia or, rather, as a state in which she cannot even exercise her basic right to a singular death. This scene demonstrates that one determinate death is impossible in the *Trauerspiel*.

This notion of indeterminacy necessitates that the plays' conclusions remain open. Benjamin writes that the *Trauerspiel*

> has 'no proper end, the stream continues on its course.' This is true of the *Trauerspiel* in general; its conclusion does not mark the end of an epoch, as the death of the tragic hero so emphatically does ... Death, as the form of tragic life, is an individual destiny; in the *Trauerspiel* it frequently takes the form of a communal fate, as if summoning all the participants before the highest court ... Whereas the tragic hero, in his 'immortality,' does not save his life, but only his name, in death the characters of the *Trauerspiel* lose only the name-bearing individuality, and not the vitality of their role. This survives undiminished in the spirit-world. (*TS*, 135–36)

As opposed to the conclusive, undeniable end of tragedy, the *Trauerspiel* seems to feature no end at all, or at least no unambiguous end. Death does not end life, and the play does not terminate with the end of the text. Benjamin lucidly explains this by considering the contradiction between individual and communal fates. The radical individuality and symbol-like closure of the tragic hero's fate leads directly to his death; this death effectively marks the essence of the hero's life, "the form of tragic life." It also marks its utter singularity in relation to the inherent multiplicity of the mythical order. The tragic hero is therefore isolated precisely because it is a "self."[57] Extreme individuality realizes itself through its termination, which is filled with meaning. The alternative proposed by the *Trauerspiel* is that of a communal fate—with this fate distributed among the characters and sometimes even the staged objects. This dissemination renders any defined resolution impossible since each figure has its own, albeit partial, power to control its own fate. Here, the lack of individuality prevents a resolute determination of fate. Friedlander claims that this model for the dispersion of meaning, which he finds in music, does not undermine a sense of resolution. On the contrary, it encompasses what can be seen as an even deeper resolution: that which is totalized precisely in the *Trauerspiel*'s lack of unity.[58]

Furthermore, in numerous instances the *Trauerspiel* also introduces ghosts of the living people that still occupy the stage. According to Benjamin this constitutes a strange duplication that again denotes the blurring between the living and the dead: "The explanation for the strange appearance of the spirits of the living is not quite so clear . . . It is . . . a remarkable testimony to the fanaticism with which even the absolutely singular, the individual character, is multiplied in the allegorical" (*TS*, 193).

In Gryphius's *Cardenio und Celinde*, for instance, the ghost of the living Olympia appears twice: once in order to speak with Cardenio and once as a walking skeleton on the stage that is suddenly transformed from a "*Lust Garten*" (garden of delight) into an "*abscheuliche Einöde*" (horrendous wasteland).[59] Instead of the living protagonist Olympia, it is her ghost who succeeds in changing Cardenio's mind and talking him out of killing Lysander, Olympia's partner, in order to win her heart (Olympia's ghost appears twice in the fourth act, in lines 1 and 193). Cardenio is transformed and "comes back to his senses" when the spectral skeleton draws a bow and arrow and threatens to kill him. It is as if Olympia could awaken Cardenio's attention only when appearing as a ghost. Her ghost turns to Cardenio to make amends before it is too late. Cardenio then meets Celinde in the midst of her attempt to rob her former lover's heart in order to brew a love potion that would arouse Cardenio's love for her. They both confess their crimes during this encounter, which becomes a transformative and reformative event.

The protagonist's ghost (in Olympia's case, the skeleton) accompanies the living individual throughout and thereby violates the clear threshold between life and death. Death, rather than ending life, becomes coterminous with life so that the living protagonists oscillate between living and dead images of themselves. Dead characters (like Hamlet's father) actively maintain their roles in the plays after the cessation of life and consequently infinitely defer their consummate end. The ghostly character of the *Trauerspiel* is its purest form—it is a play of thresholds, of liminal creatures that hover over the blurred border between life and death, consequently remaining everlasting figures of restlessness and partiality.

This liminality is also expressed in the setting of the *Trauerspiel*, which often takes place at midnight—the hour of the threshold. *Carlos Stuardus* (by Gryphius) and *Agrippina* (by Lohenstein) begin at midnight although the nocturnal quality of scenes can be communicated in various ways. *Cardenio und Celinde* (by Gryphius), not mentioned by Benjamin in this context, also takes place around midnight: Gryphius writes that the play begins in the evening and ends the next morning. The association of dramatic actions with a nocturnal ambience lies in the widespread notion that at this hour, time stands still, like "the tongue of a scale." It is in this narrow pause in the passage of time that the same ghostly image reappears (*TS*, 134–35).

A ghost can show itself only at this threshold hour since it belongs neither to day nor night but only to the elusive border between them. Hamlet's father, for instance, can only appear at midnight, the hour when one day becomes the next. He remains present only until the cock crows and day breaks, before disappearing. Another famous example is *Antigone*, not a *Trauerspiel* but definitely a play preoccupied with mourning. Antigone performs her mourning rituals beside her brother's body at midnight. Benjamin contrasts the nocturnal quality of the ghosts with that of the tragic hero, to conclude that a gulf separates the two figures and their theatrical forms (*TS*, 135). Tragedy, he writes, can never be set during night's uncertain hours because everything about it aims toward the conclusive, the lucid, and the exposed.

The temporal dimension enters here, with the threshold being time, not space—there is "an opening in the passage of time," Benjamin notes. The ghost that occupies this space functions only as a temporal creature since it is incapable of occupying any spatial sphere (to which it has been denied). Yet Benjamin curiously describes the world of spirits as "ahistorical." The ghost is ahistorical because it is entirely outside of time; it is also, however, all about time and temporality. One way to comprehend this inherent paradox is to think about the distinctive temporal structure that Benjamin describes here: past and present can exist diachronically, in parallel, only through an encounter with the ghost. In this structure the past does not necessarily appear at a moment before the present; it can coexist with the present and be gazed upon. This is possible only in the context of Benjamin's curious statement that it is vital for baroque life (in all its spheres) to transpose "the originally temporal data into a figurative spatial simultaneity" (*TS*, 81). The ghost is the embodiment of such a baroque structure in which time, being simultaneous rather than synchronic, is viewed as spatial.

The theme of thresholds is strongly present in the *Trauerspiel* book.[60] It focuses mainly on the figure of the ghost but is more generally related to the blurred boundary between life and death as they appear in the plays. The ghost represents the embodiment of this blurred boundary:

> Seen from the point of view of death, the product of the corpse is life. It is not only in the loss of limbs, not only in the changes of the aging body, but in all the processes of elimination and purification that everything corpse-like falls away from the body piece by piece. It is no accident that precisely nails and hair, which are cut away as dead matter from the living body, continue to grow on the corpse. (*TS*, 218)

This living corpse, in which the transition between life and death occurs, is a crucial image in Benjamin's work. Never reduced to merely a dead object, the corpse resides in a transitional state of continuous dying. This process emanates from a point of view in which the fact that death does not end life is considered nonpathological. Recalling my earlier claim regarding the extraction of truth from the body (the figure of the martyr being its exemplar), the mortification that culminates in the extraction of truth and meaning from the material parallels what Benjamin calls here the "processes of elimination and purification that everything corpse-like falls away piece by piece." This is the process in which the body becomes a site of meaning, where what Benjamin elsewhere calls "the material content" is slowly manipulated to unfold into "truth content."[61]

Benjamin's provocative comment regarding the continued growth of hair and nails, which is not repeated elsewhere in the *Trauerspiel* book (nor elsewhere in Benjamin's works, as far as I am aware), places this image of being not dead but no longer alive in an illuminating context. Two perspectives are relevant to the examination of the image of nails and hair as hybrid entities where life and death meet. The first is the status of nails and hair in the living body, in comparison to their status in the corpse; and the second is their special status in the framework of mourning and its customs.

As to the first perspective, we find an interesting flip in the status of nails and hair: they are regarded as dead matter when they grow on a living body and as living material when they continue to grow on a dead body. It seems that the almost spectral matter composing nails and hair continues to live on after the body's death and in that sense remains detached from the question of whether the body per se is living or dead and whether this matter has a life (or death) of its own. The distinction between life and death disappears when looking at hair and nails, which occupy the threshold between two apparently irreconcilable states. When the body is alive, this is the only part of it that we dispose of (other than waste, which is part of our bodies but not, strictly speaking, a body "part"); we do so as if trying to keep death, or dead matter, far away. We discard them without pain because pain belongs to life. As dead matter, they do not inflict any pain when cut or damaged. Only where they touch the finger or scalp do they produce pain. Only where there is an encounter between the dead and the living is pain present. Interestingly, these elements also grow at the outskirts of the body, a location contributing to their detached and even estranged position with respect to the body to which they belong.

On the second level nails and hair have a privileged position during the time of mourning, as status granted to them because of their ghostly nature. Jewish mourning customs dictate that members of the deceased's immediate family may neither cut their hair nor trim their nails in the thirty days following the interment. Both the ritual involving preparation of the deceased's body for its interment and the customs governing the family's mourning relate to the immediate period after death as a time for the slow transition from life to death. Caring for the dead body involves rites that continue its life, on the one hand, alternating with rites that mark its death, on the other—a dichotomy stressing the transitional nature of this phase.[62] Jewish tradition thus sees the mourning period as a time in which the deceased is no longer alive, not yet dead, but in transit between these two states. This represents the origin of the belief that the dead continue to hear and feel pain, symbolized by the continued growth of their hair and nails. Analogously, the mourner also occupies a transitional stage between his or her former status and a new role as orphan, widower, and so forth. The mourner may not bathe, cut his hair or nails, socialize, have intercourse, sleep in a bed, wear leather shoes, and so forth. Although he has transcended his old status, he has not yet entered his new status and should thus be treated as a child in need of help.[63]

In that sense a strong affinity persists between the deceased and the mourner: both exist in a transitional realm. This receives interesting expression in the prohibition to cut the hair and nails, those bodily elements that are, again, spectral entities situated between life and death—or, at least, they have not yet surrendered to the distinction between life and death. In other words one can say that the mourning period, as understood in Jewish tradition, is liminal in nature, a time of the undead and the spectral, a state pertaining to the deceased and the mourner alike, a time serving to unite rather than separate, or, at least, to unite in order to later separate with reconciliation. The fundamental recognition offered by the *Trauerspiel* is that there is no specific moment of closure; there is only a *process* of ending that opens up. Put otherwise, mourning begins the work directed toward denouement, toward coming into its own in an act of self-realization and putting to rest. In the plays this work remains unfulfilled, a mere presentation of the eternal return of inherited retribution and unaccounted-for debt.[64]

Understanding the ghost as undead or on the liminal threshold between life and death, past and present, announces the absence of reconciliation in the ghost itself. Death, it can be maintained, epitomizes reconciliation in that it represents the fundamental event of something coming to its own. This moment is absent in the *Trauerspiel*, as witnessed in the abundant presence of ghosts, entities whose quality of being is perpetually unresolved. Ghosts usually appear in the plays in front of a protagonist who cannot avoid the encounter. Their appearance always bodes the potential transformation of the play's reality and its protagonists' lives, and in that sense, the ghost exhibits a poignant quality that connects the ghost to the person or object it haunts.[65]

For Benjamin this connection between ghosts and the living, between past and present, is crucial not only because of the special reciprocal relationship it entails but also because of the special transverse relationship between the existent and the undead. The moment of encounter between past and present demands recognition in two senses: first, the present's acknowledgment of the past via the call of the ghost; and second, commitment stemming from such a call, that is, recognition of the commitment stemming from response to the call. This call allows grappling with the past as it "flits by" in the form of an "irretrievable image of the past which threatens to disappear in any present that does not recognize itself as intended in that image."[66] The ghostly image harbors a threat: if not retrieved and transformed into a space for work, it will disappear, before the present that does not recognize itself as being the object of the image's intentions. Benjamin perceives this potential for disappearance as inherent to historical thought: "Articulating the past historically . . . means appropriating a memory as it flashes up in a moment of danger."[67]

Appropriating the image means, here, recognizing it as legible at a specific moment. In the *Arcades Project* Benjamin discusses what he calls a "historical index" in the context of the question of legibility:

> The historical index of images not only says that they belong to a particular time; it says, above all, that they attain to legibility only at a particular time . . . Every present day is determined by the images that are synchronic with it: Each "now" is the now of a particular recognizability . . . It is not that what is past casts light on what is present, or what is present its light on what is past; rather, image is that wherein what has been comes together in a flash with the now to form a constellation.[68]

In this important formulation Benjamin is not interested in a specific point in history to which these images (or the material, for our purposes) belong. What concerns him is the moment when the image encounters us in the present and becomes something else: readable. Reformulated in terms of the ghostly figures of the *Trauerspiel*, this is the critical point at which the ghost allows itself to be read—not simply read, however, but read by a specific recipient of the present. In that sense there is a specific point of encounter in which the ghost becomes legible to the protagonist. At this moment something essential is recognized. Encountering the ghost thus means recognizing and not inventing or discovering, which is to say that we read what was always there as lost to us, having become readable only at this point of encounter with us.[69]

When Derrida discusses the notion of "inheritance," he points out that inheritance should be conceived as a task, not a given. We face this inheritance, like all other inheritors, from a state of mourning. He adds: "That we *are* heirs does not mean that we *have* or that we *receive* this or that, some inheritance that enriches us one day with this or that, but that the *being* of what we are *is* first of all inheritance, whether we like it or know it or not."[70] There is, then, a sense of urgency not only in the appearance of the ghost itself but, first and foremost, in the living's response to this appearance. The mournful inheritor is also he who is forced to address the ghost's call to undertake its inheritance. And this is unequivocally an undertaking since it does not require a quiet embrace but rather a steadfast act of responsibility and reaffirmation that Derrida entitles "the state of debt."[71]

Furthermore, thinking about this structure through the figure of the ghost renders it an encounter entailing a personal call; herein lies the import of the ghost. The ghostly apparition always has to do with the person who encounters it. The instant of recognizability occurs in a certain present moment—thus the ghost's call is never sent out arbitrarily but is always directed toward something or someone. Only under these conditions can a moment of reconciliation be possible. That is, the present moment's specificity is connected to the call, so that coming to terms with it becomes possible in that moment alone. Recognizing the call and the ethical responsibility it entails involves, therefore, a distinct, almost personal, relation.

The ghost of the dead king in *Hamlet* is an interesting example in this context. At first it appears in silence, twice before the guards and once before Horatio, and reveals nothing about the meaning of its appearance. It only speaks when Hamlet is present, after being summoned by his friends. Horatio says to them:

> Break we our watch up, and by my advice
> Let us impart what we have seen to-night
> Unto young Hamlet, for, upon my life,
> This spirit, dumb to us, will speak to him. (1.1)

Even then, the ghost only agrees to speak to Hamlet, and only when the others cannot be part of the exchange. He demands revenge for his murder and explains that he is doomed to wander the realm of ghosts until Hamlet avenges him:

> I am thy father's spirit,
> Doom'd for a certain term to walk at night,

> And for the day confin'd to fast in fires,
> Till the foul crimes done in my days of nature
> Are burnt and purg'd away . . . (1.5)

These scenes invoke an important issue. The dead king appears before the guards more than once; however, he does not speak to them. He agrees to speak only to the living Hamlet, his son. There is a clear hierarchy here between visual and sonic apparitions. Only he who is the recipient of the ghostly call can accept it. It is directed only to him. In that sense the message brought by the ghost is that of the encounter itself and not simply the communicated information. The message of the ghost does not exist independently of the encounter with its recipient and is shaped only in this encounter. There is something about the vocal apparition that is more specific than the visual one. This idea is echoed in the beautiful citation Benjamin brings from Sigmund von Birken: "Every natural occurrence in this world could be the effect or the materialization of a cosmic reverberation or sound, even the movement of the stars" (*TS*, 215).

Benjamin's historical thought has often been interpreted in visual terms;[72] here, as the citation from Birken suggests, I propose that it might be more accurate to think of it in terms of sound and voice. "Shouldn't we rather speak of events which affect us like an echo—one awakened by a sound that seems to have issued from somewhere in the darkness of past life?" writes Benjamin in "Berlin Childhood Around 1900." This sound from the past enters our consciousness as an echo—striking us as a familiar voice, long unheard, would. Through the call's very sound we enter into "the cool sepulcher of the past, from whose vault the present seems to resound only as an echo."[73] Benjamin's allusions to an echo are precise because this call resounds in no single direction. It echoes, meaning that its reverberations and consequences have their own dynamics, going back and forth between the past and present at will. In that sense the ghostly call's transformations occur in the present, as well as the past. History rereads and restages not only the meaning of the past but always and inherently its own meaning at the moment of its undertaking, and the present seems to resound only as an echo.

In a short text published in 1930 Benjamin addresses the task of the historian.[74] He writes that although the present, "today," may seem small or meager, "whatever form it takes [*Aber es mag sein wie es will*],[75] our task is to seize it by the horns so that we can interrogate [*befragen*] the past. It is the bull whose blood must fill the grave if the spirits of the departed [*Geister der Abgeschiedenen*] are to appear at its edge" (*SW*, 2:383). The bull's blood appears together with the spirits of the lost ones gathering around it. It is here that the martyr's blood and the ghost's evasive image converge. This is a moment of encounter between past and present—a moment that should be seized with fortitude, but legible and fruitful only if caught at the right moment. The commitment toward the spirits surrounding the bloody grave is one of work, of exercising (rather than exorcising) the past. In that sense historical meaning is embedded within us, within our "theories," and should become material for the philosophical work that will disclose it. However, this disclosure will not allow us to regain the past but will instead unfold it from within the present of its reading, from its "today."

Recognition of the past, by "seizing it by the horns," involves more than ghosts and the past alone, for these spirits can never exist on their own *as* the past; they are always entangled with the present. Their call to the present can resonate only if it is recognized—recognition here meaning the way the past inscribes itself in the present and is itself transformed by the act of inscription. The debt it demands of us is therefore expressed as a claim for its realization in the present. In that sense, for it to exist, the ghost requires that we take some action that will allow it to take its proper form. This can occur exclusively in the present. Thus, the ghost can only realize itself in the present.

Hence, the ghost is not a stranger, for it echoes something already present, even if concealed, something that is recognized rather than contrived. The ghost is thus realized in its call, which echoes in us like a familiar voice.[76] In the face of the ghost's need for our recognition and its power to penetrate the past into the present, which creates the said sense of familiarity, Benjamin concludes that the ghost operates only at the intersection with the living person, where disclosure of the past's meaning is necessarily transformative as it opens the present anew to the past and vice versa. In this sense the dead are never completely dead, and the past can never be hermetically closed. When we behold the ghost, we therefore bear witness and acknowledge the debt inherent in its call.

Benjamin emphasizes the danger that is always in this encounter—that of losing the opportunity to respond and come to terms with the call.[77] The point of concern here is not to exorcise the ghost but to think through it, to make the encounter ethically meaningful. Moreover, this call initiates a conversation and a responsibility to participate in it. Sometimes such an undertaking can merely amount to a recognition or a bearing witness to the ghost (or, in other cases, to actual tasks such as those Hamlet's father demands of him). Nevertheless, there is a specificity to the moment in the present that is connected to the call, so that coming to terms with it becomes possible in that moment alone.

Shifting the discussion of the ghost as a figure in the plays into the realm of meaning and truth, I claim that the importance of this image lies in how the encounter with the spectral serves as a starting point or initiation to Benjamin's philosophical work. The appearance of the ghost is meaningful, whether or not this meaning has yet been realized. The response to the ghost's call is ethically grounded and contains the potential for reconciling the haunting nature of the ghost by responding to its demand. The response can stop its recurrent appearance and virtually "put the ghost to rest," "quiet" its wanderings, and thus allow for a respite in which historical meaning can be presented.

In "Mourning and Melancholia" Freud offers the illuminating proposition that the melancholic's lost object is half-alive. Although an already lost and thereby "not living" object, it is nonetheless not completely dead since it still exists in one way or another within the melancholic conscious. This "half-alive" or "buried-alive" being can be understood as spectral. The pathology of the melancholic lies in an inability to let go, to part and bring the object to rest. Rest is also absent from the object itself, however, which hovers between life and death, powerless in the face of the destructive melancholic energy clinging to it. By relocating Freud's account into the realm of meaning created through Benjamin's transformation of the lost object's pathology, we can gain an auxiliary meaning for the terminology of stillness or rest: the ghosts of the past must be put to rest, and such rest can only be attained by answering the call of the past—which reaches us in the form of a ghost.

The achievement of rest and stillness also means rest in the sense of burial. This burial would not, however, conceal the object in order to mollify the detachment; instead, it would bury it in the sense of deepening death by bringing the ghost to a complete rest. Relocating of the Freudian discussion within the realm of meaning and truth would demonstrate that presenting meaning does not signify endowing it with life but rather bringing it to rest, to completing the process of extinction. In this sense loss is found at both ends. Because it functions as one of the conditions making the object legible in the first place, it conditions the work of expression. At the other end loss appears as a state in which the object is fully expressed and, in Benjamin's terms, drained of life. Bringing to rest, deadening, and certainly burying are also forms of loss. All the object's potential for life, all its very potentiality, is lost at the end of the process. This is, nevertheless, the only way to completely express the object at "rest."

The image of the stone that Benjamin identifies as a neglected emblem of melancholy (*TS*, 154–55) can likewise be understood as embodying such stillness. Benjamin cites Albertinus, who writes that the tears of the grieving melancholic do not soften his heart but rather encounter a callous organ that resembles a stone in that it does not absorb the tear but sweats it outward. The stone embodies the essence of melancholic philosophical work, which brings about complete actualization and saturation. Benjamin points to three instances in which the emblem of the stone is central: the heart of the grieving melancholic in Albertinus, Samuel von Butschky's funeral oration by Hallmann, and the dialogue between melancholy and joy in Filidor. The three instances remain somewhat opaque because Benjamin offers no explanation as to the relations among the three, or among them and melancholy, apart from the loose link to theological *acedia* as one of the deadly sins (*TS*, 155). I suggest reading the role of the stone in these somewhat esoteric references not only through its cold, dry features, resembling traditional melancholic traits, but also through its intimations of stillness. Here again the stone can be read as parallel to the ghost, as its equivalent.

Benjamin situates his philosophical work at the core of loss and calls for an understanding and acknowledgment of that loss, together with a strong commitment toward it and the work it requires. Hence, loss, which is the precondition to philosophical legibility and work, is likewise present at the conclusion of this work. "All purposeful manifestation[s] of life . . . have their end not in life but in the expression of its nature, in the representation of its significance" (*TT, SW*, 1:255). That said, philosophical expression takes place at the end of the object's life, at the point of the utmost loss, when work is undertaken. Philosophical work therefore imparts rest.

3

Melancholy and Language

Language and Loss: Benjamin's Concept of Expression

Benjamin's conception of philosophical truth should be explicated by means of its linguistic structure. In his early writings Benjamin repeatedly emphasizes the indispensable interconnection between truth and language. The philosophical roots of this argument appear prominently in his critical essay on Kant, "On the Program of the Coming Philosophy" (*SW*, 1:100–110 [1918]). This essay ends with a formulation of the philosophical implications of Benjamin's criticism, namely, that there is an urgent need for a complete transformation of the Kantian system, specifically its concept of experience. The core of Benjamin's argument against Kant's conception lies in Benjamin's rejection of the latter's account of experience, which, having a thoroughly mathematical and mechanical structure, fails to grasp any linguistic component, which is essential and indispensable for the concept of experience.[1]

According to Benjamin, Kant devotes hardly any attention to the fact that "all philosophical knowledge has its unique expression in language and not in formulas and numbers... A concept of knowledge gained from reflection on the linguistic nature of knowledge will create a corresponding concept of experience which will also encompass realms that Kant failed to truly systematize. The realm of religion should be mentioned as the foremost of these" (*SW*, 1:108). Incorporating the linguistic structure into the Kantian system would result in a new concept of experience, which should accordingly be understood in linguistic terms. Benjamin links this new structure of experience to the religious context of the doctrine (*Lehre*) (*SW*, 1:108). He uses the term *Lehre* in the sense of doctrine or teaching; however, in the Kantian context this term is also closely linked to what can be transmitted and can form the basis of a tradition. According to Friedlander, Benjamin attempts here to free the Kantian understanding of doctrine from its scientific disposition and turn it into the highest determination of Benjamin's own idea of philosophy.[2] He then warns against a limited understanding of doctrine that would link philosophy and religion: philosophy should not be designated as, nor be subordinated to, theology. He proposes a different constitution of this relationship in order to establish a construct in which the historical and linguistic structures are deemed more central than the mythical aspects of theology. What Benjamin offers here, in effect, is a new outlook on the role of language in philosophical thought, as well as a conviction (not entirely explicated in the text) about the importance of theology to philosophy.[3]

The crux of Benjamin's criticism of Kant is reiterated, this time positively, in the prologue to the *Trauerspiel* book. There Benjamin offers his own conception of philosophical truth, emphasizing and articulating precisely what he had missed in his earlier criticism of Kant. In the prologue he writes that "the idea is something linguistic, it is that element of the symbolic in the essence of any word" (*TS*, 36), again proclaiming what he takes to be the linguistic nature of truth. The philosopher's task is to use the method of presentation set forth in the prologue to restore the word's symbolic character that is not only not-visual but also the "opposite of all outwardly-directed communication" (*TS*, 36). What Benjamin enunciates here is a structure of truth that entails a form of expression or presentation that is neither visual nor communicative but linguistic (*TS*, 36–37). In accord with his concluding claim in the essay on Kant, he invokes the linguistic nature of truth in a theological, not mythical, context—Benjamin enthrones Adam rather than Plato as the father of philosophy. In Adam he finds a theological figure whose core is more markedly linguistic than mythical.

Benjamin's preoccupation with language and its relation to truth is especially conspicuous in 1916, the year that was by his own account the starting point for his conception of the *Trauerspiel* book.[4] This was also the year that he wrote two other important meditations on language: the posthumously published "The Role of Language in *Trauerspiel* and Tragedy," where he considers the distinction between the *Trauerspiel* and tragedy in linguistic terms; and "On Language as Such and on the Language of Man," where he sets forth the most comprehensive account of his theory of language via his interpretation of the first two chapters of Genesis.[5]

Of Benjamin's early works, "On Language as Such and on the Language of Man" has undoubtedly received the most attention in the critical literature.[6] One of the most crucial yet challenging tasks in the interpretation of Benjamin's early writings is indeed the explication of his precise engagement with language. My own reading of the text, however, is not an attempt to offer a new interpretation of Benjamin's theory of language, nor do I wish to engage in polemical disagreements with some of Benjamin's most distinguished interpreters. My aim, rather, is to reenter the text from a very distinct perspective, namely, that of the relation between language and melancholy.

In light of Benjamin's early remarks on the linguistic structure of truth, it is important to elucidate the link between language and melancholy as conjured by his interpretation of Genesis. As this chapter will establish, Benjamin not only situates language as the foundation of his structure of truth; he also views language, first, through its theological origins and, second, as what is always and fundamentally instituted on the basis of loss and melancholy. The inherent role of loss in language's structure, chiefly presented in the two aforementioned essays, is crucial to Benjamin's conception of philosophy and philosophical method. Through his reading of the place of language in the *Trauerspiel*, and his retelling of the story of Creation, Benjamin presents language as being essentially intertwined with loss, engaged in a constant interplay between existence and disappearance. Deeply saturated with melancholy and loss, language thus functions both as an expression of loss and as a site for its recuperation.

Benjamin understands language first and foremost as an expressive configuration. That is, language is not necessarily a system of articulation or communication per se but is principally defined as what bears on expression. This is already evident in the opening of "On Language as Such":

> Every expression of human mental life can be understood as a kind of language, and this understanding, in the manner of a true method, everywhere raises new questions. It is possible to talk about a language of music and of sculpture, about a language of justice that has nothing directly to do with those in which German or English legal judgments are couched, about a language of technology that is not the specialized language of technicians. Language in such contexts means the tendency inherent in the subjects concerned—technology, art, justice, or religion—toward the communication of the content of the mind. To sum up: all communication of the contents of the mind is language, communication in words being only a particular case of human language and of the justice, poetry, or whatever underlying it or founded on it. (LAN, *SW*, 1:62)

The argument here has profound implications. First, Benjamin suggests a rethinking of the linguistic system so that it is understood as something far greater than mere communication or an apparatus expressing subjective consciousness. In this structure language is deprived of any subjective consciousness whatsoever. This differentiation is also suggested by the essay's title, which distinguishes between human-communicative language and Benjamin's own conception: "language as such" and the inclination toward expression—not its articulate, communicative "language of man"—is what stands at the crux of language. Benjamin's understanding of language as a system of expression bearing on art, justice, or poetry, as well as communication, renders the speaking subject marginal in the linguistic configuration.

Second, and more importantly, Benjamin describes language not as an articulation of content, nor as a representational act, but as a "tendency inherent . . . toward the communication of the content of the mind." This means, essentially, that language is only an *inclination* to express and not necessarily an *actualization* of expression and, furthermore, that its expression's content is neither conceptual nor communicative but something Benjamin calls "content of the mind."

Benjamin expropriates linguistic expression from anything we ordinarily take it to be: it is neither a propositional nor in any way a referential structure and, furthermore, it is in no way limited to human speech. Such a radical transfiguration of the linguistic edifice allows him to consider language outside its limited, and limiting, communicative functions. Neutralizing these functions scrutinizes language as an apparatus of expression that is not limited to human speech: "There is no event or thing in either animate or inanimate nature that does not in some way partake in language, for it is in the nature of each one to communicate its mental contents . . . We cannot imagine a total absence of language in anything" (LAN, *SW,* 1:62). Benjamin thus widens the definition of language to incorporate natural and inanimate objects, as well as to human subjects.

Fenves, in pointing to an intriguing connection between Benjamin's claim and Kant's argument that space is the ground of all outer appearances, shows that, according to Kant, we cannot think of a complete absence of space, but we can think the "abyssal thought" of space becoming devoid of objects. According to Benjamin we cannot think of the absence of language, "although we can think the barren idea of languagelessness." Fenves asserts, however, that "language cannot really be like space for at least one reason: the former founds the latter; it is prior even to the *a priori* forms in which things appear."[7]

The argument that the essence of language lies in its potential rather than actual expression, even in linguistic areas where speech is not at all possible (e.g., in the realm of the inanimate), should not be taken to mean that Benjamin is implying anything mystical about language. Rather, he posits an inner-linguistic structure that is more engaged with the idea of expression and expressibility than with either a mystical world-picture, on the one hand, or with a representational-conceptual account of language, on the other.

Following Benjamin's argument in this text and his preoccupation with the expressive facets of language, I would like to link his conception of language to the idea of *expressibility* rather than *expression*. This is to say that I take it to be important to understand how language functions in Benjamin's philosophical system through its explication as the *potential* for expression, or, in Benjamin's terms, the "inclination" to express, rather than as the actualization of an act of expression.

One of the most rigorous accounts of the idea of potentiality to appear in the last decades is no doubt Giorgio Agamben's. But even before his renowned *Potentialities,* Agamben outlined some of the important threads of his thought in the preface to *Infancy and History*. There he expounds the important idea of "*experimentum linguae*," which bears on what he defines as his most fundamental, yet unwritten and thus absent, work.[8] Without going into the details of this text, which in many senses alludes to Agamben's continual preoccupation with Benjamin's thought as a whole, I would like to point to some crucial points it raises that can shed some light on Benjamin's conception of language, specifically on what I designate here as expressibility, or the preeminence of potentiality, in Benjamin's theory of language.[9]

As Agamben describes it, his own philosophical preoccupation concerns language as located outside the limits of speech. Thinking of language as existing prior to the split between language and speech, he offers a linguistic conception that is not limited to human language but to the mere possibility of language's existence. He puts forth the idea that such a linguistic undertaking can have no other possible content than the mere idea that "there is language," independent of the question of whether one (or anyone) speaks that language. He invokes the Aristotelian opposition between *dynamis* and *energia*, or potency and act. Potency has to do with the human linguistic faculty that is already defined, according to Agamben, as potential. Having a faculty, or possessing something that is merely in "one's power," essentially means having the potential to actualize such a power; it does not mean, however, that one has already done so. To possess a faculty, rather than to execute or accomplish something, means to have a privation; potential is, accordingly, not simply a negation of something actualized but an independent mode of existence that constantly bears on its own inherent privation.[10] Continuing to track the idea of potentiality and impotentiality in Aristotle's *Metaphysics*, Agamben emphasizes that potentiality is not simply non-Being, simple privation, but rather *the existence of non-Being*, the presence of an absence.

In its originary structure, *dynamis*, potentiality, maintains itself in relation to its own privation, its own *sterēsis*, its own non-Being. This relation constitutes the essence of potentiality. To be potential means: to be one's own lack, *to be in relation to one's own incapacity*. Beings that exist in the mode of potentiality *are capable of their own impotentiality*; and only in this way do they become potential. They *can be* because they are in relation to their own non-Being. In potentiality, sensation is in relation to anesthesia, knowledge to ignorance, vision to darkness.[11]

To take these ideas back to Benjamin's idea of language as expression, what Agamben offers here is an understanding of language as a potentiality to express that has two important implications: first, language is not a system of accomplished, actualized expressions but only a space of their potential; second, being such potentiality, language is in constant touch with its own unfulfillment, impotential (or impotence), and fundamental privation. Put differently, language is a realm *containing its own* inexpressibility; it encompasses not merely its expression but also its limits. Language understood as expressibility means that it is always as much about its loss and unfulfillment as it is about its enactment.

Benjamin demonstrates this idea when he extends the definition of language to include everything, animate or inanimate, every event and object—and not merely human speech (LAN, *SW*, 1:62). If language is defined as including inanimate objects or events, it is necessarily defined as potential and is thereby delineated as the inclination to express, the mere ability to express rather than a system of actualized expressive acts. If "we cannot imagine a total absence of language in anything" (LAN, *SW*, 1:62), we can only imagine language as potential.

If humanity is no longer regarded as the single dominant, defining, linguistic substance, then Benjamin can unfetter language from its sonic vocal expression, communicative functions, and intentional and propositional structure. To take Benjamin's hypothesis seriously, we should acknowledge the shared position of humanity, nature, and the inanimate in the linguistic realm. In this sense, utter silence and the sounds of nature—plants rustling, wind blowing, animals howling—are also part of the linguistic realm, since as Benjamin writes, every event or thing, animate or inanimate, partakes in language in some way (LAN, *SW*, 1:62). In their muteness these objects transform the realm of language into a space filled not only with articulate communication (which is here but one facet of language) but with muteness and speechlessness, which here prove to be the essential occupants rather than the outcasts of the linguistic realm.

What, then, ties humans to natural and inanimate phenomena in language? In what sense does language pertain to all if no expression—no speech or sound—is taking place? Benjamin answers that "it is in the nature of each one to communicate its mental content." Even if things are deprived of the formal principle of sound, they nevertheless communicate with one another immediately and infinitely, "like every linguistic communication" (LAN, *SW*, 1:67). The terms *mental content, mental essence,* and *mental entity* point to perhaps the most intricate ideas Benjamin uses to address the problem of expressibility.

Benjamin's first crucial proposition about what he calls the thing's "mental essence" (or spiritual essence) is that it should be clearly distinguished from that thing's language. Namely, there is a decisive delimitation separating the essence and its communication. This is the basis for the distinction Benjamin wants to construe between what is communicated *through* language and what is communicated *in* it:

> The German language, for example, is by no means the expression of everything that we could—theoretically—express *through* it, but is the direct expression of that which communicates *itself* in it. This "itself" is a mental entity. It is therefore obvious at once that the mental entity that communicates itself in language is not language itself but something to be distinguished from it. The view that the mental essence of a thing consists precisely in its language—this view, taken as a hypothesis, is the great abyss into which all linguistic theory threatens to fall [Benjamin's note on p. 74: "Or is it, rather, the temptation to place at the outset a hypothesis that constitutes an abyss for all philosophizing?"] and to survive suspended precisely over this abyss is its task. (LAN, *SW*, 1:63)

Mental entity is what can be communicated and expressed *in* language, not *through* it. It is not a propositional statement expressed through language or using language as a means for its transmission. The mental essence of the thing is, rather, identical with its linguistic essence but only insofar as the essence is communicable. Benjamin configures a linguistic structure in which an inseparable connection joins the essence of a thing, be it human or inanimate, with its linguistic expression. They are not, however, completely identical. What determines the dividing line between them is the question of expressibility. Language can communicate a thing's mental being only insofar as this mental being corresponds to language. That is, language does not express the thing in its entirety but can only express its linguistic being (which is, again, to be distinguished from its mental essence). The thing has a linguistic "part" to it, and it is this that is communicated in language: "Mental being is identical with linguistic being only insofar as it is capable of communication. What is communicable in a mental entity is its linguistic entity. Language therefore communicates the particular linguistic being of things, but their mental being only insofar as this is directly included in their linguistic being, insofar as it is capable of being communicated" (LAN, *SW,* 1:63).

Benjamin clarifies his intricate argument with the example of the lamp. The language of the lamp does not communicate the lamp itself, as object, for its mental being is entirely different from the lamp as such. Rather, it communicates what is linguistic about the lamp, the lamp as it is given in language, "the language-lamp, the lamp in communication, the lamp in expression" (LAN, *SW,* 1:63). This linguistic part of the lamp will be evoked later when Benjamin discusses the linguistic connection between man and nature (animate or inanimate). There it will become clear that what the lamp can communicate to humans is not its own complete mental being but only its linguistic being, that is, only what can be linguistically communicated, only what is linguistically expressible.

Benjamin warns against a tautological understanding of the claim that the linguistic being of things is their language. Rather, he claims that the communicable part of the mental entity of the thing is, in effect, its language. And "on this 'is' (equivalent to 'is immediately') everything depends" (LAN, *SW,* 1:63). This leads Benjamin's theory all the more in the direction of potentiality and expressibility, because what is really at stake here is not the thing's actual expression or expressive act but its mere potential for such expression: language is itself the capacity for communication (LAN, *SW,* 1:64). Or, as the German original clearly emphasizes: Benjamin is occupied with the *barkeit* of *Mitteilbarkeit* rather than the actual act of communication.[12] It is in this sense that Benjamin argues that "language has no speakers," since language communicates itself *in* itself (in language) and does not communicate an independent content *through* itself.

In this linguistic theory language neither fulfills a function nor serves as a means to transmit content; it is rather a space of expression and potentiality. Expression in language thus means the linguistic presentation of meaning without the communication of content. Within Benjamin's understanding of language, such a structure of expression should foremost be grasped as a tendency toward the actualization of essence in expression. This should always remain, however, a tendency, a faculty or potential. In that sense the realm of nature partakes in language not to communicate an external meaning but rather to realize its own essence and to present it in the linguistic realm.

Benjamin connects the inclination toward expression in objects "to man," who at this early stage of the essay is already viewed as possessing considerable power over mute objects. Things' inclination to express is chiefly directed toward the human: "To whom does the lamp communicate itself? The mountain? The fox?—But here the answer is: to man" (LAN, *SW,* 1:64). The human-made object (lamp), and the entities of inanimate nature (mountain) and living nature (fox), all direct the lacunae in their expression toward an addressee: man. What the inanimate communicates to man is transmitted as a *call,* as a *request from* man. To understand this call, which I will later establish as an ethical demand, Benjamin turns to the myth of Creation in Genesis.

Creation and Loss: "On Language as Such"

Benjamin's interpretation of Genesis is neither an endeavor to turn the biblical story into an object of inquiry nor an attempt to subject the Bible to objective consideration as "revealed truth." Rather, it is an attempt at a "discovery of what emerges of itself from the biblical text with regard to the nature of language" (LAN, *SW,* 1:67). Thus, his recounting of the story of Creation is meant to shed light on his linguistic theory (in the sense of "objects of theology without which truth is inconceivable," or the famous ink-blotter) and should be treated accordingly—avoiding the sometimes tempting reification of its plot. Benjamin's interpretation of the first two chapters of Genesis can therefore be taken to manifest what he meant in his essay on Kant, by the peculiar relation between philosophy and religion that he deems essential to construct. That is, he intends to substantiate the historical and linguistic structures of the theological texts, rather than provide a mythical reading of them.[13]

Benjamin's reading of Genesis yields a linguistic interpretation that vindicates his theory of language and supplies the foundation for what I will later term an ethical feeling of the linguistic commitment between man and nature. Moreover, this text emphasizes a strong kinship between language and feeling in Genesis, specifically between language and melancholy.

Language—as a realm of potentiality for expression rather than of articulation or linguistic actualization—evokes Benjamin's argument for the demarcation between the linguistic essence of objects and that of the human. If we extend the aforementioned argument regarding the "language-lamp," as Benjamin calls it, to the human realm, we find a fundamental differentiation. The linguistic being of man is his language, and he communicates this being *in* his language. Unlike other objects (such as the lamp or mountain), however, human beings speak in words: "The incomparable feature of human language is that its magical community with things is immaterial and purely mental, and the symbol of this is sound. The Bible expresses this symbolic fact when it says that God breathes his breath into man: this is at once life and mind and language" (LAN, *SW*, 1:67). Despite man's obvious sonic advantage over things, however, there exists a unique sense of sharing between humans and nature, an intimate rapport that is "immaterial and purely mental," as Benjamin writes.

To ground man's sharing of his language with natural and inanimate objects, Benjamin invokes the biblical story of Creation. There he finds the primal source from which to explicate and clarify his previous proposition regarding the expansion of language so as to include every human being or thing. The crux of the linguistic connection between man and nature lies in man's communication of his own mental essence (language) in the very first act of linguistic expression, in naming: "Man therefore communicates his own mental being (insofar as it is communicable) by *naming* all other things" (LAN, *SW*, 1:64). This inclination or potential to communicate, however, is always entangled with a fundamental incapability to completely actualize such communication—and in the context of Genesis, a *loss* of such actualized, communicative capability.

I argue here that not only do we have mere linguistic potentiality instead of actualization, but only in the context of creation is this specifically evinced as a *loss* rather than a simple negation or inverse. The inability to wholly and perfectly express is grounded specifically in the configuration of the act of naming, as well as in its degradation in the Fall. Each entity that is a part of this act essentially endures some kind of loss (though of a very different character for each) that is only deepened by the linguistic manifestation of the Fall. Put differently, Benjamin reinterprets the story of Creation from a linguistic perspective that entails the following three phases: first, we have God's language—an expression of mere immediacy and creativity, a language that produces its entities ex nihilo rather than describes them. Second, we have man's "bliss" language, manifested in the act of naming in which man expresses nature's essence in the breath of his first words. Third, there is language after the Fall, a stage in which language is no longer creative, nor blissful; it is now merely propositional communication, chatter, expressing only its inherent incapability or lost, unfulfilled potentiality.

Benjamin grounds the special linguistic relationship between man and nature in the fundamental dissimilarity in their creation (note that God does not create the inanimate, which will later be produced by man). The rhythm of the creative acts remains the same in both cases: it is a triple-structured rhythm. In the case of man, however, the place of language in the act of creation has an entirely different status than it does in the case of nature (*SW*, 1:68). When God creates nature, he uses the following threefold structure: Let there be—he made (created)—he named. This structure positions language, or the speech-act in this case, at two ends of the creative act: God announces (linguistically) the beginning of the creative act, and God completes it by naming what he has created. Language demarcates creation.

In the fashioning of humanity, however, the threefold structure is preserved without having language at both ends of the creative act. There is, rather, an odd repetition of the same act: God creates man in his image—man is created in the image of God—God creates human beings as man and woman: "And God created man in his own image, in the image of God created he him; male and female created he them" (Genesis 1:27). Hence, the triple structure in man's creation, rather than pointing to the importance of its linguistic element as is done in nature's creation, stresses its underlying lack. Benjamin explains:

God did not create man from the word, and he did not name him. He did not wish to subject him to language, but in man God set language, which had served *him* as medium of creation, free. God rested when he had left his creative power to itself in man. This creativity, relieved of its divine actuality, became knowledge. Man is the knower in the same language in which God is the creator. God created him in his image; he created the knower in the image of the creator. (LAN, *SW*, 1:68)

The role of language is presented here via the anatomy of the relationship between God and man. God delegates his creative authority to man precisely by *not* subjecting him to language. The absence of the component of language in man's creation is therefore not accidental; it indicates man's special status in the created world, and designates man as language's sole possessor. Because God did not rule over man in his creative act by subjecting man to the divine, creative language, man is the sole possessor of his own language. Benjamin continues:

> The linguistic being of things is their language; this proposition, applied to man, means: the linguistic being of man is his language. Which signifies: man communicates his own mental being in his language . . . Man therefore communicates his own mental being (insofar as it is communicable) by *naming* all other things. . . . —*It is therefore the linguistic being of man to name things.* (LAN, *SW*, 1:64)

Here Benjamin's previous attempt to connect the mental entity with the linguistic entity of things, insofar as the former is communicable, becomes more explicit. Man's fulfillment or actualization of his essence merges with the communicability of the linguistic essence of things. This amalgamation materializes itself in the act of naming. Put differently, man is not named; he is the namer. He is endowed with God's language, which was transformed from a language of creation into one of knowledge (but not yet of judgment or mere propositional communication), which is used to name and to reenact the creation of nature in the linguistic act—so as to complete God's creation with language. By raising nature out of its anonymity, Adamic language both completes and repeats the creative act of God, and translates the mental being of things into the order of names.[14] In the act of naming, man expresses his own mental being and continues the creative act he has taken upon himself as nature passes before him in anonymous procession. "And out of the ground the LORD God formed every beast of the field, and every fowl of the air; and brought them unto the man to see what he would call them: and whatsoever the man called every living creature, that was the name thereof. And the man gave names to all cattle, and to the fowl of the air, and to every beast of the field" (Genesis 2:19–20).[15] To entrust man with such naming capabilities is thus another step in the constitution of the relationship between man and nature—a relationship marked by a constant internal striving of everything to express the linguistic part of its mental essence.

There is, however, in Benjamin's interpretation an additional constituent that takes place between God's creative act and man's completion of it. For "if the lamp and the mountain and the fox did not communicate themselves to man, how should he be able to name them?" (LAN, *SW*, 1:64). Consequently, mute nature and speechless objects communicate their mental being *to man*, and he, in turn, names them according to what they have communicated to him. This act of communication should be understood as inner-linguistic; it involves language as such and does not bear on any external "content." To name them, man must be dependent on their own communication with him: he becomes their lord in the act of naming, but he also remains dependent upon their call, of which he is the addressee.

What is revealed here, and this is of the utmost importance, is that the chain of creation is also a *chain of expression*. In such a chain natural and inanimate entities are structured into a teleological hierarchy of continuous attempts to execute the internal inclination to express mental essence. The objects turn to man, and he responds to their call, endowing them with a blissful moment. Bliss (*Seligkeit*) characterizes here the moment in which the act of naming involves no subjective knowledge whatsoever. The moment is blissful only insofar as it is necessary and immediate: "In receiving the unspoken nameless language of things and converting it by name into sounds, man performs this task" (LAN, *SW*, 1:70).[16]

Man, however, does not only hold an active role in the creative act. The act of naming also fulfills a receptive function in which the human use of language as such is at the same time an expression of man's *own* linguistic essence; therefore, in naming, man manifests his own linguistic essence.[17] This receptivity, in fact, continues the creative act: with it, nature's soundless linguistic being becomes the ground upon which the word of God shines forth (LAN, *SW*, 1:69). In that sense the purpose of creation merges with the fulfillment of man's essence, which is to say, the fulfillment of the linguistic expression of an essence. The name man gives is a receptive expression of God's creative word, and with it man shares the creative act with God: "In name, the word of God has not remained creative; it has become in one part receptive, even if receptive to language. Thus fertilized, it aims to give birth to the language of things themselves, from which in turn, soundlessly, in the mute magic of nature, the word of God shines forth" (LAN *SW*, 1:69).

This shared creative act, in which man endows nature with names, is an event that perfects the language of the mute (nature in the story of Genesis, as well as inanimate objects throughout Benjamin's essay) and translates it into a more consummate linguistic expression. "[Not only is it a] translation of the mute into the sonic; it is also the translation of the nameless into the name. It is therefore the translation of an imperfect language into a more perfect one" (LAN, *SW*, 1:70)—a translation that is later guaranteed by God, thus completing the alliance and concurrence among God, man, and nature.[18]

This positive relationship, however, which seems at first glance even to be a productive collaboration, also entails a structure of strong, suppressed power relations. Nature, because it is ruled by man, also comes to be dependent on man for its expression, so man's higher position in the chain of expression turns him into an almost godlike figure in relation to nature, duplicating, in many senses, the power-relation structure that God maintains with man. Note, too, that *die Natur* in German is a feminine noun, a fact that can be read as strengthening the power structure in the act of naming. Feminine nature becomes the absorbent, mute entity, whereas man is he who gives nature her voice, who speaks *for* her.[19]

The power relations inaugurated in the story of Creation are threefold. Benjamin describes man as standing between God and nature in a continuous chain of the (power) relations structured by language, which is a configuration of degrees in which God, man, and nature stand side by side. In this chain man, "elevated above nature," is the "bearer of nature's crown" (LAN, *SW*, 1:67; RL, *SW*, 1:60):

The uninterrupted flow of this communication runs through the whole of nature, from the lowest forms of existence to man and from man to God. Man communicated himself to God through name, which he gives to nature and (in proper names) to his own kind; and to nature he gives names according to the communication that he receives from her, for the whole of nature, too, is imbued with a nameless, unspoken language, the residue of the creative word of God, which is preserved in man as the cognizing name and above man as the judgment suspended over him. (LAN, *SW*, 1:74)

This complex chain of expression, in which a linguistic relation runs continuously among God, humanity, and nature, configures language in accordance with the sense outlined at the beginning of the essay, in which Benjamin posits that language is not part of the privileged realm of communicative articulation. Although man's language is far more developed than nature's, the languages of both stand on the same continuous axis and are thereby related to each other in degree rather than kind (LAN, *SW*, 1:66). As far as language is concerned, nature is not so far from man, and its muteness resides on the same continuum as man's articulate (and, later, fallen) language. In both cases we have a linguistic potentiality, which is actualized in various degrees.

Interestingly enough, this chain and the interactive relations it entails persist in one way or another even after man's language falls into the abyss of chatter. Retelling the story of Creation this way restructures what comes after it (in the form of the Fall): the structure of the relation remains the same; however, its continuity is interrupted. The three entities still stand on the same axis, but they can no longer touch each other (this is related to the metaphor of the tangent Benjamin uses elsewhere). Understood in this way, the continuity of expression, which is violently cut after the Fall, has, we can say, an impoverishing effect on all three entities.

Adamic naming is described as knowledge; however, in this early stage—before the Fall—it still lacks understanding and conceptual analysis on the part of man. The name merely presents and is prior to a re-presentation of its objects. It is the expression of the object's utter individuality in a judgment-free manner, prior to the opening of the gap between signifier and signified. The object's essence presents itself in the name and voice that utters it. Nevertheless, the fall of human language and the expulsion from paradise cost man his original naming language. His exile stands for the loss of immediacy and creativity possessed by the Adamic language. And when stripped of the power of immediate naming, language turns into an abyss of prattle, where its communicativeness marks its exclusive function.[20] Names become signs, and immediacy reemerges as means.

Benjamin points out that the tree of knowledge, which usually marks the entry point into cognition, is not the first instance of judgment in

Genesis. Even the tree cannot conceal that its Edenic language, and specifically its place in the creative act, was already cognized: God, at the end of the first six days of the Creation, "saw that it was good"—thus marking a prior division between good and evil. Nevertheless, this division is still internal to the naming language and does not take place after its fall. In this sense it would not be accurate to say that God is judging here in the usual sense of the word, since there is no choice *between* good and evil. "Good" should not be understood here in opposition to "bad" and thus connected to an external value. Rather, it refers to an expression of the thing's internal essence. This is what "and God saw that it was good" in fact means: God conceives his creation as "good" not as opposed to "bad" but because it realizes the essence of the created thing.[21] This is how Benjamin fathoms the difference between the fallen and the expressive: fallen language is always connected to an external value to which it corresponds, whereas expressive language is centered on an inner process of realization and accomplishment (referring to the essence of created things, which parallel the aforementioned potential). Fallen meaning is thus external; but expressive meaning, which is always inherent to the linguistic sphere, is given as an echelon of the refinement of meaning.

Benjamin thus stresses the *nameless* nature of judging and propositional language rather than its division between good and evil. The snake's seduction rests not on the distinction itself but on the access to deepest, vain, nameless knowledge:[22]

Knowledge of good and evil abandons name; it is a knowledge from outside, the uncreated imitation of the creative word. Name steps outside itself in this knowledge: the Fall marks the birth of the *human word*, in which name no longer lives intact and which has stepped out of name-language, the language of knowledge, from what we may call its own immanent magic, in order to become expressly, as it were externally, magic. (LAN, *SW*, 1:71)

The abandonment of the name also entails the loss of its inherent immediacy. In it the individual, concrete name becomes a mere word, a means for communication, and an abstract linguistic statement. An immediate relation to the object is lost so as to gain the ability to generalize and judge it. The unity between signifier and signified is shattered, and arbitrariness emerges. After the Fall, any reconciliation between subject and object, any closing of the abyss between them, can be made impossible only by means of the structure of fallen, fissured language.[23] This claim for a division between subject and object arises when subjectivity enters the equation, when individual, personal knowledge penetrates language and takes over the objective power of naming. Such a division destroys immediacy and splits the reference from the object—which is to say, language and world now stand separated. This conceptualization of the structure of fallen language allows us to think of Benjamin's linguistic theory as a structuring of the relation between man and world.

Also revealed here is the basic difference between God's creative act and Adam's act of naming. Barbara Johnson points out that God's creative act brings things into material being—where word and world become one ("Let there be" begets a material entity). For Adam, however, world and language are two different, unbridgeable entities. God's reference is thus the condition in which name and thing are indissolubly one. Nevertheless, even in God's creative act, this oneness seems not to completely hold. God brings nature into language in an act that implies their original differentiation (nature was not created linguistically but, with man's assistance, was *brought into* language). In the same way, when Genesis tells us that the "word is with God," this is always already a mark of a difference inherent to the alleged primary unity. Indeed, to claim that God has created the perfect reference, if this is possible, is to destroy the concept of reference, since the latter requires a distinction between that which refers and its referent. Thus, to understand a "perfect reference" as a dissolution of this distinction is to altogether undermine the term *reference*.[24] It is important to note, however, that despite the appeal of Johnson's interpretation, it is not entirely clear that it is evidenced throughout Benjamin's essay, especially when he determines that only God's creative language guarantees the objectivity of the translation of the "nameless into name" (LAN, *SW*, 1:70).

The language essay describes two stages in the human act of naming. The first is that of the blissful name, in which the immediacy of creation still maintains itself in the Adamic name. Then, however, man is expelled from paradise, thus having his blissful naming language replaced by the empty, austere language. Here man's melancholy enters the picture. Nature now stands alone, mute, lacking its expressive human counterpart, without which it lacks the possibility to exercise or actualize, even partly, its linguistic essence. At this point of the story, after the Fall, the second stage of naming appears—which Benjamin terms "overnaming," chatter, or prattle. Both stages, writes Benjamin, induce in nature a certain melancholy, but the forms taken by such melancholy are completely different in each case.

Nature was mute before the Fall, but its muteness after the Fall and after the loss of man is wholly different. Its pre-Fall speechlessness was blissful, writes Benjamin, because nature was in intimate communion with man, who in turn named it, thereby expressing its essence and bringing it into actualization. The muteness that descends on nature after the Fall, however, is described as something utterly different—it is nature's "other muteness": "After the Fall, however, when God's word curses the ground, the appearance of nature is deeply changed. Now begins its other muteness, which is what we mean by the "deep sadness of nature" (LAN, SW, 1:72).

That which mourns feels itself thoroughly known by the unknowable. To be named—even when the namer is godlike and blissful—perhaps always remains an intimation of mourning ... There is, in the relation of human languages to that of things, something that can be approximately described as "overnaming" [*Überbenennung*]—the deepest linguistic reason for all melancholy [*Traurigkeit*] and (from the point of view of the thing) for all deliberate muteness [*Verstummens*]. (LAN, SW, 1:73)

Benjamin describes here how the relation with man has always kept nature mournful, and man's act of naming is, in turn, always imbued with melancholy. To be named (before or after the Fall) is always already to have an intimation of mourning (LAN, SW, 1:73), because such naming testifies to the need to be named by *another*, to the inability to name and express oneself, and to the dependence on another—on man. But the loss of man as a namer and the severance from nature's fleeting moment of bliss leads to an even deeper sadness. After the Fall nature cannot even be dependent on the expression of another. The stage that Benjamin calls "sorrowful" (*Traurig*)[25] marks the further deterioration of man's lost language into chatter. In the prattle that ensues after the Fall, nature is overnamed, which is even worse than not being named at all. Nature falls silent, but this time not in anticipation of being named by man but rather in the suffering of its own lack of expression, in mute forsakenness.

Recast in the aforementioned terms of potentiality, nature's inherent mournfulness bears witness to it as mere potentiality. To bear a linguistic essence that can only be given as an inclination, potential, or faculty is to be always in need of something that would bring it into actualization. This structure exists whether such actualization has occurred or can in fact come about. It merely points to its essential insufficiency and dependence. The mournfulness of nature is that of its being mere potential. There is no other way to grasp its linguistic essence; it is always a potential that exists together with its inherent privation. Yet, again, such a privation is not the negativity of expression, nor is it a contingent fact regarding expression; it is, rather, part of the fundamental structure of language itself.

The stage of overnaming, in Benjamin's terms, taking place after the Fall, makes the lack of a name only more present and distinct, as if the fundamental privation and loss of language shines forth from within endless, fallen chatter. In other words the figure of excess in *over*naming embodies and demonstrates the essential lack of content that stands behind it; it is not a new, contingent fact about language, only a starker demonstration of its inherent emptiness. The variance between the two linguistic stages of nature is not as fundamental as it may seem. It is only that the second, fallen stage has the power to demonstrate all the more clearly what is fundamental about language as such: that it is, essentially and inherently, mere potentiality, a faculty for language and not a complete and consummate act of expression. In that sense Benjamin's ostensible interpretation of the story of language in Genesis is not about the Genesis story at all; it demonstrates, rather, his essential convictions about language as such, using the narrative of the primal Fall to elucidate them.

The elemental linguistic adaptation after the Fall is therefore to be found not in nature's two stages of melancholy but rather in those of humankind. If the melancholy prior to the Fall belongs solely to nature, then the melancholy after the Fall is shared by man inherently. The name-giver himself, also in a state of loss, suddenly shares nature's endless mourning—nature endures muteness, and man is afflicted by an inflation of insufficient signifiers to express nature's linguistic essence evident in its muteness. Not only does the named not receive expression and its essence remains concealed, but the namer, too, has lost the ability to perform his task and to realize, moreover, his essence *as* a name-giver: "Man therefore communicates his own mental being (insofar as it is communicable) by *naming* all other things. . . . —*It is therefore the linguistic being of man to name things*" (LAN, *SW*, 1:64; emphasis in original). Not only can man no longer actualize another's potential (namely, nature's); he has also lost the power to express his own.

The intimate rapport between man and thing, man and nature, is grounded in the latter approaching man and calling for expression. The continuous teleological inclination of every being to actualize its mental essence in expression is the basis for this rapport with man, whose position in this equation is one of power. Man is the only possible namer and vehicle of expression for what is mute, natural, and inanimate. A linguistic alliance is established—the thing approaches and communicates itself in order to be expressed by man, and man is in turn dependent on nature and the inanimate objects around him in executing his own task of expression. Man is linguistically called on and responds in the form of the name, in what seems to be an ethical response filled with obligation toward nature and the task that he received from God. This structure, however, changes after the Fall, when man is inclined to abandon or even reject this obligation in favor of the prattle of fallen chatter:

> This immediacy in the communication of abstraction came into being as judgment, when, in the Fall, man abandoned immediacy in the communication of the concrete—that is, name—and fell into the abyss of the mediateness of all communication . . . After the Fall, which, in making language mediate, laid the foundation for its multiplicity, linguistic confusion could be only a step away. Once men had injured the purity of the name, the turning away [*Abkehr*] from that contemplation of things in which their language passes into man needed only to be completed in order to deprive men of the common foundation of an already shaken spirit of language. *Signs* must become confused when things are entangled [*verwickeln*]. The enslavement [*Verknechtung*] of language in prattle is joined by the enslavement of things in folly [*Narretei*] almost as its inevitable consequence. In this turning away from things, which was enslavement, the plan for the Tower of Babel came into being, and linguistic confusion with it. (LAN, *SW*, 1:72)

The special entanglement of man and nature, or man and thing, which existed in Benjamin's account of the Creation, was transformed into confusion (as manifested in signs and chatter) through man's turning away (*Abkehr*) from the call of things upon him. This "turning away," a word that appears twice in the passage, involves a threefold renunciation: first, man's neglecting of the task of naming, being thereby unable to actualize his own essence as namer; second, his turning away from being receptive to the language of things (i.e., the language with which they communicate themselves to man); and finally, a turning away from the concrete relation to things, exchanging it for a mediate, merely communicative relation.

In neglecting his task and renouncing this call, man not only does not name, but he also neglects and abandons his more general obligation toward nature—an obligation formed at the moment of their joint creation. Losing the ability to name has thus caused man to lose his ethical responsibility toward nature, instead of having deepened it. This, again, should be thought of in light of the difference between fallen and expressive language: in the latter there is a basic loyalty to the realization of meaning of the thing, whereas in the former, language is not expressive but rather operates within a space of judgment. Judgment thus reveals itself to be, first, external to the thing expressed, rather than pertaining to its internal essence through expression, and second, judgment is conditioned by the very structure of intentionality; that is, the language of judgment cannot communicate anything that is bereft of an intentional grip.

What is left, one may ask, at man's disposal after he loses his primordial naming language? Does man willingly refuse to continue the performance of his task, or is he incapable of fulfilling it (owing to the loss of his primordial language)? It is my suggestion here that man's obligation to nature is much more profound than the way it is presented in the act of naming itself. It lies in the intimate relationship among the elements of the triangle God-man-nature; it remains a relation even if it is not linguistically actualized. In this sense the "turning away" is always interlaced with the potential, as well as the requirement, to turn toward, to re-turn (in a structure completely different from fallenness, for example, in which the possibility to re-turn is not structurally interwoven). Thus, man remains obliged to nature even when it is impossible for him to name it, maybe even more so. This obligation relates closely to and echoes my preceding discussion of the ghost. There, also, the obligation and commitment built between the present and the past calling on it is not necessarily a commitment that needs to be resolved in a deed; rather, it is a much more general and all-encompassing pledge, in which a relationship with the past is built and an acknowledgment is given, even if not actualized.

Benjamin invokes the Babylonian tower to exemplify how man, instead of turning *toward* things (in fulfillment of God's task of naming), *turns things* into the building blocks of his own name. The signification of fallen language that turns into a language of means is echoed in the way things become the material means for man. The tower is instituted in an attempt to replicate God's creative power and to make a name and monument for humanity: "And they said, 'Come, let us build ourselves a city and a tower with its top in the heavens, and let us make ourselves a name, lest we be scattered upon the face of the entire earth'" (Genesis 11:4). Man does not name nature or things; rather, he created a name for *himself* with his building of the tower. According to Benjamin language is enslaved in prattle, and things are enslaved in folly (LAN, *SW*, 1:72), a curious remark that I take to mean that in the context of the story of Babel, both language and things are "enslaved" in that they are not present as such for man but serve only as a means to an external end—the tower aspires to reach the sky so as to eclipse God himself. To build the tower, man uses the language he shares with other men (which God deprives him of eventually), as well as the objects around him; hence, objects and men alike turn out to be of mere use-value. Not only is God's task utterly neglected, but the tower is an attempt to outdo God himself.[26]

The tower can also be seen as a clear presentation of man's forgetfulness: not only has he neglected the task he has received from God; he has forgotten it altogether. Instead of committing himself to nature, man is committed exclusively to himself—and at a cost: the natural and the inanimate have been turned into means. God's reaction is a deepening of the already fallen communicative language: he destroys what had been until then the unified language common to all men and breaks it into a multiplicity of languages so as to estrange men not only from the world around them but also from their fellow human beings.

Sadness and the loss of nature are accompanied by man's deprivation of his single, unified language. Man experiences two losses: first, he is stripped of his primordial naming language that came with his expulsion from paradise; second, after the end of the Babel story he no longer shares a unified language with his fellow humans. Man and nature share a kindred condition—one of loss and muteness. Man and nature, thus, were connected through loss, then were parted at the moment of the Fall, only to be reconnected later through their shared loss of expression.[27] In a way this loss brings them back together and restores the alliance that was lost with the exile from paradise—an alliance grounded in loss.[28]

Man's melancholy should therefore be understood as inner-linguistic, not psychological or subjective. Man is not sad or mournful for a specific loss relating to his subjective, contingent existence; his melancholy is linguistic, and it touches directly on his inability to execute his linguistic essence—that of naming nature. Adam names nature not to free it of its muteness and give it expression. He does so primarily to enact and actualize his own linguistic essence—that of being a namer. Nature's linguistic potentiality is answered by man; however, this answer also refers to man's realization of his own potential—actualized in the act of naming. Man's essence is thus intrinsically chained to that of nature, since man does not have an independent potential but only the potential he shares with nature, which, because of the Fall, can no longer be fulfilled.[29]

Lament: Language and Sadness

One of Benjamin's main concerns in his linguistic theory is the possible connection between language and feeling. Speculation about such a link appears first and foremost in his essay on language, specifically in his thoughts about the presence of melancholy, not as a content of language or its object of reference but as something that underlies its very structure. To use Benjamin's own terms, melancholy is expressed *in* language and not *through* it. Another valuable source in which Benjamin wrestles with the relationship between language and feeling is his early fragment "The Role of Language in *Trauerspiel* and Tragedy" (1916), where he poses the question, "What is the metaphysical relation of this feeling [*Trauer*] to language?" (*SW*, 1:59). The fragment examines specific questions regarding the role and structure of language in the *Trauerspiel* in comparison to tragedy, in what seems to be an excursion from the *Trauerspiel* book and the later language essay.

In this condensed, complex text Benjamin defines sadness as occupying a special role: it embodies the relation between feeling and language.

His use of the term *language* here corresponds to its definition in the opening of the language essay—as the realm of potential expression. Sadness, in turn, finds its place in the nonarticulate domain of this realm: "The sad has no main focus, and its deepest and indeed only expression is to be found neither in dramatic speech nor in speech in any sense" (RL, *SW*, 1:59). Since the *Trauerspiel* clearly shows language functioning under the conditions of sorrow, Benjamin asserts that the relation between sadness and the way it is expressed in language exemplifies "the riddle of the *Trauerspiel*."

Benjamin follows these claims by asking, "What is the metaphysical relation of this feeling to language, to the spoken word?" (RL, *SW*, 1:59), adding: "How language can fill itself with sadness, how language can express sadness, is the basic question of the *Trauerspiel*, alongside that other question: How can the feeling of sadness gain entry into the linguistic order of art?" (RL, *SW*, 1:59–60; translation altered). This fundamental question involves feeling in general and its relation to language but it also bears on *sadness* and the forms of its linguistic expression.

The question of the relation between language and feeling can be considered, I propose, through the notion of lament, which Benjamin conceives as an embodiment of the association between sorrow and language.[30] He develops this notion in both the aforementioned fragment and the language essay; in fact, a pivotal part of his argument appears in both texts using similar phrasing. I begin with Benjamin's presentation of lament in "On Language as Such," then move to the peculiar character of lament as a point of encounter between language and feeling in "The Role of Language":

It is a metaphysical truth that all nature would begin to lament if it were endowed with language (though "to endow with language" is more than "to make able to speak"). This proposition has a double meaning. It means, first, that she would lament [over[31]] language itself [*sie würde über die Sprache selbst klagen*]. Speechlessness [*Sprachlosigkeit*]: that is the great sorrow [*Leid*] of nature . . . This proposition means, second, that she would lament [*sie würde klagen*].[32] (LAN, *SW*, 1:72–73)

The double meaning presented by Benjamin in his argument is given in a conditional sentence. Its two parts are both hypothetical. *Had* language been given to nature, it *would* lament. In accordance with Benjamin's definition of language in the essay, the discussion, again, is one of potentiality, not necessarily an actualization of expression. Sorrowful, mute nature would use the language that it lacks only to lament—that is, to express its own inherent linguistic loss. It would use language only to communicate its own melancholy over the loss, and, in that sense, it would communicate the essence of nature. Nature's speechlessness is its greatest sorrow, adds Benjamin, and this is why, even if language were given to nature, it would be used solely for lament.

Nature's lament can be understood from two different angles. First, it concerns something lost, specifically lost language—or in this case, lament would respond to the *lack* rather than the loss of language. Second, this lament also signifies that nature will *merely* lament; that is, it will not express any specific objective content pertaining to its object of loss or, in fact, refer to any specific content whatsoever. "The sad has no main focus," writes Benjamin in "The Role of Language"—it is not object-oriented—and therefore signifies what it means for a lament to be nonintentional.[33] To use Freud's aforementioned conceptions (and recalling that melancholy has a nonintentional structure): it is markedly melancholic.

"Lament, however, is the most undifferentiated, impotent expression of language. It contains scarcely more than the sensuous breath; and even where there is only a rustling of plants, there is always a lament [*klingt immer eine Klage mit*]" (LAN, *SW*, 1:73). In this passage, which continues from the previous citation, the context of nature's loss is revealed. Lament is impotent because it is always already given in partial, fallen language, a language in which meaning can only be given as dispersed. In the blissful, primordial state in which nature was named by man, this expression was already an intimation of sorrow. The relationship between sorrow and language thus always remains present. Even when man named nature in his (still) blissful language, mourning was already inherent to the linguistic structure. Nature was never able to name itself—and, in that sense, its melancholy is related to its lack rather than its loss of language. Nature's dependence on man to gather its disseminated sounds (dependence construed as the power relations mentioned above) renders its existence in language fundamentally melancholic. Nature's sorrow, however, is deepened after the fall into human chatter, when nature is named "not from the one blessed paradisiacal language of names, but from the hundred languages of man, in which name has already withered [*welkte*]" (LAN, *SW*, 1:73).

In light of the Fall it becomes evident why lament is rendered impotent—it originates from a complete degradation caused by the inability to express. Though it still belongs to the linguistic realm, it is its impotent part, since the endowment of language resulting in lament "is more than 'to make able to speak.'" Nature's melancholy is now joined by that of man; a new bond is now shared between them. Mute speechlessness is accompanied by chattering speechlessness, which amounts to the same thing: two opposite responses reacting to the same lacuna. Man has lost his blissful language; nature has lost man and the blissful world where it had been so mournfully expressed. Nature thus mourns not because it cannot express itself but because it has lost the *world* in which it could have expressed itself.

Silence is the ontological state of nature and the essence of nature's linguistic being.[34] Hence, relieving nature of its muteness does not necessarily mean relieving it of its inherent melancholy: lament is always already part of chatter and thus "undifferentiated" and "impotent."[35] Created mute, nature nevertheless stammers and patters in the natural sounds it produces. This muttering should not only be thought of as nature lamenting its lack of language. The muttering is, rather, always already part of its efforts (albeit primitive and fundamental attempts) at expression. Put differently, muttering is a manifestation of the fact of mere linguistic potentiality and of the repeating failure of its actualization. Not in articulate speech, but rather in the mute facets of language, does sorrow receive expression. Sorrow's muteness, therefore, does not prevent it from being an integral part of language.

The relationship between language and lament is echoed in somewhat different terms when Benjamin writes:

Because she is mute, nature mourns. Yet the inversion of this proposition leads even further into the essence [*Wesen*] of nature; the sadness[36] [*Trauerigkeit*] of nature makes her mute [*verstummen*]. In all mourning there is the deepest inclination [*Hang*] to speechlessness [*Sprachlosigkeit*], which is infinitely more than the inability [*Unfähigkeit*] or disinclination [*Unlust*] to communicate. That which mourns feels itself thoroughly [*durch und durch*] known by the unknowable. To be named—even when the namer is godlike and blissful [*Seliger*]—perhaps always remains an intimation of mourning. But how much more melancholy it is to be named not from the one blessed paradisiacal language of names, but from the hundred languages of man, in which name has already withered [*welkte*], yet which, according to God's pronouncement, have knowledge of things. (LAN, *SW*, 1:73)

The conditional sentence in the previous paragraph involves the relation between lament and the state of being relieved of silence. Here the relationship is one of muteness (and silence) and mourning. In many senses the previous claim is of a more originary nature; taking place before the conditional claim could even be formulated, it is the prerequisite of the latter claim. The question Benjamin poses here is, Which conditions which—muteness or mourning?[37] Do muteness and linguistic lack produce mourning, or, rather, does mourning itself produce muteness? Benjamin suggests that the essence of nature is more deeply understood through the second formulation—nature's loss and melancholy cause it to be unable to possess language.

If this is true, however, what is the ground for nature's sadness? If not its loss or even its inability to express itself, what causes it to be melancholy in the first place? Nature's primary speechlessness extends further than its mere inability to speak or communicate. It has to do with the *nature* of its mourning rather than the *ground* for it (as in other texts, Benjamin refrains from positing a relational and causal relation to truth).[38]

The two stages of speechless mourning are both located in the act of naming, before and after the Fall. However, the event of the Fall seems to play no part in being a ground for nature's melancholy. Nature is created mute: speechlessness and sadness are integral to its being in a way that no event, be it historical or mythical, can be. From the moment of its creation nature is named by another—and in that sense there is no originary loss involved. For nature nothing, in fact, was ever lost: the part it plays in the scene of creation is precisely that of being speechless; thus, there is no loss at all.

Nature, created into the act of naming, was always already named and known "through and through" by another. Its original sadness is hence anchored not in loss but in knowledge. Again, a power relation is established between the knower and the known: to man, nature is completely unfolded, but nature can be unfolded only in and of itself and can never disclose another. This is the reason for nature's original sadness. Once it is created as being open to naming, nothing about it can ever remain concealed.

Mourning is therefore all about knowledge. The name opens up nature completely, knows it thoroughly, and in so doing deadens any potential life it might have. The name stabilizes meaning and completely opens up the essence of nature; however, it does so without leaving any remains in what proves here to be the mournful grounds of nature's existence. In this sense the Fall is not the reason for mourning, since it marks only the continuation of the proper name itself.

Fenves shows that the proper name is connected to fate and is thus realized only when life ceases. Only then is the reason for the choice of name unfolded. Proper names, therefore, *demand* death as price and proof of their congruence with what they name. This is also true regarding the overnaming of nature: for even when things are not yet overnamed, but only named according to their species, they must die so that their names can manifest themselves as their own. In that sense the expulsion from paradise is not a constitutive event regarding nature's mourning; it is not induced by the fall of language and the multiplicity of names. In fact, even a single name is sufficient to elicit the feeling of mourning. Having to show that this single name is one's own is reason enough for the presentiment of the "intimation of mourning."[39]

Here Benjamin links "all mourning," and not only that of nature, to an inclination to speechlessness. Something about melancholy and sorrow has to do with a tendency toward muteness, which, as Benjamin indicates throughout the language essay, is so much more than volitional or nonvolitional speechlessness (this is also argued in a different way in "The Role of Language," in which sadness, although defined as having no expression in speech, is nonetheless a part of language). This claim implies, or even proclaims, an inherent affinity between sorrow and silence. This two-sidedness of language—on the one hand, possessing an inclination to expression and, on the other, having sorrow and speechlessness as integral parts—points to a more complex image of creation, one in which muteness and sorrow assume a prominent role.

The second version of the claim regarding the relation between muteness and mournfulness appears in the *Trauerspiel* book in an almost identical phrasing. There is, however, one crucial difference. Instead of the melancholic characterization of fallen chatter, the last stage of naming, the *Trauerspiel* book claims: "But how much more so [melancholic] not to be named, only to be read, to be read uncertainly by the allegorist, and to have become highly significant thanks only to him" (*TS*, 225). Overnaming is replaced by reading, specifically allegorical reading. Not only has language fallen; its sonic expression has been succeeded by a written-allegorical one: the structure of signification replaces that of expression. Allegorical reading stands here for an even more fallen state—one in which meaning is arbitrary signification poured into the empty space of the mute object, thereby interrupting the pure flow of expression and embodying an even deeper level of degradation.

Hence, it can be maintained that there is no loss and maybe even no lack here, since it is creation itself, and nature's speechlessness is part of it. The human act of naming is also part of this scene of creation and should not be understood as responding to any sudden loss. In fact, it is not anchored in any causal relation whatsoever. Melancholy is inherent to creation, which is always already saturated with sadness and speechlessness. The indispensable role played by melancholy in the story of creation has to do with the unidentifiable and intentionless ground embodied by melancholy. It comes about not as a result of anything at all.[40]

The origination of lament is described, therefore, as being not only related to the Fall and man's betrayal of the task that had been given him. It is also portrayed, and more profoundly so, through the betrayal of language itself (not being a response to a specific loss or a disturbance of any object-relation).

"The Role of Language" explicates this structure in more detail. In this fragment lament comes into being at the point of halt or blockage that Benjamin describes as inherent to language itself. This represents a collapse and disintegration within the linguistic site otherwise marked by constant flux (language in the *Trauerspiel*, characterized as constantly changing and unstable, is evoked to contrast with the language of tragedy, with its almost overdetermined nature). The importance of the version in this essay is due to its physical, almost bodily, reference to the production of lament. Benjamin describes the process:

Words have a pure emotional life cycle in which they purify themselves by developing from the natural sound to the pure sound of feeling. For such words, language is merely a transitional phase within the entire life cycle, and in them the *Trauerspiel* finds its voice. It describes the path from natural sound via lament to music . . . Midway through its journey nature finds itself betrayed by language, and that powerful blocking of feeling turns to sorrow. (RL, *SW*, 1:60; translation altered)

The original continuity and succession, described in "On Language as Such," is presented here through its arrest. The halt and blockage in the original infinite chain of expression is that which produces lament, which manifests the internal disintegration of language. The *Trauerspiel* makes evident the potentially continuous passage from natural sounds to music, but this passage is halted midway with a lament that signifies this betrayal of the original infinite chain of expression. Lament is thus the liminal entity that stands between the sounds of nature and the production of music; it is the form of expression that symbolizes the inherent lacuna in language, grounded in sorrow.

An impediment internal to the structure of language elicits sadness and its expression in lament. Language's journey stops short midway, when natural sounds encounter language's inexpressibility, its own border of potential, and it is then that mourning and lament are called up from within the linguistic depths. Benjamin describes this moment of obstruction as the production of a blockage in the flow of expression; it is an enclosed sphere in which mourning resounds in language. Residing at the heart of this blockage, language is evoked in the interruption in the path from natural sounds to music. Lament is conjured out of this obstruction, in which mourning and sadness are elicited and become "trapped," so to speak, within language's borders. The flow of expression is physically blocked, dammed, and contained within the space of lament. Lament is thus divulged as the language of mourning, but this divulgence occurs at the border of its own expressibility. Lament, no longer natural sonic muttering, is also not yet purifying music—so, at this midpoint, "sorrow fills the sensuous world in which nature and language meet" (RL, *SW*, 1:60).

The disposition of the betrayal of language is that of the "signifying word" (RL, *SW*, 1:60)—or, put differently, fallen language. With the arrival of the signifying, mediated word, language can no longer be a sanctuary for nature, and nature is left to falter and to succumb to its own muteness. Language no longer provides comfort to nature, since sorrow cannot be expressed in signifying language. Its blockage and betrayal—and, moreover, the deprivation of comfort inherent to expression—are closely connected to the status of man and his fallen, unnaming language. This is why every act of linguistic signification inherently partakes in the melancholic disposition of language.

The use of the term "comfort" here, with regard to lament, opens up expression, specifically expression in lament *as* a form of comfort. Nature's desire to lament is also its desire to express itself in the literal *Aus-Druck*, or the releasing and ex-pressing of feeling for the purpose of relief. When nature is betrayed and expression is denied—when there is no *Druck*—pain and sorrow remain locked within the linguistic confines, echoing only themselves. Thus lament is inaugurated by the damming up of feeling described by Benjamin.

This is yet another way to understand the aforementioned "impotent" nature of lament, which attempts to express what cannot exit the confines of one's own sorrow. Nature's inability to turn lament into music also concerns the understanding of the role of hearing in Benjamin's argument: "the faculties of speech and hearing still stand equal in the scales, and ultimately everything depends on the ear for lament, for only the most profoundly heard lament can become music" (RL, *SW*, 1:61). Here, again, speechlessness and muteness enter the picture. The transformation of lament into music is impossible since lament is always silent. Lament, the silent partner of music, is only the constantly failing attempt to express and purify. Unlike music, it cannot be sung; it can only be received in hearing. Never uttered but always received, it can only echo within the confines of mournful language itself. Lament is, accordingly, a matter for the ear, not the voice. Friedlander shows insightfully that we are to understand this striking statement as being related to the fundamental dispersion of meaning in the *Trauerspiel*, which, owing to this dispersion, can never be actually sung. It can only be received as a whole from a gathering of separate voices—thus, it can only be heard.[41] In this context the echo becomes an interesting figure.

Benjamin's discussion of the echo in the *Trauerspiel* draws on a scene from *Die Glorreiche Marter Joannes von Nepomuck*.[42] This scene (no. 14) shows Zytho, one of the conspirators, echoing a speech of his victim, Quido, using the echo in an almost ironic, even "pleasing" form. Zytho's echo, repeating only Quido's last syllables, changes their meaning altogether. For instance, *erweisen* (to prove) becomes *Eisen* (iron); *liegt* (lie down) becomes *erliegt* (succumb); *mein Leben* (my life) becomes *eben* (even, just), etc. This device introduces a comic, ironic element into the dialogue, but it also presents the emptiness and meaninglessness of language and in so doing transforms Quido's plea into something utterly different and, moreover, arbitrary. After the distorting echo has been pronounced, Quido's next sentence usually begins with a reference to the mistake (here, to *Eisen*), which shifts the dialogue someplace else, again showing the meaninglessness of his original expression, together with the potential carried by its materiality. However, and more importantly, this dialogue demonstrates how meaning is never given in a single utterance but is always bestowed in a collection of individual expressions.

This structure exemplifies, according to Benjamin, the relation of the *Trauerspiel* to language and meaning: "If the echo, the true domain of the free play of sound, is now, so to speak, taken over by meaning, then it must prove to be entirely a manifestation of the linguistic, as the age understood it" (*TS*, 210). The echo is the clearest presentation of a bombastic relation to language, and in it the repetitive and the empty embody the structure of linguistic meaning in the baroque. The metaphysical order of the *Trauerspiel*, Benjamin suggests in "The Role of Language," is determined by the principles of cycle and repetition, and cycle and duality, neither of which allow the dissemination of sorrow throughout nature in the form of sound but, rather, cause unstable meaning, structured as echo, to disintegrate into sorrow (RL, *SW*, 1:60).

The disintegration of meaning into empty repetition is exemplified by the movement of the echo, which receives meaning from the outside only to merely *re*-sound it. Accordingly, it holds no content of its own but can manifest only the linguistic structure as such. The sonic structure of the echo, however, is not only repetitive; it is a figure of transmission that requires a certain physical resistance: an object encountered by sound before it turns into an echo.[43] In "The Role of Language" Benjamin describes the journey undertaken by nature—a journey starting in natural sound and moving through lament into music—as one that is stopped midway and betrayed by language itself. Nature is denied the possibility of expressing feeling in the linguistic realm, or, in Benjamin's words: "midway through its journey nature finds itself betrayed by language, and the powerful blocking of feeling turns to sorrow." Nature's sorrow is formed through an almost physical blocking of its feeling, a resistance to such feeling being expressed. Nature is unable to express or to resonate (*Ausdruck* in the sense of pressing out—*Aus-druck*). Lament is, therefore, elicited from within the wedge between natural sound and music—again, between the mute sound of creaturely beings and the most advanced expression of feeling.

Strikingly, this structure is also found in the aforementioned figure of the ghost, whose fundamental being embodies exactly this nonplace, or its inability to be anywhere present. It is, as I have shown, neither living nor dead, and belongs to neither past nor present. Its intermediate role is precisely what defines it. In a posthumously published text from his diaries, Gershom Scholem describes lament in a similar way but gives it a spatial characterization:

> Every language means a positive expression of being [*Wesen*], and its infinity lies in the two bordering lands of that which has been revealed and that which has been kept in silence, in such a way that it [language] extends over both lands in the actual sense. But this is different in the case of that language [lament] which is characterized by always being *throughout* on the border, lying precisely on the border between the two lands.[44]

Scholem presents here a topographic description where every language extends over the two lands—of the revealed and the concealed—whereas lament, which he defines as a different type of language, is not entitled to a foothold in either realm. Lament belongs to the border alone; it dwells on its thin line but is not a resident of either land that surrounds it. And precisely since it holds the place that can never be forsaken, lament can never be overcome. It stands between "revelation," as Scholem calls it in his essay, and the silent—between complete uncovering and utter lack. This liminal state may be identified as what Benjamin calls the *inclination* to express, precisely since it is, as Scholem defines it, perpetually situated on the border between complete silence and all-encompassing revelation, forever pointing at the border of expressibility of language rather than its fulfilled expressive act.[45]

In that sense lament, as Scholem describes it, cannot contain referential, propositional meaning. Just like the ghost, it is always in-between. Comprehending the nature of lament means grasping its ghostly character and its inability to contain meaning within itself. It can only point at its inability to gather meaning. Lament is, therefore, a creature of the border. Nature thus remains midway, "on the way to music" so to speak, saturated with its dammed-up sorrow. There is a blockage in the way into music, an impasse that comes about through language. Already the Greeks heard *ècho* in the word *echein* (to hold), thus linking the echo with a basic form of stoppage.[46] This blockage is the physical condition out of which the desolate, sorrowful echo emerges.

The echo is originally a natural sound, and the resistance it encounters is that of a mountain or a tree. Its iterative nature is not a reply (as it has sometimes been thought of) but rather a re-presentation of the question and, moreover, of the inability to supply it with an answer. An echo is a presentation of dispersion, emptiness, and lack. In it there is no self-expression, only a reverberation of another's expression. Nature's inability to perform signifying linguistic acts leaves it with the rustling leaves, the howling wind, and the echoing mountains—it is only able to reprise something else. The natural echo also diminishes the original sound as it is repeated. Thus it slowly restages the process of loss.

The Ghosts of Language: "The Task of the Translator"

Benjamin uses the myth of the Creation to establish his argument about the nature of language as such and specifically, as I have pointed out, about language's inherent relation to melancholy and loss. This myth, however, is to be understood neither as featuring a pure, archetypical language nor as nostalgically presenting a language that should be recaptured or retrieved. It is also not a mere presentation of language prior to its fall into chatter and the loss of its pure, creative character. What Benjamin sets forth here as the linguistic epitome of the myth of Creation serves rather to point to a *structure* of language as such.

Benjamin sets forth two models of linguistic structure in "On Language as Such and on the Language of Man." The first is what he calls "bourgeois" language, or fallen language, which is founded on the basic consciousness that a full, significant language is absent. It appears merely as "outwardly-directed communication" and is based on the eternal oscillation between lack and excess. In other words it is founded on a logic of compensation. This language is established in constant reference to the primordial Fall and is therefore structured as a system of persistent deferrals directed toward the retrieval and recovery of lost meaning, as well as the meaning of loss.

The second, quite different, linguistic model is found at the beginning of the same essay, in Benjamin's understanding of language as the realm where mental essence is being constantly perfected in its expression. There he argues for what I earlier termed the inherent potentiality of language, in which linguistic expression is always, and essentially, revealed only as an inclination to express. This inclination is what grounds the understanding of the nature of language. It does not operate within gaps and lacks, attempting at local compensations or restitution, but is rather a much broader apparatus constituting the perfection of meaning from the given—rather than its production in response to a lack. In other words nothing new is created in language, which is nonetheless a local expiation. Everything in it is given a place in a hierarchy of different levels of perfection or, put differently, in different degrees of actualization (a structure that can be read as being similar to the process that Benjamin understands in "The Role of Language" as purification).

Such a process of perfection is also articulated in the essay's closing paragraphs, in a formulation that brings together the idea of language as potentiality and the echelon of linguistic power relations formed by God, man, and nature:

The uninterrupted flow of this [linguistic] communication runs through the whole of nature, from the lowest forms of existence to man and from man to God . . . The language of nature is comparable to a secret password that each sentry passes to the next in his own language, but the meaning of the password is the sentry's language itself. All higher language is a translation of lower ones, until in ultimate clarity the word of God unfolds, which is the unity of this movement made up of language. (LAN, *SW*, 1:74)

In this structure of the perfection of meaning a perpetual chain of expression runs through the whole of nature, in a description interestingly akin to the purification process outlined in "The Role of Language." Its structure is twofold. First, the process is manifested on the individual scale of each expressive entity or each language, and second, it establishes the refinement and actualization of the linguistic structure as a whole—a structure made up of these individual expressing entities yet markedly exceeding them.[47] In a different context, discussed earlier, Benjamin formulates a similar process of perfection when he regards philosophy as "rightly" being "a struggle for the representation of a limited number of words which always remain the same—a struggle for the presentation of ideas." This interminable struggle is the attempt at perfection, and its description here runs parallel to the linguistic account in which each entity in the world is forever directed toward the linguistic expression and actualization of its essence. Benjamin's understanding of the philosophical idea as a linguistic being (*TS*, 36) is rooted in the world's inclination to express and in the all-encompassing hierarchy of all entities that are involved in one linguistic totality, aimed at the distillation of expression.

At this point the mythic account of language demands its counterpart—the historical score. Together, these two explanations shed light on the relationship among man, world, and language. The mythic account unfolds meaning as immediately and constantly present, bestowing the name as the embodiment of such immediate and present knowledge. In that sense there is no historical dimension to myth—meaning is instantly given in it. This does not suffice for the elucidation of Benjamin's conception of language, however, in which meaning has a distinct, indispensable historical dimension. Viewed with such a historical scope, meaning, for Benjamin, is not completely given at the moment of its appearance (as in the proper name) but rather is always entangled in a maturing process in which it is distilled and unfolded.

The historical dimension thus becomes the condition in which complete, actualized meaning can manifest itself. The inherent connection between the appearance of meaning and the idea of commitment should be considered, I believe, in historical terms. These can be found throughout Benjamin's writings; here, however, I would like to highlight one text in particular in his linguistic corpus, "The Task of the Translator."[48]

I suggest understanding this essay in light of my previous discussion of the figure of the ghost, which should be regarded in a historical, inner-linguistic frame of reference. The ghost introduces the moment of encounter between past and present, and specifically the call of the ghost in the past to the recipient in the present. This structure of summoning appears in "The Task of the Translator" in the intralinguistic framework, and rather than being an extralinguistic event, as it is in the *Trauerspiel*, it is inherent in the nature of language itself. In this structure, meaning, and the commitment to express derived from it, are manifested in the internal alliance between expression and that which calls for it.

The ghost's appearance marks the presentation of this moment. It appears when it beseeches to encounter us and demands to be redeemed and put to rest. The structure of this encounter should be understood as a linguistic edifice; the ghost is a linguistic ghost, a ghost internal to language. The moment of summoning is thus a step in the process of the perfection and refinement of dispersed, quivering meaning, which wishes to be concentrated and held together. The ghost of meaning in language demands to be given repose, to be brought to a standstill, or, as Benjamin puts it elsewhere, to be "inferred from the state of completion and rest" (*TS*, 47).

Benjamin introduces the term *translatability* and understands it to be the signal characteristic of certain works (TT, *SW*, 1:254). An original that possesses this property summons its own translation. To determine whether a work is translatable, it should be asked: "Does its nature *lend itself* [*zulasse*] to translation and, therefore, in view of the significance of this form, *call for it* [*verlange*]?" (TT, *SW*, 1:254; my emphasis). There are, then, two layers to translatability—the first is the work's granting permission to translate it (it lends itself, in the sense of allowing an entry into it), and the second is the way that it demands or calls for translation.

These concerns do not depend upon the *actual* event of translation; they merely concern the work's *potential* to be translatable and, more important, involve its own inherent demand to be translated. "A specific significance inherent in the original manifests itself in its translatability" (TT, *SW*, 1:254). Translatability is thus a property internal to the work itself, independent of its actualization. For Benjamin the original lends itself to translation, calls for it, and, in a way, turns to us (to the translator, to the present) with a plea—or even a claim. Akin to the world's turning to man so that he might express it, the original pleads for expression in a foreign language; the ghost demands its rest. To emphasize: translatability has to do with a certain potential, as much as language as such, according to Benjamin, is all about its expressibility—not acts of expression.[49]

The rendering of the original in another language serves as its continuation. The act of translation, therefore, is not an external undertaking performed on an object but rather the work's natural continuation so as to achieve "its latest, continually renewed, and most complete unfolding" (TT, *SW*, 1:255) (this structure is in close affinity with Benjamin's sense of the relation between the artwork and its criticism in romanticism). In light of Benjamin's phrasing here in relation to the ghostly nature of the original, it can be maintained that the latter is not complete without its translation. The untranslated original is not yet reconciled—its meaning not yet at rest. Thus its call is one of consummation and accomplishment—not of a mere transformation from one language to another.

There is, more precisely, a special vitality involved in the translation process; however, this energy is entirely different from the vitality of nature. "In the final analysis," explains Benjamin, "the range of life must be determined by the standpoint of *history rather than that of nature*" (TT, *SW*, 1:255; my emphasis). The task of philosophy, articulated in the theory of translation, is therefore to comprehend vitality and life in their historical rather than natural setting.

The term *afterlife* (*Überleben*) possesses a twofold meaning: it is the form of life that unfolds after all (natural) life is exhausted; that is, it is the survival of the work (conceived, however, not as death but as a natural continuation of life, an *after*life). Additionally, it means an expression of life and meaning, exceeding material death and the original sphere of life. It is a continuation of life, on the one hand, and of meaning and significance, on the other. In this sense it is neither life nor death—so its structure's status resembles that of the ghost, who exists after all life is gone but before death enters the scene. Thus, actual death or material death (of the original work and of the ghost) has nothing to do with the termination of its life (TT, *SW*, 1:254). This space of the afterlife is where translation takes place and actualizes the original.

Benjamin specifically notes that the notions of afterlife and continued life should not be considered metaphorical, and he unfolds their structures by reflecting that "just as the manifestations [*Äußerungen*] of life are intimately connected with the phenomenon of life without being of importance to it, a translation issues from the original—not so much from its life as from its afterlife [*Überleben*] . . . Translation marks their stage of continued life [*Fortlebens*]" (TT, *SW*, 1:254). He continues:

As an unfolding of a special and high form of life [*eigentümlich und hohen Lebens*], this process [i.e., translation that is more than simply transmission] is governed by a special high purposiveness [*Zweckmäßigkeit*]. The relationship between life and purposiveness, seemingly obvious yet almost beyond the grasp of the intellect, reveals itself only if the ultimate purpose toward which all the individual purposiveness of life tends is sought not in its own sphere but in a higher one. All purposeful manifestations of life [*Lebenserscheinungen*], including their very purposiveness, in the final analysis have their end not in life but in the expression of its nature [*Ausdruck seines Weens*], in the representation [*Darstellung*] of its significance. Translation thus ultimately serves the purpose of expressing the innermost relationship of languages to one another. It cannot possibly reveal or establish this hidden relationship itself; but it can represent it by realizing it in embryonic or intensive form [*keimhaft oder intensive verwirklicht*]. This representing of something signified through an attempt at establishing it in embryo is of so singular a nature that it is rarely met with in the sphere of nonlinguistic life. (TT, *SW*, 1:255; translation altered)

The term *afterlife* is closely connected to what Benjamin understands as the manifestations that occur after life ends. He locates life's purpose in a realm that has no bearing on life itself, thus extricating it from any causal relation. This special purposiveness, revealed in the afterlife, is a unique, high form of life.

In connecting Benjamin's theory of translation to his philosophical roots in Kantian philosophy, Friedlander links the idea of life, and its essential connection to the artwork, to Kant's purposiveness without purpose. In such a structure of meaning our reflection on the work of art is established, on the one hand, upon an inner consistency in our reflection that is not attributed to conceptual determinations (like those operating in Kant's determinate judgment). On the other hand, this liveliness of reflection comes at the price of an essential ambiguity inherent to reflection (in contrast to determination); it is therefore that "ambiguity is the condition of the aliveness of meaning in the work of art."[50] This model of the realization of meaning is vital for our understanding of its linguistic counterpart in Benjamin's text on translation. Also there, it is of utmost importance for Benjamin to trace a model of meaning that is not intentional, not conceptually determined, and, most important, transcends the simple model of translation as an activity of providing only an elementary structure of a word-for-word connection. This essential ambiguity of meaning is what produces, in turn, an instability and indeterminacy that would come to be the condition of possibility for Benjamin's idea of a "pure language."

Thus, a different sort of life takes place in the work's posthumous journey. Translation does not merely fulfill the original's aspirations but points to a higher order—taking the original out of its native sphere and carrying it into a radically different realm.[51] Moreover, this claim further professes that this purposiveness or afterlife is close to truth as Benjamin conceives it. "Truth," as he writes elsewhere, "is not timeless. It is historical,"[52] its ideal to be found not in the name's divine immediacy but rather in an understanding of truth's historical structure.[53] Understood this way, translation begins the actualization of the work's meaning. Therefore, meaning is what always resides in a different realm from life, in a sphere that unfolds after all of life's possibilities have been fully actualized. Inherent in every form of life is this special type of purposiveness, existing as a rudimentary, incipient form—a potentiality that is actualized only in the act of translation. Such a model of meaning, an aspiration to be wholly expressed, corresponds to the teleological account of the linguistic model. In the theory of translation life and meaning have their end not in themselves but in the expression of their essence—that is, beyond them or outside their living scope. This structure of meaning can only be found in linguistic life, writes Benjamin.[54]

The call of the original for translatability is intended toward life's redemption in the afterlife. In the linguistic realm Benjamin calls this a process in which even words of fixed meaning can undergo a maturing process (TT, SW, 1:256).[55] What does it mean for a work to "mature" if it has already been written? Actualized? According to Benjamin this sort of maturation involves a shift in the original's structure of meaning—what was dominant in the work when it was written is replaced by some of its other tendencies. This shift possesses a temporal dimension (time has passed, and thus changes have been visited upon the work); but it also occurs in the act of translation itself, in which the work's afterlife is unfolded.[56] Translation is thus the act that refines, realizes, and actualizes meaning.

It is also the sole literary form that fosters true commitment and loyalty toward the original, the only form "charged with the special mission of watching over the maturing process of the original language and the birth pangs of its own"—these two stages being intertwined. A good translation is thus born from the maturation of the work—hence is created out of the substantial destruction of the original. This is another version of loss being a condition of possibility for the realization of truth, understood here in its historical dimension. Destruction and the loss inhering in it are what conditions the crystallization of meaning, "one of the most powerful and fruitful historical processes" (TT, *SW*, 1:256).[57]

The internal, incipient essence that realizes itself in translation is irrelevant to the traditional theory of translation, which is bound up with notions of similarity and fidelity. It is therefore no praise to say that a translation reads as if it were written in the original; in fact, a good translation should even disregard the original. Benjamin rephrases this claim by writing that "it stands to reason that resemblance does not necessarily appear where there is kinship" (TT, *SW*, 1:259). Accordingly, a fine translation brings together the multiplicity of languages as such, bringing to light the "kinship of languages," expressing the innermost relationship binding all languages (TT, *SW*, 1:255).

The act of translation, therefore, aims at something independent of the contingent work. The existence of the discrete original serves only as the ground upon which different languages encounter one another. This encounter, detached from an individual, intentional act, exists instead in the assemblage of such acts. This special kinship between languages is brought out rather than constituted. That is, such kinship is a property of language that cannot be created ex nihilo. This goes back to Benjamin's interpretation of Genesis, in which the multiplicity of fallen languages expresses the disintegration of pure, creative language. The task of translation is, accordingly, to reflect the "great longing for linguistic complementation" (TT, *SW*, 1:260) that lies in a realm that transcends a specific original or translation.[58] In this Benjamin gives voice to the myth's opening up of the structure of meaning in language as such: "In every one of them [languages] as a whole, one and the same thing is meant. Yet this one thing is achievable not by any single language but only by the totality of their intentions supplementing one another: the pure language. Whereas all individual elements in foreign languages—words, sentences, associations—are mutually exclusive, these languages supplement one another in their intentions" (TT, *SW*, 1:257). Benjamin exemplifies this dynamic by explicating the meaning and function of intention in language. According to Benjamin we should make a distinction between what is meant in language (i.e., what language refers to, its object of intention) and how it means (i.e., what the mode of meaning is, or, in what way the object is meant).

This distinction lies at the crux of Benjamin's argument about translation, specifically with regard to the difference between two modes of what can be called a linguistic relation. First, there is language as a relation to an object of its intention; second, there is an intralinguistic relation between different languages, in which meaning springs from a relation not to the world but to language itself. By way of illustration, Benjamin gives the example of *Brot* (German) versus *pain* (French). Although both words refer to the same object—bread—each signifies this object differently. *Brot* for the German speaker is different from *pain* for the French; the difference lies, however, in more than simply the use of a different word to refer to the designated object. It lies first and foremost in the intention to express that object in a linguistically distinct way, which points not only to an isolated object (bread) but to a world and a rich constellation of meanings associated with it.

In this sense *Brot* and *pain* are not interchangeable (as the commonsense understanding of translation would have it) but rather exclude one another in that they bear within them much more than mere referential meaning. However, what this exclusion means in Benjamin's theory of translation is that both words, and consequently both languages, do not cancel each other out. Rather, they supplement each another: "Even though the way of meaning in these two words is in such conflict, it supplements itself in each of the two languages from which the words are derived; to be more specific, the way of meaning in them is supplemented in its relation to what is meant" (TT, *SW*, 1:257). The meaning revealed in the act of translation is therefore not dependent on the intention found in what Benjamin calls an individual, "unsupplemented language." In this language meaning is unstable, always in a state of flux, oscillating between various and at times contradictory or conflicting meanings. This flux ceases only when each individual language gives up its intention to fulfill a referential, utilitarian function and reaches out toward other, supplementary linguistic intentions.

Instead of meaning being extralinguistic, or established on the basis of the intentional connection between a linguistic utterance and an object to which it refers, meaning in translation is internal to language and can be founded only on the relationship between different languages and different modes of meaning. Thus, linguistic intention is immanently structured in the original, calling out to encounter what Benjamin terms "pure language," a language that would be situated beyond utilitarian and symbolic functions and would have cast off the burden of extralinguistic, referential meaning and the structures upon which it rests.[59] The work thus calls on translation not on behalf of the original but for the sake of pure language. In this sense all individual linguistic intentions—those directed toward external linguistic objects—become irrelevant with regard to the more important intentionality unfolded by translation: that which is directed toward pure language. This is an intentionality of mere potentiality; it need not be actualized.

"Pure" language should thus be understood as what stands at the intersection of these intentions—it is neither a language turned into means for communication ("bourgeois language") nor even a language to transmit mental content.[60] In being free from a propositional nature and at the same time constructed out of the relationships among the different languages, it presents itself as language as such. On this Derrida points out that what is intended by all languages is not an object or reality; it is rather language itself. This language, however, is neither universal nor natural but "the being-language of the language, tongue or language *as such*, that unity without any self-identity, which makes for the fact that there are languages and that they are languages."[61] Joining intention with language as such leaves us with a nonintentional structure, a configuration in which the aim of intention can never be consummated in a single object or word. Such a linguistic configuration can be revealed only in the act of translation. This is, in effect, what the task of the translator must reveal.

As totality and whole, all languages wish to express pure language, or language as such; this is a structure that Benjamin will use in the preface to the *Trauerspiel* book for meaning. They should be viewed as an *aggregatum* directed toward the expression of the same content, regardless of individual intentions.[62] This inclination toward expression inheres in the realm of language itself, independent of any contingent object in it. In "Language and Logic" Benjamin writes that "the multiplicity of languages ... *expresses their essential character*" (*SW*, 1:273; my emphasis). In other words the multiplicity of languages and the harmony standing at their foundation embody an essential characterization of the structure of language as such, rather than being grounded in the mythic account of a decadence originating in the Fall. Benjamin's use of the myth of the Fall expresses something internal to the structure of language itself.

For Benjamin "the language of a translation can—in fact, must—let itself go, so that it gives voice to the *intentio* of the original *not as reproduction but as harmony*, as a supplement to the language in which it expresses itself, as its own kind of *intentio*" (TT, *SW*, 1:260; my emphasis). Here the task of the translator consists not in rendering one language into another but in creating a harmony within the multilayered network of individual intentions. Pure language is the language of truth, which Benjamin defines as "tensionless" and a "silent depository"—what all languages strive for. It is this very language "in whose divination and description lies the only perfection for which a philosopher can hope, [which] is concealed in concentrated fashion in translations" (TT, *SW*, 1:259). It is in this language that meaning actualizes itself as distilled and condensed; and only in this intensive concentration can linguistic harmony offer itself.

4

Melancholy and Truth

The "Epistemo-Critical Prologue"

In a letter to Adorno of May 1931 Benjamin describes the prologue to his *Trauerspiel* book as a "self-contained exposition of the epistemo-logical foundations of my book on the Baroque Drama," a text that had been written only after those foundations "had proved their value in the material itself."[1] Indeed, many of Benjamin's readers have described the prologue as an enigmatic, self-contained text; Benjamin himself even called it "pure chutzpah."[2] Despite its inherent difficulties, however, it is also broadly acknowledged to be one of the vital contributions, perhaps even the most crucial, of the *Trauerspiel* book as a whole. Aside from its richness and philosophical complexity, it is also undoubtedly the most clear and rigorous presentation of the book's methodology and sheds light on some of the philosophical and theoretical hypotheses that would accompany Benjamin's thought until his final work, the unfinished *Arcades Project*.

The prologue's first part is devoted chiefly to methodological questions. Benjamin describes his philosophical and interpretative approach to the *Trauerspiel*, explaining why his writings about the plays are, in fact, a philosophical enterprise. He addresses questions of philosophical writing, the relation between philosophy and art, and the structure of philosophical contemplation; finally, he presents some penetrating questions about historical consciousness that will continue to occupy him in the years to come. Benjamin outlines his methodological motivations and theoretical postulations through a detailed explication of the relationship between concept and phenomena, detail and totality, and, most important, the correspondence between his research subject (the *Trauerspiel*) and what he takes to be philosophical truth—a relationship that he describes elsewhere as that between the "material content" and "truth content" (*SW*, 1:297).

These predicaments fall roughly under the rubric of what Benjamin calls the question of presentation (*Darstellung*), with which he begins the prologue. The text's first sentence reads: "It is characteristic of philosophical writing that it must continually confront the question of presentation [*Darstellung*]" (*TS*, 27; translation altered); a few pages later he describes philosophy's basic task to be "the presentation [*Darstellung*] of ideas" (*TS*, 34; translation altered). Benjamin addresses the task of *Darstellung*, which is formulated not only as a task but also as a fundamental conundrum, in numerous and varied ways in the prologue. He considers classical philosophical figures such as Plato, Kant, and Hegel, and he summons a set of metaphors or, one might say, conceptual schemes—using all these to address the theoretical foundations of the problem of philosophical presentation.

The prologue, in the uniqueness of its description and discussion of the methodological substratum of the philosophical presentation of ideas, manifests what would remain, well beyond the early *Trauerspiel* book, the hallmark of Benjamin's philosophical infrastructure. This is the philosophical exploration of the relationship between phenomena, or material, and the possible ways of its presentation in the form of truth, namely, the idea. In this text Benjamin wants to elucidate how material can be given as truth or how the phenomenal and material aspects of experience can be transformed, via their presentation, into truth. The presentation of the idea should, according to Benjamin's modus operandi, at once be committed and directly related to the material it is made of, yet at the same time it should touch on a transcendental essence that can never manifest itself in bare material as such.

This unique form of the relationship between material and truth is echoed in the historical period that provides the subject matter of the book as a whole—the seventeenth century. In the baroque we can clearly see the origins of the internal split between empiricism and idealism in the philosophical discourse, and it is precisely this division that Benjamin would like to abandon. His philosophical model shows him willing neither to give up the material (as in idealistic epistemological models) nor to lose grips with the idea or truth (as in the empiricist point of view that, roughly speaking, saw the phenomenal as the only available source of philosophical data). Instead, he seeks to avoid partitions of this kind and to hold on to both sides of the division and the essential relation between them.

This philosophical procedure—of utmost importance to grasp how Benjamin uses the *Trauerspiel* plays as material for his assertions in the book—needs to be clarified and outlined. To shed light on Benjamin's philosophical methodology, it is thus essential to understand his historical and philosophical approach to the plays of the baroque. How can these seventeenth-century plays, which do not in themselves contain truth as a whole or as a totality, become such truth or express it? And how can this truth be philosophically presented?

Close to the beginning of the text, Benjamin poses this question in detail while describing the unique complexity of the interconnection between phenomena and philosophical ideas: "For phenomena are not incorporated in ideas. They are not contained in them. Ideas are, rather, their objective, virtual arrangement, their objective interpretation. If ideas do not incorporate phenomena, and if they do not become functions of the law of phenomena, the 'hypothesis,' then the question of how they attain phenomena arises [*in welcher Art und Weise sie denn die Phänomene erreichen*]" (*TS*, 34; translation altered). Benjamin attempts here to reconstruct this interconnection so that it escapes the determinative structure of the correspondence between phenomena and concepts. He formulates such a correspondence as being the opposite of the depth of the connection of phenomena to ideas, and he grapples with this opposition through his discussion of the relation between knowledge (and concepts) and truth (and ideas). Instead of the determined, categorical structure of knowledge, philosophical ideas are given in a structure that is parallel to the phenomena they describe. That is, they are the virtual *arrangement* of such phenomena rather than what contains them. "The answer to this [i.e., the question of how ideas pertain to phenomena] is: in the presentation [*Darstellung*] of phenomena. The idea thus belongs to a fundamentally different sphere [*Bereiche*] from that which it apprehends" (*TS*, 34; translation altered).

What we should be looking for in the prologue, then, is the specific form that allows the phenomenal and the idea to operate together while being dependent on one another. This cannot be accomplished by a simple relation of sheer representation or a strictly conceptual, abstract approach. A different relation should be accounted for.

Benjamin approaches and reapproaches the problem of relationship between the phenomenal and the idea in all its complexity throughout the prologue, using a series of metaphors, images, and conceptual schemes. The abundance of such images in the text testifies to Benjamin's attempts to restate and rehearse the question of presentation of truth, of *Darstellung*. Each approaching it from its own perspective, every such image or scheme stresses the different traits of the structure of the presentation of truth; each is significant for its own reasons.

The mosaic illustrates, first and foremost, the material aspects of phenomena while stressing the constructive aspect of the philosophical method. By emphasizing the relationship between the part and the whole, the details and the complete picture, the scheme of the mosaic encompasses the totality of truth in a way that is not necessarily opposed to a structure of the disparate particles that make it up (*TS*, 28–29). The whirlpool exemplifies Benjamin's renowned concept of "origin" (*Ursprung*), which alludes to the work's material aspect and the complexity of its connection to its origin, conceived by Benjamin not as a temporal moment but rather as "that which emerges from the process of becoming and disappearance" (*TS*, 45). The figure of the mother surrounded by her children relates to the internal relationship of meaning and the decisive notion of "gathering" so pertinent to philosophical truth (*TS*, 35). The analogy of the constellation of stars puts forth the special principle of the organization and harmonization of its parts, summed up by Benjamin with the sentence: "Ideas are to objects as constellations are to stars" (*TS*, 34). Finally, Benjamin introduces the monad as the epitome of the structure of the philosophical idea, stating, without going into any detail and offering what might seem a mere hypothesis, that "the idea is a monad" (*TS*, 47).

Each of these schemes is of signal importance to the understanding of Benjamin's complex theoretical claims in the prologue and in the book that follows; however, the metaphors used have had problematic consequences, because they often draw the discussion into the realm of literary criticism—rather than being understood as part of Benjamin's rigorous philosophical framework.

We should ask, however, whether there is one specific figure among the prologue's metaphors and other schemes that best embodies Benjamin's aforementioned conception of truth. Furthermore, following the lines of the previous chapters of the present book, does one specific site among the prologue's conceptual schemes show distinctly the structural relation between melancholy and Benjamin's conception of philosophical truth? My claim in this chapter is that one such scheme indeed exists; it is to be found in Benjamin's use of Leibniz's concept of the monad. This is the only conceptual scheme that Benjamin completely and wholly conceives of *as* the idea. The monad is not a simple metaphor in the text; therefore, the idea is neither likened to the monad nor is its analogue; "the idea *is* the monad," writes Benjamin, in a phrase that appears three times in the course of one page in the prologue.[3]

For Benjamin, the monad's philosophical significance is not limited to the prologue nor to the remainder of the *Trauerspiel* book. It can be traced throughout his work, extending forward even to the late *Arcades Project* and "On the Concept of History." Despite his recurring use of the term, however, Benjamin does not elaborate on it; indeed, his explanations are chary in regard to it. One of the important places to find some further elaboration of the term is in a letter to Florence Christian Rang from December 1923: "Leibniz's entire way of thinking, his idea of the monad, which I adopt for my definition of ideas and which you evoke with your equation of ideas and numbers—since for Leibniz the discontinuity of whole numbers was a decisive importance for the theory of monads—seems to me to comprise the *summa* of a theory of ideas" (*SW*, 1:389). This formulation clearly positions Benjamin's use of the monad as a philosophical gesture, in accord with the philosophical rigor of his work as a whole—and not, as is sometimes conceived, a mere effort of literary criticism.

Furthermore, Leibniz's model is not only philosophical; it is also a baroque specimen of thought. It is therefore not surprising that the monad is precisely the scheme that Benjamin considers so crucial to his book on baroque plays (this image can also be traced in other, later texts; however, nowhere does it so strongly embody Benjamin's propositions as in the

Trauerspiel study). Because of his philosophical rigor and baroque point of view, Leibniz thus serves as the perfect example of Benjamin's philosophical method.[4]

In Leibniz's *Monadology* (1714) Benjamin finds a model to best express his conception of truth, being mindful of the inherent problematics of the connection between phenomena and ideas. Nevertheless, Leibniz is important for Benjamin for another reason: his monadological model touches on yet another crucial problem. If we consider Benjamin's concern with the relation between the phenomenal world and the philosophical enterprise in the context of the baroque, it is clear that this question raises a much broader problem: that of the inherent problematics in resolving the paradox of the gap between the direct experience of the phenomenal world and the sheer manifestation of its truth or essence. This problem has a marked presence in the philosophy as well as the science of the baroque, and can be found, to name one central figure, in Descartes's famous *Discourse on Method*. In other words this epistemological problem, although not addressed explicitly in Leibniz's philosophy, is nevertheless at work in its background. The conceptual importance of Leibniz's monad, therefore, lies in its potential to forcefully address this problem. It encompasses, in its very structure, the fundamental detachment and closure of the philosophical stance of melancholy, together with a system of great philosophical productivity and openness. For this reason it is the only model (philosophical or otherwise) to offer Benjamin a solution that incorporates isolated and detached essences that are nonetheless given in a consolidated, harmonious, and expressive system.

The monad thus incarnates a structure of basic closure coupled with expression; therefore, it provides a conceptual edifice that is vital for Benjamin. It does so for two reasons: first, it addresses the problem of the correspondence between the phenomenal and the idea; and second, it tackles the connection between philosophical truth and melancholy, exempting the latter from its historical characterization as being paralyzed and barren. For these two reasons Leibniz's monadic structure is crucial to Benjamin. The monad's structure, and specifically the unique structure of its encounter with the world, calls Benjamin to concretize the relation between melancholy and philosophy.[5]

The "Monad": Leibniz and Benjamin

The monad receives two considerations in the prologue. First, it appears in a section entitled "Philosophical Beauty," beginning with a discussion of Plato's *Symposium* and the essential link in Platonic thought between truth and beauty. This pair of concepts leads Benjamin to unfold the complexity of the transformation of beauty into truth or, more specifically, to pose the problem as a question, "Can truth do justice to beauty?" Plato's answer, according to Benjamin, is that it can if truth be made the guarantor of the existence of beauty (*TS*, 31). This raises a question with much broader implications: How is the connection established between the phenomenal and the idea? How is beauty transformed into truth?

At this point Benjamin turns to what he calls the "great philosophies," namely, the systems of Plato, Leibniz, and Hegel, where he finds an entry point into the discussion of the nature of the "idea." Plato's ideas, Leibniz's monads, and Hegel's dialectic are the three philosophical models that serve to establish his claims (*TS*, 32). Attracting Benjamin to this trio of philosophical systems is the distinct way that each offers a metaphysical structure of arrangement that is in accord with the phenomenal world. Are the Platonic ideas "abstractions" of their faint representation in phenomena? How closely does the account of history given in the Hegelian dialectic accord with actual events? Finally, in what sense can Leibniz's windowless monad be in tune with the world it represents or, in Leibniz's terms, the world it expresses?

Benjamin addresses the relation between the "order" of ideas in these philosophical systems and their attempt to represent the world as such: "If it is the task of the philosopher to practice the kind of description of the world of ideas which automatically includes and absorbs the empirical world, then he occupies an elevated position between that of the scientist and the artist" (*TS*, 32). Benjamin is searching for a philosophical stance that would combine the scientist's interest in the elimination of what is the merely empirical, and the artist's commitment to the task of presentation (*TS*, 32).

The second, more elaborate appearance of Benjamin's discussion of Leibniz's monad in the prologue, is developed in the section entitled "Monadology." In this section Benjamin makes clear why he is drawn to the monad as a concept by outlining the characteristics it shares with his own sense of the philosophical idea: "[The idea's] structure is a monadological one, imposed by totality in contrast to its own inalienable isolation. The idea is a monad" (*TS*, 47).

This short passage already contains the monad's two most important traits: first, the monad is isolated and self-absorbed (it has an "inalienable isolation"); second, the structure of the monadological system is imposed in totality. The monad's closure from the world, on the one hand, and its expression of the same world in totality, on the other, are, I claim, the two qualities at the crux of Benjamin's insistent appropriation of the monad as a model for his idea. However, not only are these two characteristics important as such. Closure and expression in totality reveal themselves to be important to Benjamin; but it is their *combination* that forms the crux.

A question therefore arises: in what sense is it at all possible to think of isolated, almost solipsistic, entities as expressing a world in its totality, the same world from which they are completely detached? How can a complete closure be coupled with a relation such as expression—and how does the transition between the two take place? Or, put differently, in terms that more closely touch on the problem from which I am approaching Benjamin's interest in Leibniz: how can melancholy, detachment, and closure work together with philosophical thought and the productivity of its attempt to express the world? To fully comprehend the complexity of the monad's structure, we must turn to Leibniz's own account of the monad.[6]

In the *Monadology* Leibniz gives a clear definition of the monad (or "substance"): "The *monad* which we are to discuss here is nothing but a simple substance which enters into compounds. Simple means without parts. There must be simple substances, since there are compounds, for the compounded is but a collection or an aggregate of simples" (MO, 643).[7] For Leibniz, then, the monad is the most basic metaphysical entity from which everything else (every compound) is structured. It is without parts, indivisible, and can never be dissolved. In the following sections Leibniz proclaims what has become a famous idiom: monads are windowless. Consequently, nothing can enter or exit their confines, and all their activity is necessarily internal and spontaneous (ibid.). In the *New System* Leibniz further explicates that the monads are immaculately independent from one another, perfectly sheltered from all possible accidents and therefore exist in utterly discrete confinement: "each mind is as a world apart and sufficient unto itself, independent of every other created being" (NS, 458). Leibniz's system of monads is, then, a system of completely discrete metaphysical entities that form one, united whole.

Monads, however, have perceptions, despite their fundamental closure and detachment from the world and from one another: "the natural changes in monads come from an *internal principle*, since an external cause could not influence [*influer dans*] their interior" (MO, 643–44). Leibniz emphasizes that this peculiar form of perception is altogether different from apperception; that is, its object is not the monad itself but rather something else. Leibniz uses the metaphor of a windmill to describe the monadic perception apparatus; namely, if one were to enter the "space" of the monad as one enters the space of a windmill, one would not find anything there except for "parts which push upon one another." Nothing there could explain or account for how exactly perception is taking place. Only perceptions and their changes can be found in the monad: "it is in this alone that the internal actions of simple substances can consist" (MO, 644). The monad's perceptions are consequential for Leibniz, since they establish those internal changes in the monad that differentiate it from any other substance. Despite their immaculate closure, monads are nevertheless involved in a continuous internal activity which is perceptive.[8] But what can such internal perception be? If the monad is completely detached from anything else, what does it perceive?

The monad's perception, and consequently its presentation of the world, is not grounded in any form of external relation it maintains with it (or to it); it lies, rather, in the monad's containment of the world, in its totality, within its confinement. In other words, the world is not an object for the monad but is part of it. It is internalized and incorporated, in what can be seen as a Freudian gesture, expressed in abbreviation (or, in other cases, Leibniz described it as miniature). Secured in its utter closure, the monad not only expresses the world: it includes it by means of expression.

According to Leibniz each simple substance maintains relations with the world and with other monads, which express all the others and forms "a perpetual mirror of the universe" (MO, 648). Leibniz uses various terms to describe the form of perception taking place in the interiority of the monad. He uses metaphors of mirrors and representations for the portrayal of the expressive nature of the monad's perception, refers to representations of the world in its totality, and writes that the monads are in "sympathy" with the world and with other monads.[9]

Such formulations lead Benjamin to comprehend the monad as containing the "image of the world"—thus linking it to the fruitful intersection mentioned above between science and art. This unique openness the monad maintains with the world, precisely from within its utter closure, can only be understood as the world's complete incorporation. Like the melancholic's lost object, no longer accessible in the form of external subject-object relations of love, the monad's world can only "live" within it. This relation is the focus of Benjamin's interest, and, following Leibniz, he explains it in the prologue:

The being that enters into it [the monad], with its past and subsequent history, brings—concealed in its own form—an indistinct abbreviation of the rest of the world of ideas, just as, according to Leibniz . . . every single monad contains, in an indistinct way, all the others . . . The idea is a monad—that means briefly: every idea contains the image of the world. The purpose [*Aufgabe*] of the presentation [*Darstellung*] of the idea is nothing less than an abbreviated outline of this image [*Bild*] of the world. (*TS*, 47–48).

The totality of the world's incorporation captivates Benjamin for another reason. The monad exemplifies what it means for the philosophical idea to touch on and circumscribe its range of possibilities. Benjamin thus writes that "the representation of an idea can under no circumstances be considered successful unless the whole range of possible extremes it contains has been virtually explored" (*TS*, 47). This structure is clearly echoed in the way that the monad bears a relation to the world as totality, encompassing it completely.

It is, however, crucial to ask at this point: how does Leibniz solve the puzzle of the relation between the phenomenal and the idea? Benjamin uses the monad as the eminent philosophical model to describe the idea, thus calling for a deeper consideration of the nature of the monad's incorporation of the world. Among the texts where Leibniz gives a comprehensive analysis of the relation of expression is a short essay from 1678 entitled "What Is an Idea?" This text gives an account of the possibility of preserving the totality of the world together with its incorporation in expression by the monad; or, in other words, it expounds on the nature of the monadic "image" of the world.

Leibniz offers seven models that describe "expression," all of which portray the expressive relation as taking place internally—that is, as what is not attained by any direct contact between the expression and its object or based on any form of similarity. What Leibniz proposes, rather, is that expression is a relation founded on a basic accord or correspondence between the expression and expressed object.[10] Leibniz writes that "we can pass from a consideration of the relations in the expression to knowledge of the corresponding properties of the thing expressed. Hence, it is clearly not necessary for that which expresses to be similar to the thing expressed, if only a certain analogy is maintained between the relations" (WI, 207–8).

Leibniz's proposal to understand "expression" as what maintains toward its object a relation of nonsimilar representation seems crucial in light of Benjamin's preoccupation in the prologue with the relation between phenomena and idea—and, more specifically, the problem of phenomena's transformation into ideas, which is not to be seen as based on similarity or any type of proximity. As we have seen, phenomena for Benjamin are neither incorporated nor contained in ideas but are related to them by way of "presentation" (*Darstellung*), which is itself an answer to the question of how ideas "attain phenomena." Leibniz's idea of proportion, ratio, or analogy is thus attractive to Benjamin since it accounts for the complexity of the unique form of "attainment" required by ideas. Leibniz touches precisely on the difficulty of the necessity of a relation between the phenomenal and the idea, together with a consideration of the essential discontinuity between the two orders. Benjamin, in contrast, is interested in articulating the correspondence between them: "The idea thus belongs to a fundamentally different sphere [*Bereiche*] from that which it apprehends" (*TS*, 34; translation altered).

When examining the intersection between the multiplicity of the monads and the totality with which they express their world, we come to an interesting focal point. Leibniz has to account for the difference between monads (to comply with his principle of "the identity of the indiscernibles," thereby addressing their different modes of expression). In Leibniz's system the multiplicity of monads express the same universe;

hence, their object of reference—the world—is one and the same. Each monad, however, "expresses the entire universe in its own way and in a certain relationship, or from that point of view, so to speak, from which it regards it" (CA, 337). And elsewhere: "each monad is a living mirror, or a mirror endowed with an internal action, and that it represents the universe according to its point of view and is regulated as completely as is the universe itself" (PNG, 637).

The individuality of the monads is defined and established via the difference in their points of view on the same world. This is what endows Leibniz's system with its expressive variety, which so captivates Benjamin. As Leibniz describes it: "the greatest variety possible, but with the greatest possible order; that is to say, this is the means of attaining as much perfection as possible" (MO, 648). In other words, despite its closure, the monad nevertheless maintains a unique accord with the world, a harmony based on its distinct point of view and consequently on the perfection of its expression—specifically, by its clarity of expression.[11]

Interestingly, it is in terms of pain that Leibniz elucidates the form of the changes in the expressive clarity of each monad. As I have shown elsewhere in detail, Leibniz explicates the uniqueness of monadic expression by using a metaphor in which the monad expresses itself more clearly "when it feels pain."[12] What is intriguing about this explanation is the connection Leibniz forms between pain and adversity and the *clarity of expression*. This juxtaposition calls to mind Freud's somewhat vague statement that the melancholic "has a keener eye for the truth than other people who are not melancholic . . . It might be, so far as we know, that he has come pretty near to understanding himself; we only wonder why a man has to be ill before he can be accessible to a truth of this kind" (*SE*, 14:246). Freud's understanding of the melancholic stance as enabling a privileged access to truth (in his case the truth of the pathological state of the patient) is echoed in the correspondence Leibniz wishes to establish between the feeling of pain and monadic expression.

A similar claim is at stake in Benjamin's aforementioned "Outline of the Psychophysical Problem," where pain, adversity, and agony are "incomparably more capable of expressing genuine diversity than the feelings of pleasure, which differ mainly in degree" (*SW*, 1:397). In linking pain and expression, however, Benjamin also connects the *continuity* and *endurance* of pain with the *flow* of expression:

Only the feeling of pain, both on the physical and metaphysical planes, is capable of such an uninterrupted flow—what might be termed a "thematic treatment." Man is the most consummate instrument of pain: only in human suffering does pain find its adequate expression; only in human life does it flow to its destination, of all the corporeal feelings, pain alone is like a navigable river which never dried up and which leads man down to the sea. (*SW*, 1:397)

In Leibniz and in Benjamin pain is characterized as being continuous and overflowing. This structure is also maintained in each thinker's conception of expression as such, whose nature is of a constant progression. In the *Monadology* Leibniz describes the continuity of monads and his principle of *plenum* via the metaphor of a river: "For all bodies are in a perpetual flux, like rivers, and parts are passing in and out from them continually" (MO, 650). In Benjamin's language essay this uninterrupted flow is formulated as abounding "through the whole of nature, from the lowest form of existence to man and from man to God" (LAN, *SW*, 1:74). The streaming that runs through all entities taking part in expressing also entails a continual movement toward the standstill of perfection. Such motility, extending from what Benjamin conceives as the lowest forms of nature all the way up to God, embodies a constant flux of refinement and distillation, until the ultimate crystallization of meaning.

Toward the end of the prologue Benjamin describes the idea as a monad:

The higher the order of the ideas, the more perfect the representation contained within them. And so the real world could well constitute a task, in the sense that it would be a question of penetrating so deeply into everything real as to reveal thereby an objective interpretation of the world. In the light of such a task of penetration it is not surprising that the philosopher of the *Monadology* was also the founder of infinitesimal calculus. (*TS*, 47–48)

This elucidation unfolds in a different conceptual framework at the end of the language essay: "All higher language is a translation of lower ones, until in ultimate clarity the word of God unfolds, which is the unity of this movement made up of language" (LAN, *SW*, 1:74).

Taken together, these quotes show that for Benjamin the system of monads should be understood as a linguistic edifice providing the foundation of his conception of the idea: "the idea is a monad," on the one hand, and "the idea is something linguistic," on the other (*TS*, 47; 36). I therefore propose that the idea be apprehended as a *linguistic monad*.

These enunciations, along with the conceptions of flow and perfection, are strikingly similar to Leibniz's formation of the monad. Expression in each monad is continually perfected so as to maximize the clarity of expression in the entire system. In constant movement so as to refine such expression, each part leads in turn to perfection in the entire system. This model is related to the discussion of happiness in the last paragraphs of the *Monadology*, where every creature inclines toward a maximization of expression that is directly intimated to God. Expressing the world within the confines of the monad is in fact an expression of the glory of God and his "best of possible worlds." This teleological structure of expression turns out to be the foundation of Leibniz's often criticized optimism. However, neither the teleology nor the optimism belong to a personal dimension. Rather, the system of monads is a structure that directs itself toward happiness in the sense of the maximization of expression.[13] Similarly, the model proposed by Benjamin in his "Task of the Translator" posits a special "high purposiveness," always beyond the individual purpose, to be sought in a higher sphere than that of individual life (TT, 255).

The Monads' Configuration as a Hierarchy

The description of the system of monads in the closing passages of the *Monadology* carries strong theo-political overtones. Leibniz describes a hierarchic assemblage of monads that make up what he calls "a city of God," which is ruled by "the perfect monarch" (MO, 651). This hierarchy is constructed according to the different grades and classes of the clarity of expression: God represents the clearest, most exhaustive expression, and the entelechies below him constitute echelons of different ranks of clarity. Leibniz formulates this anatomy in various texts: "There are also infinite degrees . . . in the monads, some of which dominate more or less over others" (PNG, 637); "a dominant monad would detract [nothing] from the existence of other monads, since there is really no interaction between them but merely an agreement (consensus)"; and so forth.[14] The *Monadology* supplies us with an array of metaphors describing this harmonious hierarchy: God is the inventor of his machine, a prince to his subjects, a father to his children (§84), an architect of the machine of the universe (§87, §89), and the monarch of the divine city of spirits (§87).

All these titles convey the sense of a hierarchically ordered system that operates through a principle of power in which there is evidently no direct contact among the different levels. The echelon of perfection designates that not only does God control the entire system; there is also a complex organization of power relations that dictates that each separate level rules over the one below it. Every aggregate of monads (a group of monads in accord) possesses a dominant entelechy (MO, 650); every such dominating monad knows the system of the universe, according to Leibniz, and imitates it through its own samples of architectonic endeavor, "each spirit being like a little divinity within its own sphere" (MO, 651). The criteria for domination is the level of clarity in the prevailing monad, which serves as a small deity (or "little divinity," as Leibniz calls it) in its own realm. Expressing itself more clearly than others, it has access to the other monads and their perceptions.[15] Hence, each level of the hierarchy duplicates the structure of the system, with God at its top. The function of power and control is therefore replicated in the sphere of each aggregate in this pyramidal structure.[16]

This construct becomes essential to Benjamin, inasmuch as Leibniz maintains that the power system offered in the *Monadology* is *based on expression*, whose criteria determine the definition of its sovereignty. In that sense the dominant monad has access to expression in the levels dominated by it. This is why God functions as part of the system and is not external to it: "This is what makes it possible for minds to enter into a kind of community with God, and it is what makes him with respect to them not only what an inventor is to his machine . . . but also what a prince is to his subjects, and indeed what a father is to his children" (MO, 651). We find here a system of control based on different hierarchies of refinement and perfection of expression, which together constitute a complete expressive compound.

Benjamin addresses this unique hierarchical apparatus principally in the linguistic context. In the language essay he describes the different levels in nature as an expressive hierarchy, comprising different grades of clarity: "All higher language is a translation of lower ones, until in ultimate clarity the word of God unfolds, which is the unity of this movement made up of language" (LAN, *SW,* 1:74). As in Leibniz's conception, God stands at the top of the expressive pyramid. In his 1920–21 essay "Language and Logic" Benjamin discusses (without specifically addressing Leibniz) the scale of the linguistic structure as being identical to the monadological setup, though he excludes God from the equation and addresses only the internal, hierarchical structure of the monadic aggregates. Benjamin understands the morphology of the relation between essences as exercised by means of power and authority, a configuration that is radically different from the model in which concepts consume each other:

The lower concepts are contained in the higher ones—that is to say, in one sense or another what is known loses its autonomy for the sake of what it is known as. In the sphere of essences, the higher does not devour the lower. Instead, *it rules over it.* This explains why the regional separation between them, their disparateness, remains as *irreducible as the gulf between monarch and people.* The legitimacy that characterizes their relations possesses canonical validity for the relation between the unity of essence and the multiplicity of essences . . . The relation between monarch and people makes very clear that in the sphere of essence questions of legitimacy are questions of authenticity and ultimately of origins. (*SW,* 1:272–73; my emphasis)

The essences and the monads, then, are governed by systems structured on the basis of being composed of disparate parts. The system constituted by these elements is not founded on subsumption or a causal relation of any kind. It is rather what Benjamin calls "a system of control" (ibid.), founded upon the essential independence of the monads, which demands the introduction of power in the system. Where direct connection is not feasible, power and authority enter the picture.

Benjamin's two most renowned images in the prologue, the mosaic and the constellation, both engage with the problem of the connection between meaning and dispersion established by him and articulate the structure of meaning and dispersion in terms of power and control, as well as those of harmony. Since truth cannot be exclusively conveyed at a single site—cannot be contained in a single phenomenal object—this structure can be manifested only in the configuration and accord of its partial elements. The mosaic and the constellation offer different versions of such a configuration of meaning; however, both metaphors maintain the same principle—an arrangement of dispersed fragments of meaning becomes the expression of the idea:

> Just as mosaics preserve their majesty despite their fragmentation into capricious particles, so philosophical contemplation is not lacking in momentum. Both are made up of the distinct and the disparate; and nothing could bear more powerful testimony to the transcendent force of the sacred image and the truth itself... The relationship between the minute precision of the work and the proportions of the sculptural or intellectual whole demonstrates that truth content is only to be grasped through immersion in the most minute details of subject-matter. (*TS*, 28–29)

The material fragments making up the mosaic image are isolated and self-consumed. Only when arranged and brought to equilibrium—only when held together—do they constitute the multifarious image itself. In fact, they become laden with meaning only when put together (while keeping, nevertheless, their initial form): "The value of fragments of thought is all the greater the less direct their relationship to the underlying idea," Benjamin stresses. In other words truth manifests itself in the idea—always from within the form of arrangement of the disparate elements, never out of its independent components. Truth is thus presented in the relations and configuration of its parts and can only be given at a distance from their original phenomenal appearance.

Nevertheless, there is a basic difficulty with Benjamin's figure of the mosaic, which puts the indispensable *material aspect* of truth at its center. The layout of the image of the mosaic does not comply entirely with Benjamin's understanding of the idea's configuration. A mosaic is intentionally fashioned, sometimes according to a pregiven pattern. It emerges out of a careful process of arrangement and a meticulous work of correspondence among disparate fragments. The mosaic, hence, stresses power, control, and the holding-together of its material fragments, but it lacks in its description the transformation of material (phenomena) into idea (truth). This transformation is emphasized in the scheme of the constellation:

> The idea thus belongs to a fundamentally different sphere [*Bereiche*] from that which it apprehends... [This] can be illustrated with an analogy. Ideas are to objects as constellations [*Sternbilder*] are to stars. This means, in the first

place, that they are neither their concepts nor their laws. They do not contribute to the knowledge of phenomena, and in no way can the latter be criteria with which to judge the existence of ideas. The significance of phenomena for ideas is confined to their conceptual elements. Whereas phenomena determine the scope and content of the concepts which encompass them, by their existence, by what they have in common, and by their differences, their relationship to ideas is the opposite of this inasmuch as the idea, the objective interpretation of phenomena—or rather their elements—determines their relationship to each other. Ideas are timeless constellations, and by virtue of the elements' being seen as points in such constellations, phenomena are subdivided and at the same time redeemed. (*TS*, 34)

Here a transition takes place between the orders of the individual star and of the presentation of the constellation—or, as Benjamin makes evident, between the phenomena and the idea. This transition is clarified when Benjamin writes: "Phenomena do not, however, enter into the realm of ideas whole, in their crude empirical state, adulterated by appearances, but only in their basic elements, redeemed. They are divested of their false unity so that, thus divided, they might partake of the genuine unity of truth" (*TS*, 33). The destruction of phenomena as a precondition to their entry into the sphere of the idea detaches them from their original context of life, making their loss inherent to their presentation in the higher sphere of the idea. In their representation in the realm of truth, phenomena are in turn absolved from the original loss underlying their transformation. It is a moment when the loss and destruction of the particular coexist simultaneously with the presentation of totality—in the idea: the structure of the idea, Benjamin explains, is "imposed by totality in contrast to its own inalienable isolation" (*TS*, 47).

This process of destruction and retrieval requires conceptual work:

In this their division, phenomena are subordinate to concepts, for it is the latter which effect the resolution of objects into their constituent elements . . . Through their mediating role concepts enable phenomena to participate in the existence of ideas. It is this same mediating role which fits them for the other equally basic task of philosophy, the representation of ideas . . . For ideas are not represented in themselves, but solely and exclusively in an arrangement of concrete elements in the concept: as the configuration of these elements. (*TS*, 33–34)

The concept is what performs the work of destruction and loss. In the conceptual analysis, phenomena, divested of their adulterated appearances, are revealed to be extremes (*TS*, 35).[17] The concept stands as mediator between the phenomena and the idea, showing the differentiation and variation between phenomena rather than their similarities. The concept thus departs from its traditional conception as what establishes the similarities and common traits of groups of phenomena.[18] This extreme, conceptual analysis, as Benjamin sees it here, is aimed precisely at the singularization of the idea, compounded from shattered phenomena.

This move unfolds Leibniz's categories of power and control. Describing the intentional aspect of the idea in the prologue, Benjamin writes: "Truth is not an intent which realizes itself in empirical reality; it is the formative power [*prägende Gewalt*] which determines the essence of this empirical reality" (*TS*, 36; translation altered). Here, the Leibnizian power-relation reemerges. There is a fundamental *Gewalt* inherent in the phenomena's transformation into the constituent of the idea. Something in the material needs to be destroyed, then "held together" and arranged, for it to be revealed as truth.

Loss, then, becomes a condition of possibility for the phenomena's presentation as truth. In fact, phenomena are first lost and then released from the melancholy of that loss so as to enter a higher order in which their essence is presented—in a structure similar to that of "The Task of the Translator," where the purposiveness of life always lies beyond it, in its loss.[19] A melancholic dependence on the object conditions the destructive and synthetic process undergone by phenomena; however, this melancholic absorption in the object is later eschewed in favor of the higher order of meaning. Along these same lines Benjamin writes, in a 1923 letter to Florence Christian Rang, that "the ideas are stars, in contrast to the sun of revelation. They do not appear in the daylight of history; they are at work in history only invisibly" (*SW*, 1:389). The "invisibility" of ideas is only pertinent when ideas are searched for in the phenomenal order. They become visible and operate only on their own plane, transcended from what is purely phenomenal.

The constellation's appearance is hence based on the recognition of the relation among the stars that form the image, a relation that nevertheless preserves the existence of each individual star. Each redeemed star stands as an extreme in a collection of zeniths forming the image of the constellation in the sky, akin to the way the mother (standing for the idea) has her children (extreme phenomena) gather around her and bring her to life (*TS*, 35). There appears a higher order that cannot be grasped within the confines of each individual star and can only become manifest in the organization and relationships of the stars in the image of the constellation. The constellation's stars have no preordained, objective relationship to each other; their association is not predetermined by objective facts, common space, or temporal or causal rules. Each star acts only for itself, moving in its regular path without being influenced by other stars in its vicinity (and if it is affected by other stars, the effect is internalized in its path; hence it is an influence internalized). The constellation's power resides precisely in never being grounded in any factual or spatial data pertaining to any star or the conceptual relations among them—it is grounded only in feeling. The constellation does not exist in and of itself; it depends on the isolated stars gathered in it in a certain pattern or accord that can be grasped only in feeling.

Benjamin proposes here a parallel between stars and phenomena and between the constellation and the idea. Just as the stars are not objectively connected to one another before being placed in a constellation, phenomena are independent of each other and are unrelated to other phenomena—they sustain themselves. Phenomena, like stars, follow certain laws, through which it is possible to see them realizing certain aspects of themselves and moving in accordance with given laws. Ideas and phenomena are also mutually dependent, like the stars and their constellations, and every configuration or presentation of the idea will always be bound up with the phenomena in its realm. The idea cannot be presented without the phenomena in its realm; phenomena, however, can exist without the idea, albeit differently: unredeemed. Observing a single star's path reveals nothing other than mere information about the laws determining its celestial movement—so, too, the conceptual observation of the phenomenon prohibits us from examining it in relation to anything else. We can regard it only in terms of itself, which will significantly narrow the framework of discussion and the meaning that can be derived from it.

In relation to the predicament (discussed above) of the figure of the mosaic in which the image is intentionally produced, the constellation provides a model according to which the harmony expressed within the stars and their configuration is identified and exposed; but it is not generated and is thus experienced just as musical harmony is experienced. To gaze at the constellation in the sky is thus to recognize only what is already there.[20]

There is a moment (albeit not a temporal one) when the synthetic conceptual work, in which relations are determined by power, is arrested—and something independent of it emerges. The meticulous work of conceptual analysis and synthesis is thus always accompanied by something that is fundamentally revealed, not produced. In the example of the constellation this moment will occur when the image of the constellated stars emerges and reveals anew the skies to us. This is expressed more clearly and emphatically in the concept of harmony, which will prove essential to Benjamin's conception of truth, as well as to the *Monadology*.

A Preestablished Harmony: Benjamin's Conception of Truth as Harmony

Benjamin and Leibniz both define as harmonious the relation between the detached, isolated parts of their philosophical and metaphysical systems. As Benjamin writes in the prologue: "The harmonious relationship between such essences is what constitutes truth" (*TS*, 37). Again, the foundation of the harmony called for here is the basic discontinuity between its parts: to present truth, these parts should not be united but rather *harmonized*.

In the remainder of this chapter I argue that the relation between the discrete and isolated should be conceived in terms of harmony. The system of power thus provides only one version of the relationship among isolated entities; another is characterized by harmony. The act of holding together can be based on dominance and power or on agreement and accord. I find that both Leibniz and Benjamin posit a special type of harmony in which detached, isolated entities are held together in a unified structure: Leibniz in his preestablished harmony, and Benjamin in a somewhat different type of harmony, which I will present in what follows. It is important to note, however, that both in Leibniz and in Benjamin, power and harmony do not exclude each other; rather, they are manifested on different levels of the system.

Deleuze claims that the monads' harmonic foundation "allow[s] us to understand certain traits of the theory of monads, and first of all why we go, not from monads to harmony but from harmony to monads. Harmony is monadological, but because monads are initially harmonic."[21] Here Deleuze establishes the principle of harmony as essential and internal to the understanding of the monad, not merely as an external organizing principle of the system. The unique harmonic accord between the monads is based on the fact that there are no external relations whatsoever, neither between the monad and the world nor between itself and other substances. This basic structure of detachment and impediment is what reinforces Leibniz's *requirement* of the component of preestablishment in his theory. The monads have no other way to operate as a system; they must function according to a principle of *internal* accord and attunement that is not based on any causal relation. Leibniz's alternative is his principle of concomitance and preestablished agreement, which he defines as follows: "The *way of preestablished harmony*, according to which God has made each of the two substances from the beginning in such a way that though each follows only its own laws which it has received with its being, each agrees throughout with the other, entirely as if they were mutually influenced or as if God were always putting forth his hand, beyond his general concurrence" (NS2, 460). No direct communication or contact is taking place among the monads; moreover, the type of harmony offered by Leibniz does not involve a continuous divine intervention. After being initiated by God, each monad, self-absorbed and never causally related to anything, is at work only from within itself, in what can be seen as internal energy at work.

To illustrate this conception, Leibniz employs his famous metaphor of two clocks working in perfect agreement. In a letter to Basnage de Beauval of 1696, he puts forward three ways to account for their concomitance. First, a natural influence runs between the clocks; namely, they directly and causally operate each other—an explanation Leibniz deems to be "common philosophy." Second, a skilled craftsman is constantly adjusting and setting the two clocks in agreement—which Leibniz calls "a way of assistance." Third, to harmonize the clocks, one must "construct these two time-pieces at the beginning with such skill and accuracy that one can be assured of their subsequent agreement" (NS2, 460). The third way is Leibniz's hypothesis, which he calls "the way of preestablished harmony." After God creates and sets the clocks, they work in perfect agreement even though they are completely isolated from one another (NS2, 459).[22]

A harmony likewise underlies Benjamin's structure of truth. In an earlier version of the prologue (not translated into English) harmony is a more central concept than it would be in the published version; moreover, it is articulated not as mere harmony but rather as a *preestablished* harmony. In this version Benjamin defines the relation between essences as that of suns that do not touch one another. This unbridgeable distance performs as a precondition of their harmony, or, put differently, the very fact of the essences' being completely isolated and secluded from one another is what determines their ability to be given in harmony (*GS*, vol. 1, pt. 3, 928).

This early version of the text is important because of the centrality of the idea of "preestablished" harmony to it. The relationship between the suns here is defined precisely as a relationship between monads: occupying a safe distance from each other, they do not touch but are nevertheless in deep correspondence, based on harmony. Benjamin defines the harmonic relations in this version of the prologue as "objective in the highest sense," an objectivity that arises precisely from within the fundamental detachment at the heart of the harmonic. Drawing on the previously mentioned constellation of stars, Benjamin alludes here to the "melody of the spheres" that arises from within the independent track of every individual star (*GS*, vol. 1, pt. 3, 928). Music, that is, arises from within the opening between the nontouching, independent, albeit harmonically constituted essences. In both the published and unpublished versions of the prologue, harmony and preestablished harmony are grounded in the basic independence of the essences that compose it. These constructions of harmony are based on the essential melancholic character of detachment and closure.

This is analogous to the way that Leibniz uses his preestablished harmony as the only apparatus through which the isolated monads can maintain contact with each other and thus form a system. The distance between the stars and the immaculate autonomy of essences are what call for such harmony. Furthermore, the concept of preestablished harmony alludes to the structure of the appearance of the idea, or the structure of truth, in which a pattern or configuration is recognized in feeling in the existent, and so is not intentionally produced. We should also conceive the proposition "truth is the death of intention" to underlie Benjamin's notion of harmony.

The monadic scheme is apprehended by Benjamin as an idea, that is, as a structure of truth and meaning. It is important to note, however, that although Benjamin refers to Leibniz's discussion of the monad as if it appears in his *Discourse of Metaphysics*, Leibniz in fact, never mentions the term in this text. Hence, we can assume that Benjamin is referring to Leibniz's *Monadology*, and this probably from memory. Presenting the idea as a monad, Benjamin in fact claims that the world arranges itself around the idea. The idea expresses the world in conveying the structure of this orchestration. The Leibnizian world parallels the Benjaminian phenomena, and perspective correlates with arrangement. The diverse viewpoints of the monads are reiterated by Benjamin as the different forms of arrangement of the phenomena around each idea. There are as many ideas as there are monads, and there are infinite possible configurations of the world—and, therefore, infinite forms of expressing it.

It follows, then, that what philosophy presents is not an object but the totality of the world itself. The nonintentional structure of truth, elaborated early on, points precisely at there being no specific intentional relation to an object of desire—rather, the world is harmonically arranged around the idea *as* a totality. Being open to a world, as the monad is, is entirely different from being attached to a single object in a relation of desire. Ideas, like monads, stand in a constant relation of expression to what is around them—or, rather, to what is internalized by them—and maintain incessant contact with the world (which, in some contexts in Benjamin's writings, can be understood as a historical contact).[23]

The harmony suggested by Leibniz is grasped not only by the divine eye, by God's all-encompassing gaze upon his best-of-all-possible systems of monads. Harmony, rather, is potentially grasped in *every* expression of *each* single monad. Inherent in the expression of the world is an expression of what composes it—that is, other monads and their perceptions. As Benjamin himself reformulates Leibniz: "every single monad contains, in an indistinct way, all the others" (*TS*, 47).[24] The more perfectly the world is expressed in an individual perspective, the more clearly does the monad or the idea include all other expressions in its own realm. A distinct perception of the world includes its perfect harmonious structure, and God is therefore not the only being with access to harmony; hence, harmony is internal to each monad and idea, and it is not a construct grasped only from an external, divine point of view. Each idea contains the abbreviation of the world—in the sense not only of representing the world but also of incorporating its harmony within this representation.

Harmony, however, also exists on another level. Not only is there a harmony at stake in the encounter between the idea and the world it expresses, but this structure also exists in the relationships between the ideas themselves. Several times in the prologue Benjamin specifically claims that the world of ideas is essentially discontinuous (*TS*, 33, 37). He then adds a detailed description of this world (in a passage similar to one previously cited):

> And so ideas subscribe to the law which states: all essences exist in complete and immaculate independence, not only from phenomena, but especially, from each other. Just as the harmony of the spheres depends on the orbits of stars which do not come into contact with each other, so the existence of *mundus intelligibilis* depends on the unbridgeable distance between pure essences. Every idea is a sun related to other ideas just as suns are related to each other. The harmonious relationship between such essences is what constitutes truth. (*TS*, 37)

In this crucial quote Benjamin presents the structure of the relationship between essences as the ground for the presentation of truth. Because of the basically discontinuous, isolated nature of the essences, their configuration can only be established via an *internal accord*. Since no external relations are feasible between them, only such an accord can constitute a harmony while still maintaining the independent existence of each essence. The harmonious configuration neither unites the essences nor welds them into each other—it rather places them in a congruent structure and arrangement. This is what Benjamin refers to in the prologue as the "virtual arrangement" of phenomena. Moreover, the presentation of ideas in harmony depends on the specific structure of impediment and the melancholic isolation standing at its core. What Benjamin here calls "the harmony of the spheres" is another rendering of his "melody of the spheres." Terms of musical harmony are thus essential to how Benjamin sees the relation between essences. It should be noted, however, that at this point Benjamin does not specifically make the connection to Leibniz's idea of preestablished harmony.

For Benjamin truth is constituted by the structure of discontinuous, self-sufficient suns configured in harmony. When one idea is presented from within its redeemed phenomenal elements, it is also put in a relation to other ideas and unfolds them. In that sense the nature of truth is all-encompassing, and in it ideas are not only individually unfolded but reveal one another.[25] When the idea of the *Trauerspiel* is presented, for instance, it also reveals the idea of the tragic or of melancholy.

This structure diverges from that of power and control. Crucially, there are no hierarchies here, nor is there a center attracting and concentrating everything to it. All essences coexist on the same level, parallel and in equal valence with each other. This is, again, a form resembling musical harmony, in which each sound retains its individuality but at the same time operates in relation to other sounds within the melodious structure.

A musical structure of meaning and reference within the musical context of harmony also appears in Benjamin's "Language and Logic," where he argues as follows:

And so the characteristics of human beings are to be counterpoised as alien to one another, and so the *harmony* of the spheres *resounds* from their orbits, which do not come into contact with one another. Every essential being is a sun and related to beings like itself, as suns in fact relate to one another. This also applies to the realm of philosophy, which is the only realm in which the *truth becomes manifest, namely with a sound like music*. And this is the *harmonic concept of truth*, which we must acquire so that the false quality of watertightness that characterizes its delusion vanishes from the authentic concept, the concept of truth. The truth is not watertight. Much that we expect to find in it slips through the net. (*SW*, 1:272; my emphasis)

Here, harmony is founded on the essentially partial nature of each element of truth. Arguing that "truth is not watertight," Benjamin proposes instead that there is no hermetic, immaculate truth.[26] This solemn conception should be dismissed in favor of the harmonization of its parts. The stars of the constellation, originally alien to one another, begin to resound across their separate orbits, so as to form a musical accord; and the essences, alien to and isolated from each other, are given in a structure of resounding and echo one another to occupy a comprehensive system of truth. Truth is manifested in sound, writes Benjamin. The anatomy of truth does not entail a unity between its scattered parts; it signifies, rather, the necessity to view this *dispersion as a totality*, in which the independence of the elements is maintained, yet they are configured into a harmonious structure.[27] Just as the musical notes in harmony follow their original score, so, too, do essences remain isolated even within the structure. They are given as a configuration of multiplicity and simultaneity.[28]

Friedlander offers a thesis that situates the pattern of Benjamin's structure of meaning within the recovery of musical echoes, and he claims that only music makes possible the fulfillment of meaning in the *Trauerspiel*.[29] Benjamin describes the *Trauerspiel*'s linguistic and dramatic principles as having been "symphonically laid"; they constitute the foundation on which the play's dispersed characters, and the diverse scale of feelings they represent, are to be put together, or "held together," as Friedlander suggests. This is exemplified by the unity of echoes that, despite their essential dissociation, can still be assembled into a harmonious structure. I find that this telling interpretation of Benjamin's reading of the *Trauerspiel* also refers implicitly to some of the crucial elements in the prologue, especially to its reference to the idea as a monad.

To go back to the previously mentioned examples, both the mosaic and the constellation present a form of holding together what is scattered; more specifically, this holding together resembles what musical harmony does with its disparate components. Holding together, however, can be articulated not only as a relation of control but also as harmony and attunement. In that sense the stars constituting the constellation and the material particles of the mosaic are to be attuned to one another in order to construct the overall image or a special form in which expression is arranged.[30] The articulation of meaning in terms of harmony should be understood in connection to musical harmony; it should also be grasped within the context of harmony regarded as an accord between disparate elements, a harmony capable, but only when given in concomitance, of being the presentation of truth.

Stimmung: Philosophy and Mood

The harmonious construction of meaning found in Leibniz as well as in Benjamin is not well served by the English term *harmony*, which lacks the resonance of *attunement*, *accord*, or particularly the German word *Stimmung* (a word that Leo Spitzer describes as virtually untranslatable).³¹ The translation of *Stimmung* as "mood" leaves out the important musical implications of the German word, whereas its translation as "harmony" disregards the subjective connotations of mood. But what the rendering of the word specifically shuns is the special interconnection between the musical and psychological, the external and internal. However, not only does the word in English translation fail to encompass both denotations at the same time; it also cannot encompass the unique intertwinement of the two found in *Stimmung*. As Agamben shows, the term expresses a unity between a subjective feeling and the human accord with the surrounding environment (with a landscape, for instance), and it presents a conceptual integration of the objective or factual with the subjective and psychological—which are brought into a harmonious unity.³²

This special structure of *Stimmung* challenges notions of psychological "inner" and objective "outer" states; it evokes a structure of meaning with an inherent harmony or accord between subject and world. This is precisely the structure given by Heidegger in *Being and Time*, when he evokes *Stimmung* as Dasein's primary way of entering the world.³³ In his analysis of *Stimmung* Heidegger argues that mood is neither internal nor external (*BT*, 176 [136]) but operates exactly at the intersection between the two states, namely, at the intersection between man and world; in Heidegger's terms mood is what determines Dasein's Being-in-the-World. Agamben explicates this structure by writing that *Stimmung*'s position "is neither within interiority nor in the world, but at their limit. Thus being-there, insofar as it is essentially its own opening, is always already in a *Stimmung*, is always already emotively oriented . . . We can say, then, that the *Stimmung*, rather than being itself in a place, is the very opening of the world, the very place of being."³⁴

This opening, however, is to be understood not as a spatial description of the situation within the world but rather, in concordance with the dual structure of *Stimmung* itself, as what lies neither inside nor outside, neither in the subject nor in the world, but instead constitutes their interconnection: "Having a mood is not related to the psychical in the first instance, and is not itself an inner condition which then reaches forth in an enigmatical way and puts its mark on Things and persons" (*BT*, 176 [137]). Heidegger terms this interconnection between Dasein and the world "*Befindlichkeit*," or affectedness.[35] *Befindlichkeit* refers to the way Dasein becomes affected (*Betroffenwerdens*) by the world and finds itself always already in the world as what matters to it. Being in a certain mood determines the different ways that the world affects Dasein, carries specific import for it and touches it: "the fact that this sort of thing can 'matter' to it is grounded in one's affectedness . . . Dasein's openness to the world is constituted existentially by the attunement of affectedness" (*BT*, 176 [136]; translation altered).

The connection between Heidegger's uses of *Stimmung* and *Befindlichkeit* becomes clear when we go back to the aforementioned musical and harmonic connotations of *Stimmung* (originating from the Latin *concentus* and *temperamentum* and to the Greek *harmonia*).[36] When referring to music, *Stimmung* means the tuning of an instrument or the bringing of several sounds or voices into accord; whereas in Heidegger's use of *Stimmung* as mood, there is a clear correspondence with the way Dasein attunes itself or is always given in an accord with the world. Moods operate, in effect, precisely, to bring about such an accord, in setting Dasein and the world in which it always already exists in a "*Gestimmeheit*," an accord or attunement.[37]

There is a striking correspondence between Heidegger's idea of *Stimmung* and the unique structure of the monadic system, as I have described it here. Most important, this link is found in the accord between Dasein and the world, paralleled by the monad's special way of "encountering" the world by way of expression. Leibniz describes the changes in the perception of the monad, which involve, in effect, its incessant expressive movements as an "internal principle" or its "internal actions" (MO, 644). This internal expressive activity in the monads is elucidated as being in correlation or correspondence to the thing expressed, in a way that the expressing monad is not similar to what it expresses, nor is it given in any direct relation to it. The monad, rather, *corresponds* to it and expresses it in a relation that Leibniz understands as analogy or proportion (WI, 207). What Leibniz stresses here is that given the monad's immaculate, pristine closure and detachment from the world, its expression of the world can never be taken to be causally structured, and the monad is therefore not directly affected by the world. Its expression of the world demonstrates rather the special *accord* it maintains with it, as established in Leibniz's principle of preestablished harmony. Leibniz's use of accord here is similar to Heidegger's description of Dasein's accord with the world as manifested in its mood.

Furthermore, Heidegger's affectedness finds an analogue in Leibniz's explanation of the monad's activity of expression. The monad is not only in accord with the world as totality, but its expression of the world depends on how the world pertains to it: "Although each created monad represents the whole universe, it represents more distinctly the body which is particularly affected by it" (MO, 649).[38] My aim here is not to argue that the monad is in fact a human entity or in any way similar to the Heideggerian Dasein. My claim is that there is, rather, a similar principle at work in both cases, namely, that both in the monad and in the structure of *Stimmung* or mood there is a special type of accord with the world, rooted in its possibility to affect or to matter in different ways to what is in relation to it.

Stimmung must then be viewed as a basic element of the monad: its being given in a preestablished harmony alludes to a musically harmonious structure in its encounter with the world, as well as to a special attunement or mood, through which it encounters the world as the object of its expression. As in Heidegger's account of moods, so too in the monad—the world is encountered in and through mood. In Leibniz this mood is termed "an individual perspective" from which each monad is in accord with and expresses the world; this perspective determines precisely how the world is taken in, just as anxiety or nostalgia determines the disclosure of the world in affect (again, it is the world as such, as totality, that is revealed, and not an object of intention placed in it). When Heidegger mentions the monad in his account of Dasein in *The Basic Problems of Phenomenology*, he writes, strikingly, that Dasein, like a monad, needs no window to look out toward something external to itself. It can do so, however, not because, as Leibniz professes, all beings are already accessible from within their capsule but rather because the monad, the Dasein, in its own being is already outside, among other beings. The Dasein is not in a capsule, and because of Dasein's original transcendence, a window would be superfluous for it.[39]

The importance of the figure of the monad lies precisely in this structure that I have defined as melancholic. The encounter with the world originates from complete closure, detachment, and self-absorption, from which the monad is attuned with the world (attunement understood here as being internally constituted). Its overcoming of the categories of inner and outer (which explicitly appears in Freud's account of the melancholic's pathological internalization of the lost object) demonstrates a blurring, or maybe—as in Heidegger—an overcoming, of the inner-outer border constitutive of its expressive function. The monad is a radical interiority intimately bound up and interlaced with its complete exteriority—the world itself. This structure is manifest, as in Benjamin's idea, through the category of expression that stands at its foundation.

The monadic structure is crucial to Benjamin's elucidation of truth and the idea in the prologue. There are common traits shared by this structure and the configuration of both the idea and the monad—which are expressive structures being in accord with the world, structures through which the world is revealed and distinguished. The expressive monad and the Benjaminian idea both make manifest different forms of accord with the world, of being attuned with the world. Benjamin's turn to the monad, therefore, is grounded not only in its closure, detachment, or even its chiefly expressive character (all of which occupy a prominent role in the idea). It is, rather, underpinned by the relationship between the monad and the world it expresses and in the crystallization of meaning and the presentation of truth, specifically, in the monad embodying the structure of mood as such.[40]

Since Benjamin proclaims that the "idea is the monad," it follows that a philosophically expressive encounter with the world in the idea has a primary element of *Stimmung* (in both its denotations) through which it encounters the world and according to which the world is arranged around it. The monad serves as an exemplary instance to examine the question of mood, in general, and melancholy, specifically. It has a certain mood, an attunement, through which it approaches the world and takes it in, and it is through this attunement that the nature of this encounter is determined.

Benjamin has been brought together with Heidegger by way of encounters with Freud and Leibniz. Now it becomes more readily explicit how we can establish philosophically the relationship between truth and melancholy. Their correspondence can unfold and be spread out only via a long detour, in which questions of language, presentation, and intention are reconsidered. Adopting a Benjaminian perspective, we can say that even though moods condition our ability to be in the world and to use language—and are, in that sense, prior to any possibility of discussing language or truth in the first place—we cannot examine the role and importance of moods only by delving into the philosophical structures of language and the presentation of truth. Precisely here lies the strength of Heidegger's theorization of moods: their precedence and preeminence does not obscure the ontological elements they make room for. Their characterization as opening up Dasein to the world and conditioning the way the world is revealed and matters to Dasein is also reflected in their conceptual structure: their philosophical predominance entails not a shrouding but rather an unfolding, an opening up. This is also how I suggest we see the relationship formed among Heidegger's theory of moods, Freud's psychoanalytic analysis of melancholia, and Benjamin's philosophical (and not theatrical or literary) reconsideration of truth, intention, and language. This interconnection not only opens up a novel view of the possibility of a metaphysics of melancholy, as this book has aimed to show, but also carves out the way for further exploration of the role played by moods in general in the history of philosophy.

Notes

INTRODUCTION

1. Here and throughout this work, wherever the German word *Darstellung* is used in the original, I have replaced the English translation "representation" with "presentation." In "Der Ursprung des deutschen *Trauerspiels*" Benjamin makes a point, especially in his preface, of distinguishing between these two meanings, and, in this sense, John Osborne's translation in *The Origin of German Tragic Drama* of *Darstellung* into "representation" is problematic.

2. For some illuminating genealogies of this type, see the canonical text by R. Klibansky, E. Panofsky, and F. Saxl, *Saturn and Melancholy: Studies in the History of Natural Philosophy, Religion and Art* (London: Nelson, 1964); Max Pensky, *Melancholy Dialectics: Walter Benjamin and the Play of Mourning* (Amherst: University of Massachusetts Press, 2001); and Julia Kristeva, *Black Sun: Depression and Melancholia*, trans. L. S. Roudiez (New York: Columbia University Press, 1992). For a useful anthology dealing with melancholy, containing an illuminating introduction to the different approaches to the term, see Jennifer Radden, ed., *The Nature of Melancholy: From Aristotle to Kristeva* (Oxford: Oxford University Press, 2000).

3. Genius stands out in this list because of its productive traits. The issue of melancholy's productiveness has always had a prominent place in its meaning. The prevailing passivity and hardship of melancholy, paired with the astounding bouts of creative productivity it seems to produce, was constantly addressed by its theorists.

4. For an important description of this and the surprising continuity of accounts of melancholy up to Freud see Giorgio Agamben, *Stanzas: Word and Phantasm in Western Culture*, trans. R. L. Martinez (Minneapolis: University of Minnesota Press, 1992), 3–19.

5. See Robert Burton, *The Anatomy of Melancholy*, ed. T. Faulkner, N. Kiessling, and R. Blair (Oxford: Clarendon, 1989).

6. See Klibansky, Panofsky, and Saxl, *Saturn and Melancholy*, 349. For Benjamin's discussion of this engraving see *TS*, 140.

7. David Hume, *A Treatise of Human Nature*, ed. D. F. Norton and M. J. Norton (Oxford: Clarendon, 2007), 175.

8. Martin Heidegger, *The Fundamental Concepts of Metaphysics: World, Finitude, Solitude*, trans. W. McNeill and N. Walker (Bloomington: Indiana University Press, 1995), 60.

9. See Martin Heidegger, *History of the Concept of Time*, trans. Theodore Kisiel (Bloomington: Indiana University Press, 2009), 255–56; and Martin Heidegger, *Zollikon Seminars*, ed. Medard Boss, trans. F. Mayr and R. Askay (Evanston, IL: Northwestern University Press, 2001), 196, 202–3, 211.

10. Martin Heidegger, *Being and Time*, trans. J. Macquarrie and E. Robinson (San Francisco: Harper and Row, 1962), 255–56. In references to Heidegger's *Being and Time* I provide the English pagination followed by the German pagination in brackets.

11. In *The Fundamental Concepts of Metaphysics* Heidegger declares that what he calls "profound boredom" is a "fundamental attunement" of *Dasein*. This is not the first time that he deals with the concept of fundamental attunement; his description of anxiety (*Angst*) in *Being and Time* can also be seen as an important treatment of the subject.

12. See Quentin Smith, "On Heidegger's Theory of Moods," *Modern Schoolman* 58 (1981): 211–35.

13. For a discussion of the inherent relationship between moods and philosophy see Hagi Kenaan and Ilit Ferber, "Moods and Philosophy," in *Philosophy's Moods: The Affective Grounds of Thinking*, ed. Hagi Kenaan and Ilit Ferber (Dordrecht: Springer, 2011), 3–10.

14. See Ilit Ferber, "*Stimmung*: Heidegger and Benjamin," in *Sparks Will Fly: Walter Benjamin and Martin Heidegger*, ed. A. Benjamin and D. Vardoulakis (New York: State University of New York Press, 2014).

15. Theodor Adorno, "A Portrait of Walter Benjamin," in *Prisms*, trans. Samuel and Shierry Weber (Cambridge, MA: MIT Press, 1981), 227–41.

16. Originally published under the title "The Origin of German Tragic Drama." When discussing Benjamin's book hereafter, I use the original German term *Trauerspiel* instead of John Osborne's translation, "Tragic Drama." Osborne's translation ignores the consequential distinction Benjamin makes between *Trauerspiel* and tragedy, a distinction that lies, in many senses, at the heart of his book. I elaborate on this distinction in Chapter 2.

17. All these texts can be found in *SW*, 1:55–74. Between 1916 and 1924 Benjamin also wrote his dissertation, "On the Concept of Criticism in German Romanticism" (*SW*, 1:116–200), a work that lies beyond the scope of the present volume.

18. For some interesting comments on the process of composing the book see Benjamin's letters to Scholem from 1924 to 1925, especially March 5, 1924; Sept.

16, 1924; Dec. 22, 1924; and Feb. 19, 1925 (Walter Benjamin, *The Correspondence of Walter Benjamin, 1910–1940*, ed. G. Scholem and T. W. Adorno, trans. M. R. Jacobson and E. M Jacobson [Chicago: University of Chicago Press, 1994]).

19. For a detailed description of the rejection of Benjamin's habilitation see George Steiner, introduction to *The Origin of German Tragic Drama*, trans. John Osborne (London: Verso, 1998), 8–11; and Bernd Witte, *Walter Benjamin: An Intellectual Biography*, trans. James Rolleston (Detroit: Wayne State University Press, 1997), 86–87.

20. Heidegger's project entails a break from the objective-subjective dichotomy (which traditionally underlies the modernist notion of subjectivity). This may in part be why moods are so essential to him: they present a model in which the polarities subjective-objective, internal-external, and passive-active are challenged.

21. The discussion of mood is attractive to Benjamin because, among other things, it allows him to discuss the subject without carrying the discussion into the subjective realm of concepts; in other words mood allows him to ignore subjectivity without completely surrendering the subject. Benjamin's general shying away from subjectivity can also be viewed as a response to the extreme individuality rooted in psychoanalysis, among other spheres (see also Max Pensky's *Melancholy Dialectics*, which offers an illuminating discussion of the question of subjectivity in the *Trauerspiel*).

CHAPTER I

1. An earlier and shorter version of this chapter was published under the title "Melancholy Philosophy: Freud and Benjamin," in *EREA (Revue d'études anglophones)* 4, no. 1 (spring 2006): 66–74.

2. This change in the form of the name is in itself of utmost importance for the understanding of the difference in Benjamin's and Freud's relationships to melancholy. I return to this change later.

3. Benjamin writes in the book's dedication that it was "conceived" in 1916 and written in 1925. Freud's text was written in 1915 and published two years later.

4. See Radden, *The Nature of Melancholy*, 4, 45–51.

5. For discussion purposes, I state this claim somewhat generally here. A careful reading of the original text reveals greater complexity. For Freud some states that can be considered normal and even important stages of development tend to turn pathological on occasion (narcissism, for example).

6. See, respectively, Rainer Nägele, *Theater, Theory, Speculation* (Baltimore: Johns Hopkins University Press, 1991), 57; Laurence A. Rickels, "Suicitation: Benjamin and Freud," in *Benjamin's Ghosts: Interventions in Contemporary Literary and Cultural Theory*, ed. Gerhard Richter (Stanford: Stanford University Press,

2002), 149; Beatrice Hanssen, "Portrait of Melancholy (Benjamin, Warburg, Panofsky)," *MLN* 114, no. 5 (1999): 991–1013 (this essay also appears in *Benjamin's Ghosts*, 169–88); Sarah Ley Roff, "Benjamin and Psychoanalysis," *The Cambridge Companion to Walter Benjamin*, ed. David S. Ferris (Cambridge, UK: Cambridge University Press, 2004), 115–33. Nägele seeks to place Freud and Benjamin into a single constellation, claiming that to do so does not imply direct influence between the two (although Benjamin did refer to Freud in his writings) because "a constellation is not a question of influence." Hanssen writes that Benjamin proves to be "especially dependent on Freud's model of the unconscious, recasting the historical-materialist analysis of utopia into Freudian wish and dream images" (995). A more genealogical perspective is taken by Sigrid Weigel in her *Body- and Image-Space: Re-reading Walter Benjamin*, trans. Georgia Paul (London: Routledge, 1996), where she divides Benjamin's relationship to Freud into different periods: 1918–19 (first acquaintance with psychoanalysis), 1928–29, and 1935–39 (memory).

7. Nägele, *Theater, Theory, Speculation*, 54, 60.

8. Ley Roff, "Benjamin and Psychoanalysis," 118. Ley Roff concludes by suggesting that Benjamin's use of psychoanalysis is characterized by structures of annihilation and reinscription, which mark his attitude to texts and textuality in general. She thus infers that translation between discourses (as between Benjamin's and Freud's) can never be either seamless or complete (133). See also Ley Roff's interesting discussion of a forgotten 1932 essay by Alexander Matte, who detects a connection between Freud and Benjamin through the latter's differentiation between tragedy and *Trauerspiel*.

9. Rickels, "Suicitation," 143.

10. See also Freud, *Constructions in Analysis*, *SE*, 23:296; and Freud, *Moses and Monotheism*, Essay III, Chapter G ("Historical Truth"), *SE*, 23:127–32.

11. For an interesting parallel consider Benjamin's analysis of the critics' response to the genre of *Trauerspiel*: "Just as a man lying sick with fever transforms all the words which he hears in the extravagant images of delirium, so it is that the spirit of the present age seizes on the manifestations of past or distant spiritual worlds, in order to take possession of them and unfeelingly incorporate them into its own self-absorbed fantasizing" (*TS*, 53).

12. Jean Laplanche remarks that "Mourning and Melancholia" presents a central *aporia* regarding mourning: "Mourning is described as the 'normal prototype' of melancholia—it is that which sheds light on, and thus that on which there would be no light to be shed; how could light be illuminated?" (Jean Laplanche, *Essays on Otherness*, trans. Luke Thurston [London: Routledge, 1999], 248).

13. The economic lexicon used by Freud in relation to the self is intriguing. The melancholic stance does not surrender to this logic of capitalism—the libido as "capital" that should be released for "production" (of life) to continue.

14. Hanssen argues that Benjamin remains seemingly "oblivious" to the distinctions between mourning and melancholia. Hanssen thus insinuates that Benjamin was actually acquainted with the distinction but chose to ignore it, or merely forgot it (Hanssen, "Portrait of Melancholy," 1003).

15. Some citations in the *Trauerspiel* book illustrate this usage: "*Mourning* is the state of mind in which feeling revives the empty world in the form of a mask . . . Accordingly the theory of mourning . . . can only be developed in the description of that world which is revealed under the gaze of the melancholic man" (*TS*, 139; my emphasis). Benjamin cites Filidor in writing that "Die *traurige Melankoley* wohnt mehrenteiles in Pallästen" [*Mournful melancholy* mostly dwells in palaces] (*TS*, 144; emphasis added). He adds that "the 'Trauergeist' [spirit of mourning] which figures in Harsdörffer, is presumably none other than the devil. The same melancholy, whose domination over man is marked by shudders of fear, is regarded by scholars as the source of those manifestations which form the obligatory accompaniment when despots meet their end" (*TS*, 144). Others are found in his description of the history of the term *melancholy*. Benjamin cites Constantinus Africanus as characterizing the *melancholic as mournful* (*TS*, 145; emphasis added); he quotes Julius Caesar Scaliger, who depicts the kings and princes in the Haupt- und Staatsaktionen as "very melancholic and mournful" (*TS*, 123); he describes Cronos, who was considered the melancholy god because he mourned his children, whom he had himself devoured in an exemplary act of melancholy destruction; and he describes Hamlet as the melancholic figure who treats his life as the object of mourning: "His life, the exemplary object of mourning, points, before its extinction, to the Christian providence in whose bosom his mournful images are transformed into a blessed existence. Only in a princely life such as this is melancholy redeemed, by being confronted with itself" (*TS*, 158). Another interesting claim built on the interchangeability of the terms is Benjamin's discussion of the tenacious self-absorption characteristic of melancholy, which he accompanies with a correspondence between melancholy and betrayal of the world for the sake of knowledge (*TS*, 157).

16. Max Pensky, one of the few writers who have profoundly and extensively dealt with melancholy and the *Trauerspiel*, claims that "as a feeling situating itself on the frontier between subject and object, *Trauer* only exists in its historical specificity. Yet, insofar as the dialectic contained in *Trauer* is nothing other than the real structure of human history itself, *Trauer* is itself transhistorical, messianic. Melancholy is nothing other than *Trauer* from the point of view of the historically situated subject" (Pensky, *Melancholy Dialectics*, 94).

17. Rebecca Comay, "Perverse History: Fetishism and Dialectic in Walter Benjamin," *Research in Phenomenology* 29 (1999): 52.

18. In "Portrait of Melancholy" Hanssen explains that she is attempting to "broaden the reception of Benjamin as a philosopher of melancholia" (994).

She convincingly describes how Benjamin relates to melancholy, yet she fails to discuss his important claims regarding truth—which are intimately related to melancholy—as elaborated in the preface to the *Trauerspiel* book.

19. This idea appears in many later psychoanalytic texts, including those of Lacan, Kristeva, and Klein.

20. On this change in Freud's views see also Tammy Clewell, "Mourning Beyond Melancholia: Freud's Psychoanalysis of Loss," *Journal of American Psychoanalytic Association* 52, no. 1 (2004), 61–63; and Judith Butler, "Thresholds of Melancholy," in *The Prism of the Self: Philosophical Essays in Honor of Maurice Natanson*, ed. Steven Galt Crowell (Dordrecht: Springer, 1995), 8–12.

21. Helga Geyer-Ryan, "Effects of Abjection in the Texts of Walter Benjamin," *MLN* 107, no. 3 (April 1992): 502.

22. Freud's famous description of the "fort-da" game in *Beyond the Pleasure Principle* (*SE*, 18:14–15) exemplifies the idea of loss as essential to healthy development of the self. Freud articulates this idea in numerous places; for instance, in *Three Essays on Sexuality* he writes that "the pathway to reality is marked off with lost objects" (*SE*, 7:222); and in the last section of "Inhibitions, Symptoms and Anxiety" he discusses how a child "learns to lose" (*SE*, 20:169).

23. On the notion of mortification in Benjamin and the connection between philosophy and literature see Michael Jennings, *Dialectical Images: Walter Benjamin's Theory of Literary Criticism* (Ithaca, NY: Cornell University Press, 1987), esp. chap. 4 (121–63).

24. The work's dazzling brilliance is also what blinds us in states of ecstasy. Benjamin is therefore proposing to transform this dazzlement into "sober light"—with soberness functioning as the state allowing one to approach a work without being dazzled. See "The Concept of Criticism in German Romanticism" (*SW*, 1:185).

25. See Walter Benjamin, "Goethe's *Elective Affinities*," *SW*, 1:297–360.

26. Judith Butler, "Afterword: After Loss, What Then?" in *Loss: The Politics of Mourning*, ed. David L. Eng and David Kazanjian (Berkeley: University of California Press, 2003), 469.

27. Peter Fenves defines *eschatology* as "the name for gathering together of last things" (Peter Fenves, "Tragedy and Prophecy in Benjamin's *Origin of the German Mourning Play*," in *Benjamin's Ghosts*, 245).

28. Georg Lukács, "On Walter Benjamin," *New Left Review* 110 (1978): 83–88.

29. Peter Fenves, "Marx, Mourning, Messianicity," in *Violence, Identity, and Self-Determination*, ed. Hent de Vries and Samuel Weber (Stanford: Stanford University Press, 1997), 259.

30. I elaborate on Benjamin's use of Hamlet in Chapter 2.

31. In his 1932 seminar on Benjamin's *Trauerspiel* book Adorno compares Benjamin's "empty world" to Lukács's notion of "*Zweiten Natur*," which Lukács

elaborates in his "Theory of the Novel." See Theodor W. Adorno, "Adornos Seminar von Sommersemester 1932 über Benjamins Ursprung des deutschen *Trauerspiels*, Protokolle," *Frankfurter Adorno Blätter* IV, Herausgegeben vom Theodor W. Adorno Archiv (Frankfurt: edition text + kritik, 1995), 54–55.

32. Another important image is that of a mold, specifically, the stamp and its imprint in "Goethe's *Elective Affinities*." There, Benjamin discusses the question of material content and truth content through the wax and mold, raising the question of the relationship between emptiness and material. See *SW*, 1:300.

33. As in many other cases, the distinction between normality and pathology in Freud remains fragile. The moment at which the normal stage of a child's development becomes an adult pathology is especially interesting in cases of the internalization of the external world or, in this case, the lost object. In *An Outline of Psychoanalysis* (1940) Freud discusses the internal world and the formation of subjectivity in the young child (the first period of childhood, which he locates around the age of five). Until this stage the ego mediates between the id and external realty, but at the age of five the child gives up a portion of the external world as an external object and takes it into the ego, so that it becomes an integral part of the internal apparatus. This internalization is very similar to that of the melancholic. The functions carried out by the external world (judgment, punishment, or being a source of orders) until this point are now managed by the superego, which is formed at this stage (*SE*, 23:205–7).

34. Laplanche, *Essays on Otherness*, 256.

35. Clewell, "Mourning Beyond Melancholia," 60.

36. Nicolas Abraham and Maria Torok, "Mourning *or* Melancholia: Introjection *versus* Incorporation," in *The Shell and the Kernel*, vol. 1., ed. and trans. Nicholas T. Rand (Chicago: University of Chicago Press, 1994), 126–27.

37. Ibid., 130–31.

38. Agamben, *Stanzas*, 21.

39. Kristeva argues that our subjectivity depends on "killing off," or separating from, the mother. She argues that for a normal subject to be formed, the self has to identify with someone else (rather than the lost one). The failure to mourn the mother results in inadequate integration into society, a process that Kristeva clearly associates with women (see Clewell, "Mourning Beyond Melancholia," 51–52).

40. Comay, "Perverse History," 51–52.

41. Ibid., 52–53.

42. Samuel Weber, *Benjamin's -abilities* (Cambridge, MA: Harvard University Press, 2008), 189–93.

43. Susan Sontag, "The Last Intellectual," *New York Review of Books*, Oct. 12, 1978.

44. Pensky, *Melancholy Dialectics*, 105–6.

45. Loyalty to materiality and to objects, which appears in another Benjaminian context, that of childhood, is especially interesting in the present context. Whereas loyalty is present there, its obverse—betrayal—is absent; in that sense the introduction of objects and the relationships maintained with them during childhood are more distant from allegory and perhaps closer to another stance that Benjamin discusses—that of the collector. Pensky refers to Susan Buck-Morss's claim that Benjamin's position regarding relationships to objects is located between the two extremes of the allegorist (or, the *Grübler*) and the collector, suggesting that Benjamin's materialist criticism is actually located in the space between these two positions (Pensky, *Melancholy Dialectics*, 246). For the collector, like the allegorist, any declaration of loyalty to the material becomes destructive since the (desired) object, once subjected to these feelings, must change. It is transformed into something altogether different while ensconced within the intense feeling addressed to it, which in one case empties it out and in the other tears it away from everything that is not consummate infatuation.

46. Sontag, "The Last Intellectual."

47. Agamben, *Stanzas*, 20–21.

48. Ibid., 21.

49. Benjamin read Husserl around 1913 and wrote a fragment on Scotus in 1920. See "According to the Theory of Duns Scotus" (*SW*, 1:228). Another relevant fragment from 1922–23 is "Stages of Intention" (*SW*, 1:391–92).

50. Weber, *Benjamin's -abilities*, 71.

51. Pensky, *Melancholy Dialectics*, 92.

52. This paragraph is a further example of Benjamin's lack of distinction between mourning and melancholy: he again describes mourning as having melancholic traits.

53. Adorno, "Adornos Seminar von Sommersemester 1932," 54.

54. Another example of this movement can be found in Lohenstein's *Sophonisbe*, where the oscillation between desire and hate controls the scene (see *TS*, 83).

55. *GS*, vol. 2, pt. 1, 79. Cited in Nägele, *Theater, Theory, Speculation*, 66. My discussion of Benjamin's relation to empathy is, for the most part, based on Nägele's account (64–68).

56. Benjamin also mentions R. M. Meyer and his empathic method as a contrast to his own methodology in the *Trauerspiel* book: "[The] subjective state of the recipient projected into the work; that is what the empathy, which Meyer regards as the keystone of his method, amounts to. This method . . . is the opposite of the one to be used in the course of the current investigation" (*TS*, 42).

57. Nägele, *Theater, Theory, Speculation*, 189. On Benjamin's critique of Oskar Walzel's concept of empathy in literary criticism see ibid., 66.

58. See note 1 in the Introduction.

59. For a discussion of Heidegger's distinction between anxiety and fear and its importance to his theory of moods see Stephen Mulhall, "Attunement and Disorientation: The Moods of Philosophy in Heidegger and Sartre," in Kenaan and Ferber, *Philosophy's Moods*, 123–39, esp. 123–130.

60. For an elaborate account of the relationship between Benjamin and Heidegger see Ferber, "*Stimmung*: Heidegger and Benjamin," in Benjamin and Vardoulakis, *Sparks Will Fly*.

61. Laplanche, *Essays on Otherness*, 251–52. Nägele discusses the myth of Penelope in the context of "*Nachträglichkeit*," a concept common to Freud and Benjamin. For the latter this is a historical force, creating a rupture in the continuity of time and memory. Nägele points to the myth of Penelope's work as something that ties thinkers together (and marks a difference with Habermas) in that they are more interested in the work of forgetting than in finding a superficially powerful method of remembering. They are unweaving rather than weaving. See Nägele, *Theater, Theory Speculation*, 76–77.

62. Werner Hamacher, "Working Through Working," trans. Matthew T. Hartman, *Modernism/Modernity* 3, no.1 (Jan. 1996): 24. This compelling article discusses the concept of work along several axes: National Socialism and Hitler (the "labor" party); Auschwitz as a workplace; Heidegger and his speech to the unemployed in 1933; Ernst Jünger; and more.

63. There is an interesting difference between mourning and melancholia in this context. *Melancholia* is a noun, whereas *mourning* is usually used as a verb or a verbal noun indicating a state of being (e.g., someone is in a state of mourning). This distinction can be related to the "work" done in mourning—i.e., its active nature—that contrasts with the passivity abounding in melancholy. This passivity is not present only in Freud; it is part of many more historical accounts of the term.

64. Sontag, "The Last Intellectual." Sontag likewise refers to Benjamin's own melancholy and his constant allusions to "recipes" for work, as in his *One-Way Street*, which describes the best conditions for work, its timing, utensils, etc., and in a large part of his correspondence, which Sontag claims was motivated by his need to chronicle, report on, and confirm the existence of his work.

65. This quality of "heaviness" appears in the book several times. Apart from the "heaviness of soul" attributed to Luther, Benjamin also mentions the "heaviness of things, indeed of beings" in a quote from Daniel Halévy, who alludes to Péguy. Benjamin also mentions the heaviness of heart attributed to melancholics in the context of his discussion of the melancholic emblem of the stone (*TS*, 155).

66. Benjamin claims that the exemplar of this relationship can be found in Calderon's plays, in which "the very precision with which the 'mourning' [*Trauer*] and the 'play' [*Spiel*] can harmonize with one another gives its exemplary validity—the validity of the word and of the thing alike" (*TS*, 81).

67. Hamacher argues that Freud, in his *remembering, repeating, and working through*, maintains that overcoming the resistance of the patient to his condition and to the analysis entails *naming* (thus acknowledging) these resistances to the patient (Hamacher, "Working Through Working," 45). The power of naming is crucial to Benjamin as well, as I point out in my third chapter.

68. Or, in Nägele's translation: "Thus philosophical contemplation does not worry about its élan" (*Theater, Theory, Speculation*, 198).

69. In the first version of the preface Benjamin uses *Wert* (value), and in the second, published version, he uses *Glanz* (brilliance, shine).

70. The central problematic in Benjamin's use of this image is the fact that mosaics are usually composed after the empty outline of the image has been drawn. There is a sketch, to which the little particles adhere. This analogy presupposes, then, a picture that exists before the material, whereas Benjamin's Idea is that which springs from the material itself, incapable of being established independently of the material.

71. Adorno, "Adornos Seminar von Sommersemester 1932," 55.

CHAPTER 2

1. Christine Buci-Glucksmann, *Baroque Reason: The Aesthetics of Modernity* (London: Sage, 1994).

2. William Egginton, *The Theater and Truth: The Ideology of (Neo)Baroque Aesthetics* (Stanford: Stanford University Press, 2010), 39.

3. In a letter to Benjamin from August 1935, Adorno writes that "baroque drama found its fulfillment in Hamlet" (Theodor Adorno and Walter Benjamin, *Adorno and Benjamin: The Complete Correspondence, 1928–1940*, ed. Henri Lonitz, trans. Nicholas Walker [Cambridge, MA: Harvard University Press, 1999], 108). On Benjamin's sometimes problematic use of *Hamlet* see Jane O. Newman, "'Hamlet ist Saturnkind': Citationality, Lutheranism, and German Identity in Walter Benjamin's 'Ursprung des deutschen *Trauerspiels*,'" in *Benjamin-Studien* 1, ed. D. Weidner and S. Weigel (Munich: Wilhelm Fink, 2008), esp. 179–82.

4. For a detailed background on Benjamin's historical motivations see Jane O. Newman, "Periodization, Modernity, Nation: Benjamin Between Renaissance and Baroque," *Journal of the Northern Renaissance* 1, no.1 (spring 2009): 27–42. Newman also notes that Benjamin, in fact, takes on a project similar to the one undertaken by Heinrich Wölfflin nearly thirty years earlier in his *Renaissance and Baroque* (1888) (ibid., 31).

5. See Jennings, *Dialectical Images*, 55n10.

6. I elaborate on the distinction between ideas and concepts, and their reciprocal relations, in Chapter 4.

7. On this difficulty in the translation see Weber, *Benjamin's -abilities*, 143.

8. See Weber, *Benjamin's -abilities*, 143–51; and Eli Friedlander, *Walter Benjamin: A Philosophical Portrait* (Cambridge, MA: Harvard University Press, 2012), 125–29.

9. Louis G. Wysocki, "Andreas Gryphius et la tragédie allemande au XVIIe siècle" (Thèse de doctorat, Paris, 1892), 14 (cited by Benjamin in *TS*, 53).

10. I am using the term *content* based on the early language essays. I elaborate on this term, together with the issue of expression in its linguistic context, in Chapter 3.

11. J.-B. Pontalis, "On Psychic Pain," in *Frontiers in Psychoanalysis: Between the Dream and Psychic Pain*, trans. Catherine Cullen and Philip Cullen (New York: International Universities Press, 1981), 197–99, 205.

12. This can be found, among other places, where Benjamin invokes Filidor's claim that "mournful melancholy mostly dwells in palaces," to which he responds: "These statements apply as much to the internal disposition of the sovereign as to his external situation" (*TS*, 144).

13. Leibniz, one of Benjamin's major philosophical inspirations—especially in regard to the melancholic foundations of his thought—makes an intriguing remark about the relation between grief and joy. He cites Plato's observation, made in the *Phaedo*, that "grief occupies the extremes of joy" and adds: "So one need not be surprised at this transition; pleasure seems sometimes to be only a composite of little perceptions, each of which would be a grief if it were great" ("Reply to the Thoughts on the System of Preestablished Harmony Contained in the Second Edition of Mr. Bayle's Critical Dictionary, Article Rorarius" [1702], in *PPL*, 579–80).

14. Judith Butler reads the respective sentence insightfully but replaces *comedy* with *mourning*, stating that mourning is the lining of comedy, instead of the other way around. However, some of Butler's beautiful insights regarding mourning can, in fact, be helpful in thinking about the role of comedy in the *Trauerspiel*. As she writes in "After Loss, What Then?" mourning is "likened to an 'interior' region of clothing that is suddenly, and perhaps with some embarrassment, exposed, not to the public eye, but to the flesh itself . . . [It] emerges as the lining of the dress, where the dress is, as it were, laughing" (470).

15. Cited in Geyer-Ryan, "Effects of Abjection in the Texts of Walter Benjamin," 510.

16. On this and Benjamin's unfinished project on comedy see Adriana Bontea, "A Project in Its Context: Walter Benjamin on Comedy," *MLN* 121 (2006): 1041–71. On the affinities among jokes, cruelty, and violence see also Geyer-Ryan, "Effects of Abjection in the Texts of Walter Benjamin," 499–520.

17. For a discussion of this text and an elaboration on the distinction Benjamin makes between *Leib* and *Körper*, two different significations of "body," see Friedlander, *Walter Benjamin*, 74–89.

18. This will become highly relevant in my discussion of the status of pain in Leibniz, in whose texts I find pain related to clarity of expression.

19. I thank Arnd Wedemeyer for our conversations on pain, which contributed considerably to these understandings.

20. I elaborate on the structure of expression in the language essay in Chapter 4.

21. The relationship between melancholy and proliferation or excess of expression has an indirect albeit powerful presence in Freud's definition of melancholy, where he states that melancholy is a response to a loss that can be "some abstraction which has taken the place of one, such as one's country, liberty, an ideal, *and so on*" (*SE*, 14:243; emphasis added). This "and so on" marks, according to David L. Eng and David Kazanjian, a melancholic excess and an abundance fundamental to any notion of remains. The authors view the latter as what surpasses the restrictiveness of melancholia as pathology or negation. See David L. Eng and David Kazanjian, "Introduction: Mourning Remains," in *Loss: The Politics of Mourning*, ed. David L. Eng and David Kazanjian (Berkeley: University of California Press, 2003), 5.

22. Fried provides one of the most important observations dealing with the relationship between absorption and theatricality in French painting of the eighteenth century. See Michael Fried, *Absorption and Theatricality: Painting and Beholder in the Age of Diderot* (Berkeley: University of California Press, 1980).

23. In "Some Points for a Comparative Study of Organic and Hysterical Motor Paralyses" Freud discusses the relationship between paralysis and hysteria—conditions that appear to be completely opposite at first glance. Paralysis, which for a long time characterized melancholia, is coupled in this text peculiarly with what can be seen as its opposite, namely, hysteria. Moreover, Freud's hysterics seem similar to the ostentatious and extravagant characters in the *Trauerspiel* (see *SE*, 1:164). Freud also links the structure of hysteria specifically to that of melancholy when he describes their common cyclical structure, which is rooted in the damming up related to melancholy, a damming up that causes an outburst of a hysterical nature (see "Draft E," *SE*, 1:189; *SE*, 1:39).

24. Buci-Glucksmann, *Baroque Reason*, 130.

25. Ibid., 139–41.

26. Friedlander, *Walter Benjamin*, 126.

27. Jennings, *Dialectical Images*, 170–79, esp. 170–71. For other detailed accounts of the role of allegory in Benjamin's book see Samuel Weber, "Genealogy of Modernity: History, Myth and Allegory in Benjamin's Origin of the German Mourning Play," in *MLN* 106, no. 3 (1991): 465–500 (also published in Weber, *Benjamin's -abilities*, 131–63); and Pensky, *Melancholy Dialectics*, 108–50 (most useful for understanding the crucial question of subjectivity in allegory).

28. Weber, *Benjamin's -abilities*, 160.

29. A citation Benjamin takes from Wysocki's "Andreas Gryphius et la tragédie allemande au XVIIe siècle."

30. Benjamin makes another relevant reference to pantomime when he mentions gestures in fighting that are another form of the bombastic and an almost pantomimic manner in which the fight is executed (see *TS*, 68).

31. Butler, "Afterword," 470.

32. In *Leo Armenius*, for instance, there are five mute characters (*Stumme Personen*). For a fascinating discussion of silence's role in the baroque theater see Claudia Benthien, *Barockes Schweigen: Rhetorik und Performativität des Sprachlosen im 17. Jahrhundert* (München: Wilhelm Fink, 2006).

33. See Shakespeare, *Hamlet*, act 3, scene 2, where Hamlet gives direction to the players: "Speak the speech, I pray you, as I pronounced it to you, trippingly on the tongue"; "you must acquire and beget a temperance that may give it smoothness"; and "Be not too tame neither, but let your own discretion be your tutor: suit the action to the word, the word to the action." For a compelling interpretation of this scene, in light of his philosophical analysis of the play, see Stanley Cavell, "Hamlet's Burden of Proof," in *Disowning Knowledge in Seven Plays of Shakespeare* (Cambridge: Cambridge University Press, 2003), 179–91.

34. See especially *TS*, 176–77, 192.

35. The role of "*Reyen*" is similar. The *Reyen* was the versified part in the *Trauerspiel* in which allegorical or mythological characters comment on the plot's events while singing and dancing (see Bontea, "A Project in Its Context," 1068n5).

36. The relationship between Benjamin and Schmitt, together with the implications of the phrase "state of emergency" for Benjamin's writings, has been extensively discussed. See especially Giorgio Agamben's *State of Exception*, trans. Kevin Attell (Chicago: University of Chicago Press, 2005); Giorgio Agamben, *Homo Sacer: Sovereign Power and Bare Life*, trans. Daniel Heller-Roazen (Stanford: Stanford University Press, 1995); Samuel Weber, "Taking Exception to Decision," in *Benjamin's -abilities*, esp. 176–94; and Lutz Koepnick, "The Spectacle, the *Trauerspiel*, and the Politics of Resolution: Benjamin Reading the Baroque Reading Weimar," *Critical Inquiry* 22 (winter 1996): 280–86.

37. Weber, *Benjamin's -abilities*, 186–87.

38. Giorgio Agamben, *Potentialities: Collected Essays in Philosophy*, trans. Daniel Heller-Roazen (Stanford: Stanford University Press, 1999), 161–62.

39. Cited in ibid., 162.

40. See, for instance, the beautiful opening scene of *Catharina von Georgien*, in which the stage is depicted as filled with "*Leichen Bilder / Cronen / Zepter / Schwerdter etc.*"—all uselessly lying about. Above the stage *der Himmel* opens up

while below it we find *Helle. Ewigkeit* descends from heaven, to stand at the center of the stage (Andreas Gryphius, *Catharina von Georgien* [Stuttgart: Reclam, 1975], act 1, line 13).

41. See Koepnick, "The Spectacle," 289.
42. Friedlander, *Walter Benjamin*, 136–37.
43. Harsdörffer, *Poetischen Trichters zweyter Theil*, cited by Benjamin in *TS*, 72.
44. Other notable female martyrs mentioned by Benjamin are those in *Sophia* and *Mariamne*, by Hallmann, and in *Maria Stuarda*, by Haugwitz.
45. Another somewhat more complex example is that of *Leo Armenius*. King Leo Armenius postpones the execution of his former close friend and present conspirator against him, Michael Balbus, in order not to desecrate Christmas with murder. This decision, which Leo makes at his wife's request, is what finally brings on his own death, as Michael Balbus flees his prison chains during the celebration and stabs the king in church. It is here that the king's decision to postpone the execution, a decision made in the name of Christianity, turns against him. On the play's structure as tragedy, and not as *Trauerspiel*, see Peter Szondi, *An Essay on the Tragic* (Stanford: Stanford University Press, 2002), 74–77.
46. See Gryphius, *Catharina von Georgien*, act 5, lines 70–103.
47. Geyer-Ryan points to the connection between allegory, sexual violence, and rape in "Effects of Abjection in the Texts of Walter Benjamin," 510.
48. "The Passions of the Soul," in *The Philosophical Writings of Descartes*, ed. and trans. J. Cottingham, R. Stoothoff, and D. Murdoch (Cambridge: Cambridge University Press, 1985), 1:328–404. Descartes's text is an invaluable source for understanding the philosophical preoccupation with the relationship between emotion and thought in the seventeenth century and is also an important, although often underestimated, countertext to his own renowned "Meditations on First Philosophy."
49. Nicolas Abraham, "Notes on the Phantom: A Complement to Freud's Metapsychology," in Abraham and Torok, *The Shell and the Kernel*, 171, 174.
50. Jacques Derrida, *Specters of Marx: The State of the Debt, the Work of Mourning and the New International*, trans. Peggy Kamuf (London: Routledge, 2006), 11.
51. The principal explanation for the predominance of ghost figures in the plays lies in the period's violent character and its response to the pervasiveness of unnatural death, especially attributed to the bloody Thirty Years' War (1618–48).
52. The nature of repetition is thus not only related to death in the *Trauerspiel*—Benjamin describes repetition as one of the strong characteristics of the plays' more general structure: "Again and again, the *Trauerspiel* of the seventeenth century treat the same subjects, and treat them in such a way as to permit, indeed necessitate, repetition" (*TS*, 137).

53. Benjamin's discussion of the death of Socrates is most interesting within this context. Benjamin describes Socrates's death as nontragic since it marks no end, in contrast to tragic death. Furthermore, tragic death also differs from the *Trauerspiel* in that it does not remain fluid, endless, but functions as a continuation or even a new beginning. Socrates's death does not mark a boundary for the philosopher since he believes in life after death, a belief unavailable to the tragic hero (see *TS*, 114).

54. Note the similarity to Leibniz's use of terms (set of mirrors, hyperbolic relation, etc.) in the *Monadology* (discussed in Chapter 4).

55. Nicolas Abraham, "The Phantom of Hamlet or the Sixth Act Preceded by the Intermission of 'Truth,'" in Abraham and Torok, *The Shell and the Kernel*, 187.

56. I find in Benjamin's "Berlin Childhood Around 1900" many points of intersection with the theme of the ghost. One example is in Benjamin's description of his grandmother's apartment in Berlin: the apartment, which does not allow a space for death, is also the site in which the ghost, homeless, appears, its presence felt even if it does not actively interfere with Benjamin the child going up the stairs (see *SW*, 3:621–22). This half-felt presence, in which the ghost is no longer alive (thus is not active) but is also not yet dead (and so has a presence in the house), will prove to be typical of the baroque *Trauerspiel*.

57. Weber, *Benjamin's -abilities*, 144, 152.

58. Eli Friedlander, "On the Musical Gathering of Echoes of the Voice: Walter Benjamin on Opera and the *Trauerspiel*," *Opera Quarterly* 21, no. 4 (2005): 639. I return to this claim in my last chapter, where I discuss the notion of harmony as a model of meaning.

59. Gryphius, *Cardenio und Celinde* (Stuttgart: Reclam, 1968), 64–65.

60. Following Menninghaus, Richter claims that Benjamin incessantly alludes to the world of thresholds and transitory spaces. The *Passagenwerk* is understood in that sense as a "ghost book," and is linked to a literary tradition in which Paris is the city of ghosts. Richter elaborates on the theme of unclosed doors which serve as "transitory spaces in which images of the past, thought to be gone for good, come back to haunt the present" (Richter, "Introduction," in *Benjamin's Ghosts*, 4–5).

61. Benjamin, "Goethe's *Elective Affinities*," *SW*, 1:297–300.

62. There are several explanations for this custom. They include the imperative not to damage the body that, during mourning, is closer to the dead and thus to God. Cutting the hair or nails is therefore considered an act of "breaking of the vessels." Thus, damaging the mourner's body entails damaging an image of God. One possible source is ancient Egyptian practices of self-denial and detachment from daily life during mourning, customs meant to bring the family closer to the lost one. For instructive explanations about these and other

mourning customs see Nissan Rubin, *The End of Life: Rites of Burial and Mourning in the Talmud and Midrash* (Ha'Kibutz Ha'meuchad, 1997) [Hebrew]; Rabbi Abner Weisee, *Death and Bereavement: A Halakhic Guide* (Hoboken, NJ: Ktav, 1991); Aharon Berekhyah mi-Modena, *Sefer Ma'avar Yabok* (Jerusalem: Ahavat Shalom, 1995) [Hebrew]; Yehi'el Mikhal ben Aharon Tukazinski, *The Bridge of Life* (Jerusalem: N. A. Tukazinski, 1960) [Hebrew].

63. Rubin, *The End of Life*, 161.

64. Fenves traces this pattern in the plays and professes that there is never a rest or resolution, only an everlasting fateful retribution and eternal return of the same inherited debt. The *Trauerspiel* presents no end to this debt, and it is "never anything but this play—thus consist[ing] in an interminable interplay of vengeance and expiation" (Fenves, "Marx, Mourning, Messianicity," 260).

65. Gerhard Richter discusses Benjamin and the figure of the ghost by reading the legacy of Benjamin himself as ghostlike. He understands Benjamin's impact on such a diverse range of disciplines and the basic resistance of his texts to assimilation as a haunting characteristic of his thought, which he characterizes as "ghostly" since it returns time and again to haunt us as soon as we turn our back to it. See Richter, "Introduction," in *Benjamin's Ghosts*, 3. My point in discussing the ghost is, however, somewhat different: it is not located in the spectral character of Benjamin's own writings and their legacy but in the role the figure of the ghost plays for Benjamin, in its meaning for him.

66. Benjamin, "On the Concept of History," *SW*, 4:390–91.

67. A similar idea appears in Benjamin's famous phrase: "Perhaps revolutions are an attempt by the passengers on this train—namely, the human race—to activate the emergency brake" (*SW*, 4:402).

68. Walter Benjamin, *The Arcades Project*, trans. Howard Eiland and Kevin McLaughlin (Cambridge, MA: Harvard University Press, 1999), 462–63.

69. For a suggestive analysis and discussion of Benjamin's "On the Concept of History," especially in relation to the temporal structure the essay puts forth, the idea of debt, and how it weaves the web of correspondences between past and present in Benjamin's thought on historical time, see Werner Hamacher, "'Now': Walter Benjamin on Historical Time," in *Walter Benjamin and History*, ed. Andrew Benjamin (London: Continuum, 2005), 38–68.

70. Derrida, *Specters of Marx*, 54.

71. Ibid., 91. I elaborate on Derrida's idea of debt in the context of Benjamin's theory of language in the next chapter.

72. See, for instance, Eduardo Cadava, *Words of Light: Theses on the Photography of History* (Princeton, NJ: Princeton University Press, 1997); and Ariella Azoulay, *Once upon a Time: Photography Following Walter Benjamin* (Ramat-Gan: Bar-Ilan University Press, 2007 [Hebrew]). In *Specters of Marx* Derrida mentions an interesting visual constituent of the ghost: "the specter first of all

sees *us*. From the other side of the eye, *visor effect*, it looks at us even before we see *it* or even before we see period. We feel ourselves observed, sometimes under surveillance by it even before any apparition" (101).

73. Here Benjamin describes this encounter between the past and the present in terms of a voice and not an image. Benjamin starts the passage (entitled "News of Death") by challenging the concept of déjà vu, taken from the visual realm, with that of sound and echo. I see the model of the ghost as closer to that of sound and echo (and "call") than of image (*SW*, 2:389–90).

74. Benjamin, "Against a Masterpiece." Criticism written on *Der Dichter als Führer in der deutschen Klassik*, by Max Kommerell (*SW*, 2:378–85).

75. The German expression *Aber es mag sein wie es will* imparts a more active part to the past, which "decides" for itself, or is independent regarding the form it ventures to take. In the English translation something of this movement is lost.

76. "A ghost had appeared to me. I would have had a hard time describing the place where the specter went about its business. Still, it resembled a setting that was known to me, though likewise inaccessible" (Benjamin, "A Ghost," *SW*, 3:376).

77. Elsewhere Benjamin writes about the difference between forgiveness and reconciliation. In "Meaning of Time in the Moral Universe" he discusses the temporal aspect of forgiveness (and the "storm of forgiveness"), which is distinct from reconciliation and can take place without the latter. This pair of terms is described there in relation to the parting from the dead (see *SW*, 1:286–87).

CHAPTER 3

1. Another interesting source for Benjamin's discussion of the inherent relations between language and truth is his dissertation on the romantic conception of critique, "The Concept of Criticism in German Romanticism" (1919) (*SW*, 1:116–200). Benjamin criticizes the romantics' structure of truth, which is principally that of a reflecting consciousness, and offers instead to account for the linguistic character of truth. Cited by Rainer Nägele in *Echoes of Translation: Reading Between Texts* (Baltimore: Johns Hopkins University Press, 1997), 7.

2. Friedlander, *Walter Benjamin*, 32. Friedlander provides a thought-provoking account of Benjamin's relation to Kant in ibid., 27–36.

3. Benjamin elaborates on the relation between philosophy and theology in the "Addendum" to his essay on Kant. See *SW*, 1:108–10.

4. In the dedication to the *Trauerspiel* book he writes that it was "conceived 1916 written 1925."

5. *SW*, 1:59–61 and *SW*, 1:62–74, respectively. To help differentiate between the two essays I am referring to here, I have abbreviated "The Role of Language" as RL, and "On Language as Such" as LAN.

6. Most notably Rodolphe Gasché, "Saturnine Vision and the Question of Difference: Reflections on Walter Benjamin's Theory of Language," in *Benjamin's Ground: New Readings of Walter Benjamin*, ed. Rainer Nägele (Detroit: Wayne State University Press, 1988), 83–104; Beatrice Hanssen, "Language and Mimesis in Walter Benjamin's Work," in *The Cambridge Companion to Walter Benjamin*, ed. David S. Ferris (Cambridge: Cambridge University Press, 2004), 54–72; Peter Fenves, "The Genesis of Judgment: Spatiality, Analogy, and Metaphor in Benjamin's 'On Language as Such and on Human Language,'" in *Walter Benjamin: Theoretical Questions*, ed. David S. Ferris (Stanford: Stanford University Press, 1996), 75–93; Friedlander, *Walter Benjamin*, 14–19; and Winfried Menninghaus, *Walter Benjamins Theorie der Sprachmagie* (Frankfurt am Main: Suhrkamp, 1980).

7. See Fenves, *Arresting Language: From Leibniz to Benjamin* (Stanford: Stanford University Press, 2001), 203–4.

8. Giorgio Agamben, *Infancy and History: The Destruction of Experience*, trans. Liz Heron (London: Verso, 1993), 3–10.

9. Another important account of the notion of possibility is no doubt Derrida's. In his discussion of spoken vs. written language in "Limited Inc a b c," he describes the relationship between presence, absence, and the possibility. His discussion is close to Agamben's in that he attends to the structure of possibility qua possibility while pointing at its essential independence from necessity or actualization. See Jacques Derrida, *Limited Inc*, trans. Samuel Weber (Evanston, IL: Northwestern University Press, 1988), 47–50.

10. Agamben, *Potentialities*, 178–79.

11. Ibid., 182.

12. Samuel Weber's book *Benjamin's -abilities* centers on the suffix *-barkeit* (-ability) in Benjamin's writings and deals with the idea of possibility in general in Benjamin's work; however, it is in the two chapters on translation and the idea of *translatability* that Weber's argument is at its best. See Weber, *Benjamin's -abilities*, 53–94.

13. See the "Addendum" to "On the Program of the Coming Philosophy," in *SW*, 1:108–10.

14. Pensky, *Melancholy Dialectics*, 48.

15. The human act of naming can also be considered when thinking of the voice, and naming can be regarded as a voice-ly act. The place of human beings in the chain of creation entails that God's physical creation is given a vocal expression. This stresses the place of the voice-ly in the relation between humanity and nature.

16. On blissfulness and immediacy see Pensky, *Melancholy Dialectics*, 50.

17. Fenves claims that human language is limited in its creativity—it is only creative in its giving of proper names. With everything else it is merely cognitive.

In the case of proper names language can be creative only as long as no reason is applied in deciding to call someone in one way or another. If there is such a reason, then no decision is made. A proper name should be created ex nihilo, "not from *earth*, as in the case of Adam; not from *man* or *life*, as in the case of Eve; and not even—one might suppose—from the tautology 'I will be what I will be,' as in the case of God (Exod. 3:14)" (Fenves, *Arresting Language*, 217).

18. Benjamin's reference here to the movement between languages as translation is related to his theory of translation in "The Task of the Translator" (discussed in the last part of this chapter).

19. The feminine-masculine aspect of the act of naming, and—in my interpretation—the power relations inherent in Benjamin's account, can also be found in the history of melancholy. Writers such as Kristeva, Butler, and Irigaray have located the loss of speech within a feminist context. In "On Language as Such" feminine nature is silenced by its own sadness; this is a continuation of the structure so dominant in the history of melancholy. Jennifer Radden claims that in contemporary feminist writings there is a structural pattern in melancholy that relates to gender differences: loquacious male melancholy is set in contrast to the mute suffering (or mourning) of women. Women's estrangement from language, in turn, is explained by what can be seen as self-estrangement (see Radden, *The Nature of Melancholy*, 34–35).

20. Pensky, *Melancholy Dialectics*, 49. Pensky also links the notion of *Ursprache* (representing immediacy and blissfulness) and Jewish mysticism, on the one hand, and German romantic theories, on the other. He describes the latter as revelatory and noninstrumental, leading to theological-historical speculations about lost poetic language (ibid., 50–51).

21. This can also be found to be true regarding God's assertion that "it is not good that the man should be alone; I will make him a helper fit for him" (Genesis 2:18), which is, again, not propositional, being prior to the introduction of evil into the story.

22. Benjamin points to the tree of knowledge as that which stood in the garden of Eden as the emblem of judgment, thus marking the mythical origin of law (*SW*, 1:72).

23. Nägele, *Theater, Theory, Speculation*, 199–200.

24. Barbara Johnson, *Mother Tongues: Sexuality, Trials, Motherhood, Translation* (Cambridge, MA: Harvard University Press, 2003), 52 (cited and discussed by Judith Butler in "Betrayal's Felicity," *Diacritics* 34, no. 1 [spring 2004]: 85n1).

25. In the English translation it is "melancholy," which is not altogether wrong, considering Benjamin's blurring of melancholy, sorrow, and mourning.

26. See also Jacques Derrida's momentous discussion of the Babylonian tower in the context of Benjamin's theory of language in his "Des tours de Babel," in *Acts of Religion*, ed. Gil Anidjar (Routledge: New York, 2002), 104–33.

27. Pensky addresses the question of the retrieval of the continuity between man and nature in claiming that criticism takes the place of naming; he shows how Benjamin implies that the redemption of things is not limited to a restitution of a lost unity but also has a revelatory function. Emerging as a counterpart to *Trauer* and loss, criticism is directed against *Trauer* so as to destroy and redeem it at the same time. Critical language hence becomes a struggle against *Trauer*. See Pensky, *Melancholy Dialectics*, 58–59.

28. A figure worth noting in this context is Nebuchadnezzar, the Babylonian king, discussed in the *Trauerspiel* book with regard to Hunold's play named for him. Nebuchadnezzar was known as a melancholic figure, constantly having bad dreams (interpreted by Daniel) and eventually dethroned for a period when he virtually turns into a beast. After Daniel's prophecy comes true, Nebuchadnezzar falls ill, in what seems to be a version of acute melancholy, and retires far away from human beings. He eats grass, his body grows feathers, and his nails are transformed into long claws (see Daniel 4:28–33). Interpreters have claimed that perhaps the king was put in isolation after he thought he was an animal (this evolved into the medieval legend of the werewolf). Condensed within the story of Nebuchadnezzar is melancholy, mourning, the loss of language (Babel), a fall of a king similar to the deterioration of the baroque tyrant, and the external signs of mourning mentioned above in the context of the ghost (long nails and hair). Nebuchadnezzar's story exemplifies the more general alliance between man and animal and the fact that the border between them is anchored in melancholy, as Benjamin writes: "In fact, it is the most genuinely creaturely of the contemplative impulses, and it has always been noticed that its power need be no less in the gaze of a dog than in the attitude of a pensive genius. 'Sir, sorrow was not ordained for beasts but men, yet if men exceed in it they become beasts,' says Sancho Panza to Don Quixote" (*TS*, 146).

29. Man's inability to actualize his own mental being, to give it complete expression, stands in contrast to his place in the creaturely hierarchy. Although he possesses all the highest qualities and potentials, he cannot execute them. This is similar to the behavioral structure of the tyrant in the *Trauerspiel*. The tyrant, observes Benjamin, is the ruler who, because his infinite power stands in contrast to his human limitations, is a frustrated, paralyzed figure, unable to exercise the authority and supremacy endowed on him by his status and rank. Writing about Herod, Benjamin describes this conflict clearly: "he falls victim to the disproportion between the unlimited hierarchical dignity, with which he is divinely invested, and the humble estate of his humanity" (*TS*, 70). This antithesis between the ruler's power and his ability to exercise it produces indecisiveness and paralysis (*TS*, 71), which are also among the most profound characteristics of the melancholic. Like the tyrant, man, too, after the Fall, encompasses an internal conflict that leaves him speechless and distanced from his original task. He possesses the highest of

powers—language—but he cannot avail himself of it. The extensive degradation of his blissful language into impotence leaves man in a state analogous to that of the tyrant—their ostensible powers are empty and unutilized.

Another aspect shared by Adam in Genesis and the tyrant of the *Trauerspiel* is the way their fates are entangled with those dependent on them. Thus the latter's fall is inherently bound up with the demise of his rule. Benjamin writes that the baroque ruler, "the summit of creation, erupt[s] into madness like a volcano and destroy[s] himself and his entire court" (*TS*, 70); and "the tyrant falls, not simply in his own name, as an individual, but as a ruler and in the name of mankind and history" (*TS*, 72). In the same way, the degradation of Adam's language always has to do with how nature, experiencing a loss as well, is influenced by such a dissolution.

30. As far as I am aware, the only interpretive account centering on Benjamin's fragment "The Role of Language in *Trauerspiel* and Tragedy" is Friedlander's "On the Musical Gathering." There is, however, no interpretation specifically devoted to Benjamin's notion of "lament" in this text.

31. My addition. I find that the difference between the two meanings is better understood when adding "over" to translate "*über die Sprache*" more accurately.

32. This claim appears in three places in Benjamin. Apart from the above-cited paragraph from "On Language as Such," Benjamin also uses these same words in the *Trauerspiel* book (*TS*, 224–25) and in "The Role of Language," where he writes that "it was already defined in the ancient wise saying that the whole of nature would begin to lament if it were but granted the gift of language" (RL, *SW*, 1:60).

33. See my discussion of the intentionless and its importance to melancholy in Chapter 1.

34. See Pensky, *Melancholy Dialectics*, 53.

35. The "undifferentiated" nature of lament is precisely this unidentifiable and impotent expression, as lament is customarily a form of song used to express sorrow. In the Jewish tradition a lament was a repetitive, often chant-like song, whose content was irrelevant to the specific loss and rather referred to loss as such. The form of expression in the lament is that one woman (usually) is speaking-singing, and the others rely on her recitation of the verse and echo after her. See Rubin, *The End of Life*.

36. In the same sentence in the *Trauerspiel* book the word *Trauerigkeit* is also translated by Osborne as "mournfulness."

37. Nägele explains Benjamin's odd use of the paradoxical inversion of the sentence in grammatical terms. He suggests that the inversion annuls the grammatical logic of the first sentence, since the causal structure does not permit such an inversion. However, the syntactical inversion is prepared in the first sentence by the prolepsis of the pronoun, that is, the placeholder of a noun yet to come. Since

in the German the pronoun referring to nature is *she*, and not *it*, the scene is set for the allegorical personification of a mourning nature before the term actually occurs. Nägele claims that the inversion is thus not a poetical figure but rather a stylistic device to break up speech, in which the abruption of language ruptures the appearance of a causal connection. See Nägele, *Theater, Theory, Speculation*, 196–97.

38. See, e.g., the prologue to the *Trauerspiel* book.

39. Fenves, *Arresting Language*, 217–18.

40. The coupling of the inclination to expression and speechlessness renders language to be a realm that simultaneously contains expression and the expressionless [*Ausdruckslose*]. This structure is present both after the fall into chatter and before it, inhering in paradisiacal language and specifically in the act of naming. Expression, in both cases, is an intimation of mourning and the inability to immediately express. All expression, hence, is always also intrinsically expressionless.

41. See Friedlander, "On the Musical Gathering," 641–42.

42. Fritz Homeyer, *Stranitzkys Drama vom "Heiligen Nepomuck"* (Berlin: Mayer and Müller, 1907).

43. Nägele, *Echoes of Translation*, 10; see especially the chapter "Echolalia," which examines the figure of the echo and its relation to translation.

44. Gershom Scholem, "Über Klage und Klagelied," *Tagebücher*, vol. 2, *1917–1923* (Frankfurt am Main: Jüdischer, 2000), 128–33. This essay, unpublished in Scholem's lifetime, is part of his recently published diaries. There is as yet no English translation for the text; therefore, all translations here are my own. Benjamin read Scholem's text after he had written his own "Role of Language." In 1918 he wrote to Scholem about the crucial impact the latter's text had made on him: "without you knowing that I wrestled with the same problem two years ago, you have made a significant contribution to clarifying it for me . . . I applied the following question to the *Trauerspiel* in a short essay entitled: 'The role of language in *Trauerspiel* and Tragedy': 'how can language as such fulfill itself in mourning and how can it be the expression of mourning?' In so doing, I arrived at an insight that approximates yours in its particulars and in its entirety" (Benjamin, *The Correspondence of Walter Benjamin, 1910–1940*, 120–21).

45. For a detailed interpretation of Scholem's text, as well as a discussion of its proximity to Benjamin's fragments on language and lament, see Ilit Ferber, "A Language of the Border: On Scholem's Theory of Lament," *Journal of Jewish Thought and Philosophy*, forthcoming.

46. Nägele, *Echoes of Translation*, 47.

47. This model is akin to Leibniz's metaphysical model, which I will discuss in detail in the next chapter.

48. *SW*, 1:253–63, hereafter TT. This text has been widely discussed in the secondary literature. See especially Derrida, "Des tours de Babel"; Paul de Man,

"'Conclusions' Walter Benjamin's 'The Task of the Translator' Messenger Lecture, Cornell University, March 4, 1983," *Yale French Studies* 69 (1985): 25–46; Gasché, "Saturnine Vision and the Question of Difference," 90–96; Andrew Benjamin, *Translation and the Nature of Philosophy* (London: Routledge, 1989), 86–108; Friedlander, *Walter Benjamin*, 17–27.

49. Samuel Weber provides a thorough discussion of "translatability" in Benjamin's theory of translation in Weber, *Benjamin's -abilities*, 53–94.

50. Friedlander, *Walter Benjamin*, 18–21.

51. Gasché understands translatability in this context as a call for the liberation of the work of art from itself ("Saturnine Vision," 90).

52. Walter Benjamin, "On the Topic of Individual Disciplines and Philosophy," *SW*, 1:404.

53. The best example of these claims regarding the afterlife of works is found in Benjamin's own criticism of the *Trauerspiel*, which accurately demonstrates what *afterlife* means. The *Trauerspiel* can only unfold the way it does, in Benjamin's account of it, after its life has ended and its works have been mortified. Its special purposiveness, with its "truth content," can be revealed only after it has been (violently) detached from its original life-sphere, and after its interior configuration has undergone a shift. This example shows, above all, the special affinity fashioned by Benjamin between translation and criticism.

54. This structure is the exact opposite of the structure of time in tragedy, in which death produces an end point to meaning rather than unfolds it. This explains in part why the temporal structure of the *Trauerspiel* is so appealing to Benjamin.

55. This again echoes Benjamin's presentation of the purification process that language undergoes in RL.

56. A similar structure shows itself at the beginning of Benjamin's "Goethe's *Elective Affinities*," in which the terms *material content* and *truth content* appear. There he writes of the way in which this pair, bound up together in the beginning of the life of the work, are in time separated from each other, rendering the truth content presentable or readable. Again—the question of separation and the loss of the original state proves itself to be a condition of legibility. The separation between the two is present, together with their eternal dependence. The scene of the funeral pyre mentioned in the text—a scene of loss and farewell—takes place within another framework of such a loss: that of historical loss. See Benjamin's "Goethe's *Elective Affinities*," in *SW*, 1:297–360. For a detailed discussion of the relation between material content and truth content see also Anson Rabinbach, "Critique and Commentary / Alchemy and Chemistry," *New German Critique* 17 (spring 1979): 3–14. For another version of Benjamin's discussion of truth content and material content in the context of philosophical criticism see *TS*, 182.

57. It is important to refer here to the famous debate around Paul de Man's discussion in "The Task of the Translator," specifically the debate around his alleged mistake in understanding the German *Wehen* to mean death-pangs instead of birth-pangs. See de Man, "'Conclusions' Walter Benjamin's 'The Task of the Translator.'"

58. Benjamin explains this via a simile of a broken vessel being glued together:

> Fragments of a vessel that are to be glued together must match one another in the smallest detail, although they need not be like one another. In the same way a translation, instead of imitating the sense of the original, must lovingly and in detail incorporate the original's way of meaning, thus making both the original and the translation recognizable as fragments of a greater language, just as fragments are part of a vessel. For this very reason translation must in large measure refrain from wanting to communicate something, from rendering the sense, and in this the original is important to it only insofar as it has already relieved the translator and his translation of the effort of assembling and expressing what is to be conveyed. (TT, SW, 1:260)

This simile is taken from the famous Lurianic myth of the broken vessels.

59. See Gasché, "Saturnine Vision," 92.

60. Fenves notes this important point in *Arresting Language*, 222.

61. Derrida, "Des tours de Babel," 131.

62. Gasché claims a connection between this type of intention and what he calls "the difference" that language as language makes—a difference structurally close to the difference philosophy itself makes (see "Saturnine Vision," 95). He also makes a claim regarding the intrinsic relation of translation to philosophy, by explaining that the special mode of intention in translation is "not a reference to one particular philosophical problem [but] to philosophy itself . . . Naming and translating, because they reflect cognitively on difference, are of the order of philosophy" (ibid.). Gasché makes a point of saying that the manifestation of this shared intentionality is conditioned by the denaturalization of language, which is the task par excellence of translation. This is achieved by translation's focusing not on the objects intended in language but on the mode of its intending, or what the Scholastics called *modus significandi*—the mode, or intention, of meaning (ibid., 93).

CHAPTER 4

1. Benjamin to Adorno, May 31, 1931, in Adorno and Benjamin, *Adorno and Benjamin: The Complete Correspondence, 1928–1940*, 89.

2. Benjamin, *The Correspondence of Walter Benjamin*, 261, cited in SW, 1:511.

3. See TS, 47–48. All other schemes are presented as metaphoric or analogical. See, e.g.: "*Just as* mosaics . . . *so* philosophical contemplation" (TS, 28; my

emphasis); "Ideas are to objects *as* constellations are to stars" (*TS*, 34; my emphasis); "*Just as* the mother . . . *so do* ideas come to life" (*TS*, 35; my emphasis).

4. For a discussion of Leibniz as a philosopher of the baroque, and for some illuminating observations on the structure of the monad, see Gilles Deleuze, *The Fold: Leibniz and the Baroque*, trans. Tom Conley (Minneapolis: University of Minnesota Press, 1993). Deleuze compellingly links the structure of the monad to that of allegory. He describes allegory through terms such as *concentration*, *isolation*, and *detachment*—all of which can be found in the monad (144–51).

5. It is important to emphasize here that Benjamin's interest in the monad does not extend to all of Leibniz's philosophy but, specifically, to his conception of the monad (appearing in its most concentrated form in Leibniz's *Monadology*, but structured in other, earlier texts, which will be discussed in the next sections).The relation between the two thinkers was compellingly discussed by Fenves in his *Arresting Language*, a book that focuses on the theory of language in Benjamin and Leibniz, among other thinkers. Fenves also develops the concept of "arrest," which he finds in both Leibniz and Benjamin, in relation to the crystallization of meaning (see Fenves, "Of Philosophical Style— from Leibniz to Benjamin," *boundary 2* 30, no. 1 [2003]: 67–87). Another trenchant account of this relation is in Rainer Nägele, "Das Beben des Barock in der Moderne: Walter Benjamins Monadologie," *MLN* 106, no. 3 (1991): 501–27; and in his *Literarische Vexierbilder: Drei Versuche zu einer Figur* (Eggingen: Isele, 2001), where he discusses the monad as an important figure for Benjamin's *Berliner Kindheit* and for the concept of interruption in his autobiographical writings (see esp., 36–37). Finally, see also Rolf Tiedemann, who concentrates on understanding the monad as "Bild" and stresses the importance of this term to Benjamin's conception of truth (see his *Studien zur Philosophie Walter Benjamins*, 60–65).

6. For a more elaborate version of the melancholic traits in Leibniz's system of monads, as well as on the productivity of the relation between melancholy and philosophy, see Ilit Ferber, "Leibniz's Monad: A Study in Melancholy and Harmony," in Kenaan and Ferber, *Philosophy's Moods*, 53–68.

7. Most of Leibniz's texts cited here are taken from *PPL*. For each citation I have provided the initials of the text title and page numbers in the Loemker edition. Abbreviations are as follows: CA: "Correspondence with Arnauld" (331–50); DAC: "Dissertation on the Art of Combinations" (74–78); FT: "First Truths" (267–71); MO: "The Monadology" (643–53); MW: Letter to Magnus Wedderkopf, May 1671 (146–47); NS: "A New System of the Nature of Substances and Their Communication, and of the Union Which Exists Between the Soul and Body" (451–59); NS2: "Second Explanation of the New System" (postscript of a letter to Basnage de Beauval, January 3/13, 1696) (459–61); PNG: "The Principles of Nature and Grace, Based on Reason" (636–42); RPH: "Reply to the Thoughts

on the System of Preestablished Harmony Contained in the Second Edition of Mr. Bayle's Critical Dictionary" (574–85); and WI: "What Is an Idea?" (207–8).

8. On the difference between "part" and "detail" in Leibniz's account of the monads see Weber, *Benjamin's -abilities*, 244–46.

9. See, e.g., MO, 648; and CA, 339.

10. See, e.g., in the *Monadology*, where Leibniz describes a relation of proportion or ratio (MO, 644).

11. See, e.g., MO, 644–45; and CA, 360.

12. CA, 339. For an elaboration on this metaphor see Ferber, "Leibniz's Monad," 57–61.

13. Deleuze describes the clear and distinct expression in the monad as follows: "At its highest degree a monad produces major and perfect accords: these occur where the small solicitations of anxiety, far from disappearing, are integrated in a pleasure that can be continued, prolonged, renewed, multiplied; that can proliferate, be reflexive and attractive for other accords, that give us the force to go further and further. This pleasure is a 'felicity' specific to the soul; it is harmonic par excellence" (*The Fold*, 150). Here it is clear that felicity is attributed to the function of expression or, more accurately, the amount of clear and distinct expression in the monad.

14. Leibniz, *Die philosophischen Schriften von G. W. Leibniz*, ed. C. I. Gerhardt (Berlin, 1890), 452.

15. For an explanation of this structure see Nicholas Rescher, *Leibniz: An Introduction to His Philosophy* (Totowa, NJ: Rowan and Littlefield, 1979), 110–17.

16. In PNG Leibniz describes this structure of a dominating monad slightly differently: "Each outstanding simple substance or monad which forms the center of a compound substance (such as an animal, for example), and is the principle of its uniqueness, is surrounded by a mass composed of an infinity of other monads which constitute the body belonging to this central monad, corresponding to the affections by which it represents, as in a kind of the center, the things which are outside of it" (PNG, 637).

17. Pensky points out that the constellation's phenomena are not "mere" phenomena; however, they still maintain their individual status (*Melancholy Dialectics*, 70).

18. See Weber, *Benjamin's -abilities*, 7. Weber claims that this conceptual work is what allows the phenomenon to "part company with itself" (8). In this assertion he gives an account of the complex relation between remaining the same as it was and, at the same time, invoking an internal movement of meaning.

19. See Chapter 2.

20. A noteworthy anecdote comes from Benjamin's inclusion of a letter whose topic is a constellation of stars. In his "German Men and Women" [*Deutsche Menschen*], a collection of letters edited by Benjamin under the pseudonym

Detlef Holz, he includes a letter written by Wilhelm Grimm to Jenny von Droste-Hülshoff. Grimm mentions that the last time they met, he had shown her the Cassiopeian constellation and she promised never to forget it. Now he wishes to acquaint her with another group of stars. Grimm describes the Orion group and its configuration, adding an illustration of its arrangement (*SW*, 3:198).

21. Deleuze, *The Fold*, 148.

22. For a detailed elaboration of Leibniz's conception of harmony, in all its levels, see Leroy E. Loemker, *Struggle for Synthesis: The Seventeenth Century Background of Leibniz's Synthesis of Order and Freedom* (Cambridge, MA: Harvard University Press, 1972), 177–202.

23. In its relation to the world the melancholic state can be understood as redefining the borders of the self. Freud's incorporation of the lost object also means thinking anew about one's borders. Nevertheless, what happens when there is no border with the world at all? Or when such a border disappears? In the case of the idea and the monad there is an expression from within interiority. In this sense the model of the monad—the creature of interiority that nevertheless expresses the world—stands in contradiction to the Freudian model.

24. As I mentioned earlier, Benjamin indicates that Leibniz's argument appears in *Discourse of Metaphysics*; however, it seems that he is actually citing Leibniz's *Monadology* here, probably §61.

25. Deleuze describes Leibniz's dynamics as related to his harmony. He describes the latter's perfect accords not as pauses but rather as "dynamisms which can pass into other accords, which can attract them, which can reappear, and which can be infinitely combined" (Deleuze, *The Fold*, 150). This is a variant of my claim here regarding the mutual dependence of ideas, a dependence in which they reveal one another in a constant movement of reverberation.

26. In "Truth and Truths / Knowledge and Elements of Knowledge," Benjamin makes similar claims when he discusses truth as what can only be expressed in works of art: "There are as many ultimate truths as there are authentic works of art. These ultimate truths are not elements but genuine parts, pieces, or fragments of the truth; in themselves, however, they offer no possibility of interconnection and are not to be completed through one another" (*SW*, 1:278).

27. In relation to unity and harmony Leibniz writes: "Every relation is either one of *union* or one of *harmony* [*convenientia*]. In union the things between which there is this relation are called *parts*, and taken together with their union, a *whole*. This happens whenever we take many things simultaneously as *one*" (DAC, 76).

28. This configuration and what follows are also related to another image in the prologue: that of the mother gathering her children around her: "Just as a mother is seen to begin to live in the fullness of her power only when the circle of her children, inspired by the feeling of her proximity, close around her, so do

ideas come to life only when extremes are assembled around them. Ideas—or, to use Goethe's term, ideals—are the Faustian 'Mothers.' They remain obscure so long as phenomena do not declare their faith to them and gather around them" (*TS*, 35). Here the mother articulates the way that the idea "comes to life" from its elements and, moreover, from the gathering of its parts around it.

29. See Friedlander, "On the Musical Gathering," esp. 639.

30. Leibniz also uses musical metaphors and phrases with musical associations to describe harmony, and not by chance. In his German texts Leibniz describes the system of monads as operating under the principles of *Zusammenstimmung* (harmony) and *Übereinstimmung* (accord), summoning metaphors of choirs, notes, and song (see G. W. Leibniz, *Discourse on Metaphysics, Correspondence with Arnauld, Monadology*, trans. George R. Montgomery [LaSalle, IL: Open Court, 1973], 188). (This citation is not included in the Loemker edition.) Leibniz's principle of harmony should hence not be viewed merely as a synonym for perfection and order, but should be linked more concretely with its musical connotations. For a more detailed account of the musical suggestions in his concept of preestablished harmony see Ferber, "Leibniz's Monad," 65–67. See also Deleuze's discussion of the link between Leibniz's concept of harmony and the specific musical genres of the baroque, in *The Fold* (150–51).

31. Leo Spitzer, "Classical and Christian Ideas of World Harmony: Prolegomena to an Interpretation of the Word 'Stimmung,'" cited in David E. Wellbery's entry "Stimmung," in *Ästhetische Grundbegriffe: Historisches Wörterbuch in sieben Bänden*, vol. 5, ed. Karlheinz Barck (Stuttgart: J. B. Metzler, 2003), 703.

32. Giorgio Agamben, "Vocation and Voice," *Qui Parle* 10, no. 2 (1997): 89. On the meaning of *Stimmung* see also Wellbery, "Stimmung," 703–33; Giorgio Agamben, *Language and Death: The Place of Negativity*, trans. Karen E. Pinkus with Michael Hardt (Minneapolis: University of Minnesota Press, 1999), 55, where Agamben links *Stimmung* and *Stimme* and makes the claim that *Stimme* is more originary than *Stimmung*, pointing to the structure of the voice as being the most original and negative metaphysical foundation (59).

33. For a further discussion of the relationship between Benjamin and Heidegger in light of their discussion of *Stimmung*, see Ferber, "*Stimmung*: Heidegger and Benjamin," in Benjamin and Vardoulakis, *Sparks Will Fly*.

34. Agamben, "Vocation and Voice," 92.

35. *Befindlichkeit* is rendered in Macquarrie and Robinson's translation as "state of mind," a misleading translation in the context of Heidegger's argument. On the problematic translation of *Befindlichkeit* see Hubert L. Dreyfus, *Being-in-the-World: A Commentary on Heidegger's "Being and Time," Division I* (Cambridge, MA: MIT Press, 1991), 168; Theodore Kisiel, *Heidegger's Way of Thought* (New York: Continuum, 2002); and William Large, *Heidegger's Being and Time* (Bloomington: Indiana University Press, 2008), 123–34.

36. See Agamben, "Vocation and Voice," 89.

37. See also Macquarrie and Robinson's note 3 in *BT,* 172.

38. Deleuze describes this in terms of "striking a chord": each monad is distinguished by its unique chord, which he defines as the monad's "inner actions" (Deleuze, *The Fold*, 150).

39. See Yoko Arisaka, "On Heidegger's Theory of Space: A Critique of Dreyfus," *Inquiry* 38, no. 4 (Dec. 1995): 455–67.

40. Novalis has an interesting comment pertinent to this context in *Notes for a Romantic Encyclopaedia*: "The mood of consciousness—of every kind of presentation, is the mood of crystallization, of formation—and diversification—i.e., it is arrested repose—a static force—a rationalizing (equilibrating) force—and proportional force of evolution—a constant quantity amid variable change. (Point of rest on a lever.)" (Novalis, *Notes for a Romantic Encyclopaedia: Das Allgemeine Brouillon*, trans. and ed. David W. Wood [Albany: State University of New York Press, 2007], 153).

Bibliography

Abraham, Nicolas. "Notes on the Phantom: A Complement to Freud's Metapsychology." In Abraham and Torok, *The Shell and the Kernel*, 171–76.
———. "The Phantom of Hamlet *or* The Sixth Act, *Preceded by* The Intermission of 'Truth.'" In Abraham and Torok, *The Shell and the Kernel*, 187–205.
Abraham, Nicolas, and Maria Torok. *The Shell and the Kernel.* Vol. 1. Edited and translated by Nicholas T. Rand. Chicago: University of Chicago Press, 1994.
Adorno, Theodor. "A Portrait of Walter Benjamin." In *Prisms.* Translated by Samuel Weber and Shierry Weber, 227–41. Cambridge, MA: MIT Press, 1981.
———. "Adornos Seminar von Sommersemester 1932 über Benjamins 'Ursprung des deutschen *Trauerspiels*, Protokolle.'" In *Frankfurter Adorno Blätter* IV. Herausgegeben vom. Edited by Rolf Tiedemann. Theodor W. Adorno Archiv, 52–77. Frankfurt: edition text + kritik, 1995.
Adorno, Theodor, and Walter Benjamin. *Adorno and Benjamin: The Complete Correspondence, 1928–1940.* Edited by Henri Lonitz. Translated by Nicholas Walker. Cambridge, MA: Harvard University Press, 1999.
Agamben, Giorgio. *Homo Sacer: Sovereign Power and Bare Life.* Translated by Daniel Heller-Roazen. Stanford: Stanford University Press, 1995.
———. *Infancy and History: The Destruction of Experience.* Translated by Liz Heron. London: Verso, 1993.
———. *Language and Death: The Place of Negativity.* Translated by Karen E. Pinkus with Michael Hardt. Minneapolis: University of Minnesota Press, 1991.
———. *Potentialities: Collected Essays in Philosophy.* Edited and translated by Daniel Heller-Roazen. Stanford: Stanford University Press, 1999.
———. *Stanzas: Word and Phantasm in Western Culture.* Translated by R. L. Martinez. Minneapolis: University of Minnesota Press, 1992.
———. *State of Exception.* Translated by Kevin Attell. Chicago: University of Chicago Press, 2005.
———. "Vocation and Voice." *Qui Parle* 10, no. 2 (spring/summer 1997): 89–100.
Arisaka, Yoko. "On Heidegger's Theory of Space: A Critique of Dreyfus." *Inquiry* 38, no. 4 (Dec. 1995): 455–67.

Azoulay, Ariella. *Once upon a Time: Photography Following Walter Benjamin*. Ramat-Gan: Bar-Ilan University Press, 2007.

Benjamin, Andrew. *Translation and the Nature of Philosophy*. London: Routledge, 1989.

Benjamin, Walter. *The Arcades Project*. Translated by Howard Eiland and Kevin McLaughlin. Cambridge, MA: Harvard University Press, 1999.

———. *The Correspondence of Walter Benjamin, 1910–1940*. Edited by G. Scholem and T. W. Adorno. Translated by M. R. Jacobson and E. M Jacobson. Chicago: University of Chicago Press, 1994.

———. *The Origin of German Tragic Drama*. Translated by John Osborne. London: Verso, 1998. Translation of "Der Ursprung des deutschen *Trauerspiels*" (1925), in *Gesammelte Schriften*. Vol. 1.1. Frankfurt: Suhrkamp, 1991.

———. *Selected Writings*. Vol. 1, *1913–1926*. Edited by Marcus Bullock and Michael W. Jennings. Translated by Edmund Jephcott et al. Cambridge, MA: Harvard University Press, 1996.

———. *Selected Writings*. Vol. 2, *1927–1934*. Edited by Michael W. Jennings, Howard Eiland, and Gary Smith. Translated by Rodney Livingstone et al. Cambridge, MA: Harvard University Press, 1999.

———. *Selected Writings*. Vol. 3, *1935–1938*. Edited by Howard Eiland and Michael W. Jennings. Translated by Edmund Jephcott et al. Cambridge, MA: Harvard University Press, 2002.

———. *Selected Writings*. Vol. 4, *1938–1940*. Edited by Howard Eiland and Michael W. Jennings. Translated by Edmund Jephcott et al. Cambridge, MA: Harvard University Press, 2003.

Benthien, Claudia. *Barockes Schweigen: Rhetorik und Performativität des Sprachlosen im 17. Jahrhundert*. München: Wilhelm Fink, 2006.

Berekhyah mi-Modena, Aharon. *Sefer Ma'avar Yabok*. Jerusalem: Ahavat Shalom, 1995.

Bontea, Adriana. "A Project in Its Context: Walter Benjamin on Comedy." *MLN* 121 (2006): 1041–71.

Buci-Glucksmann, Christine. *Baroque Reason: The Aesthetics of Modernity*. London: Sage, 1994.

Burton, Robert. *The Anatomy of Melancholy*. Edited by T. Faulkner, N. Kiessling, and R. Blair. Oxford: Clarendon, 1989.

Butler, Judith. "Afterword: After Loss, What Then?" In *Loss: The Politics of Mourning*, edited by David Eng, 467–73. Berkeley: University of California Press, 2002.

———. "Betrayal's Felicity." *Diacritics* 34, no.1 (spring 2004): 82–87.

———. "Thresholds of Melancholy." In *The Prism of the Self: Philosophical Essays in Honor of Maurice Natanson*, edited by Steven Galt Crowell, 8–12. Dordrecht: Kluwer, 1995.

Cadava, Eduardo. *Words of Light: Theses on the Photography of History*. Princeton, NJ: Princeton University Press, 1997.
Cavell, Stanley. "Hamlet's Burden of Proof." In *Disowning Knowledge in Seven Plays of Shakespeare*, 179–91. Cambridge: Cambridge University Press, 2003.
Clewell, Tammy. "Mourning Beyond Melancholia: Freud's Psychoanalysis of Loss." *Journal of American Psychoanalytic Association* 52, no. 1 (2004): 43–67.
Comay, Rebecca, "Perverse History: Fetishism and Dialectic in Walter Benjamin." *Research in Phenomenology* 29 (1999): 51–62.
Deleuze, Gilles. *The Fold: Leibniz and the Baroque*. Translated by Tom Conley. Minneapolis: University of Minnesota Press, 1993.
de Man, Paul. "'Conclusions' Walter Benjamin's 'The Task of the Translator' Messenger Lecture, Cornell University, March 4, 1983." *Yale French Studies* 69 (1985): 25–46.
Derrida, Jacques. *Acts of Religion*. Edited by Gil Anidjar. New York: Routledge, 2002.
———. "Des tours de Babel." In Derrida, *Acts of Religion*, 104–33.
———. *Limited Inc*. Translated by Samuel Weber. Evanston, IL: Northwestern University Press, 1988.
———. *Specters of Marx: The State of Debt, the Work of Mourning and the New International*. Translated by Peggy Kamuf. London: Routledge, 2006.
Descartes, René. "The Passions of the Soul." In *The Philosophical Writings of Descartes*. Vol. 1. Translated and edited by J. Cottingham, R. Stoothoff, and D. Murdoch, 328–404. Cambridge: Cambridge University Press, 1985.
Dreyfus, Hubert L. *Being-in-the-World: A Commentary on Heidegger's "Being and Time," Division I*. Cambridge, MA: MIT Press, 1991.
Egginton, William. *The Theater and Truth: The Ideology of (Neo)Baroque Aesthetics*. Stanford: Stanford University Press, 2010.
Eng, David L., and David Kazanjian. "Introduction: Mourning Remains." In *Loss: The Politics of Mourning*, edited by David L. Eng and David Kazanjian, 1–25. Berkeley: University of California Press, 2003.
Fenves, Peter. *Arresting Language: From Leibniz to Benjamin*. Stanford: Stanford University Press, 2001.
———. "The Genesis of Judgment: Spatiality, Analogy, and Metaphor in Benjamin's 'On Language as Such and on Human Language.'" In *Walter Benjamin: Theoretical Questions*, edited by David S. Ferris, 75–93. Stanford: Stanford University Press, 1996.
———. "Marx, Mourning, Messianicity." In *Violence, Identity, and Self-Determination*, edited by Hent de Vries and Samuel Weber, 253–70. Stanford: Stanford University Press, 1997.
———. "Of Philosophical Style—from Leibniz to Benjamin." *boundary 2* 30, no. 1 (2003): 67–87.

———. "Tragedy and Prophecy in Benjamin's *Origin of the German Mourning Play*." In Richter, *Benjamin's Ghosts*, 237–59.
Ferber, Ilit. "A Language of the Border: On Scholem's Theory of Lament." *Journal of Jewish Thought and Philosophy*, forthcoming.
———. "Leibniz's Monad: A Study in Melancholy and Harmony." In Kenaan and Ferber, *Philosophy's Moods*, 53–68.
———. "Melancholy Philosophy: Freud and Benjamin." *EREA (Revue d'études anglophones)* 4, no. 1 (spring 2006): 66–74.
———. "*Stimmung*: Heidegger and Benjamin." In *Sparks Will Fly: Benjamin and Heidegger*, edited by A. Benjamin and D. Vardoulakis. Albany: State University of New York Press, 2014.
Ferris, David S., ed. *Walter Benjamin: Theoretical Questions*. Stanford: Stanford University Press, 1996.
Fried, Michael. *Absorption and Theatricality: Painting and Beholder in the Age of Diderot*. Berkeley: University of California Press, 1980.
Friedlander, Eli. "On the Musical Gathering of Echoes of the Voice: Walter Benjamin on Opera and the *Trauerspiel*." *Opera Quarterly* 21, no. 4 (2005): 631–46.
———. *Walter Benjamin: A Philosophical Portrait*. Cambridge, MA: Harvard University Press, 2012.
Freud, Sigmund. *The Standard Edition of the Complete Psychological Works of Sigmund Freud*. Edited and translated by James Strachey. London: Hogarth, 1957–66.
Gasché, Rodolphe. "Saturnine Vision and the Question of Difference: Reflections on Walter Benjamin's Theory of Language." In Nägele, *Benjamin's Ground*, 83–104.
Geyer-Ryan, Helga. "Effects of Abjection in the Texts of Walter Benjamin." *MLN* 107, no. 3 (April 1992): 499–520.
Gryphius, Andreas. *Cardenio und Celinde*. Stuttgart: Reclam, 1968.
———. *Catharina von Georgien*. Stuttgart: Reclam, 1975.
———. *Leo Armenius*. Stuttgart: Reclam, 1971.
Hamacher, Werner. "'Now': Walter Benjamin on Historical Time." In *Walter Benjamin and History*, edited by Andrew Benjamin, 38–68. London: Continuum, 2005.
———. "Working Through Working." *Modernism/Modernity* 3, no. 1 (Jan. 1996): 23–56.
Hanssen, Beatrice. "Language and Mimesis in Walter Benjamin's Work." In *The Cambridge Companion to Walter Benjamin*, edited by David S. Ferris, 54–72. Cambridge: Cambridge University Press, 2004.
———. "Portrait of Melancholy (Benjamin, Warburg, Panofsky)." *MLN* 114, no. 5 (1999): 991–1013. Reprinted in Richter, *Benjamin's Ghosts*, 169–88.
Heidegger, Martin. *Being and Time*. Translated by J. Macquarrie and E. Robinson. San Francisco: Harper and Row, 1962.

———. *The Fundamental Concepts of Metaphysics: World, Finitude, Solitude.* Translated by W. McNeill and N. Walker. Bloomington: Indiana University Press, 1995.

———. *History of the Concept of Time.* Translated by Theodore Kisiel. Bloomington: Indiana University Press, 2009.

———. *Sein und Zeit.* 17th ed. Tübingen: Max Niemeyer, 1993.

———. *Zollikon Seminars.* Edited by Medard Boss. Translated by F. Mayr and R. Askay. Evanston, IL: Northwestern University Press, 2001.

Homeyer, Fritz. *Stranitzkys Drama vom "Heiligen Nepomuk."* Berlin: Mayer and Müller, 1907.

Hume, David. *A Treatise of Human Nature.* Edited by D. F. Norton and M. J. Norton. Oxford: Clarendon, 2007.

Jennings, Michael W. *Dialectical Images: Walter Benjamin's Theory of Literary Criticism.* Ithaca, NY: Cornell University Press, 1987.

Johnson, Barbara. *Mother Tongues: Sexuality, Trials, Motherhood, Translation.* Cambridge, MA: Harvard University Press, 2003.

Kenaan, Hagi, and Ilit Ferber. "Moods and Philosophy." In Kenaan and Ferber, *Philosophy's Moods*, 3–10.

———, eds. *Philosophy's Moods: The Affective Grounds of Thinking.* Dordrecht: Springer, 2011.

Kisiel, Theodore. *Heidegger's Way of Thought.* New York: Continuum, 2002.

Klibansky, R., E. Panofsky, and F. Saxl. *Saturn and Melancholy: Studies in the History of Natural Philosophy, Religion and Art.* London: Nelson, 1964.

Koepnick, Lutz L. "The Spectacle, the *Trauerspiel*, and the Politics of Resolution: Benjamin Reading the Baroque Reading Weimar." *Critical Inquiry* 22 (winter 1996): 268–91.

Kristeva, Julia. *Black Sun: Depression and Melancholia.* Translated by L. S. Roudiez. New York: Columbia University Press, 1992.

Laplanche, Jean. *Essays on Otherness.* Translated by Luke Thurston. London: Routledge, 1999.

Large, William. *Heidegger's Being and Time.* Bloomington: Indiana University Press, 2008.

Leibniz, G. W. *Die philosophischen Schriften von G. W. Leibniz.* Edited by C. I. Gerhardt. 1890. Hildesheim: G. Olms, 1960–61.

———. *Discourse on Metaphysics, Correspondence with Arnauld, Monadology.* Translated by George R. Montgomery. LaSalle, IL: Open Court, 1973.

———. *Philosophical Papers and Letters.* Edited and translated by Leroy E. Loemker. 2nd ed. Dordrecht: Kluwer, 1969.

Ley Roff, Sarah. "Benjamin and Psychoanalysis." In *The Cambridge Companion to Walter Benjamin*, edited by David S. Ferris, 115–33. Cambridge: Cambridge University Press, 2004.

Loemker, Leroy E. *Struggle for Synthesis: The Seventeenth Century Background of Leibniz's Synthesis of Order and Freedom*. Cambridge, MA: Harvard University Press, 1972.

Lohenstein, Daniel Casper von. *Sophonisbe*. Stuttgart: Reclam, 1970.

Lukács, Georg. "On Walter Benjamin." *New Left Review* 110 (1978): 83–88.

Menninghaus, Winfried. *Walter Benjamins Theorie der Sprachmagie*. Frankfurt am Main: Suhrkamp, 1995.

Mulhall, Stephen. "Attunement and Disorientation: The Moods of Philosophy in Heidegger and Sartre." In Kenaan and Ferber, *Philosophy's Moods*, 123–39.

Nägele, Rainer, ed. *Benjamin's Ground: New Readings of Walter Benjamin*. Detroit: Wayne State University Press, 1988.

———. "Das Beben des Barock in der Moderne: Walter Benjamins Monadologie." *MLN* 106, no. 3 (April 1991): 501–27.

———. *Echoes of Translation: Reading Between Texts*. Baltimore: Johns Hopkins University Press, 1997.

———. *Literarische Vexierbilder: Drei Versuche zu einer Figur*. Eggingen: Isele, 2001.

———. *Theater, Theory, Speculation: Walter Benjamin and the Scenes of Modernity*. Baltimore: Johns Hopkins University Press, 1991.

Newman, Jane O. "'Hamlet ist Saturnkind': Citationality, Lutheranism, and German Identity in Walter Benjamin's 'Ursprung des deutschen *Trauerspiels*.'" In *Benjamin-Studien* 1, edited by D. Weidner and S. Weigel, 171–88. Munich: Wilhelm Fink, 2008.

———. "Periodization, Modernity, Nation: Benjamin Between Renaissance and Baroque." *Journal of the Northern Renaissance* 1, no. 1 (spring 2009): 27–42.

Novalis. *Notes for a Romantic Encyclopaedia: Das Allgemeine Brouillon*. Translated and edited by David W. Wood. Albany: State University of New York Press, 2007.

Pensky, Max. *Melancholy Dialectics: Walter Benjamin and the Play of Mourning*. Amherst: University of Massachusetts Press, 2001.

Pontalis, Jean-Bartrand. "On Psychic Pain." In *Frontiers in Psychoanalysis: Between the Dream and Psychic Pain*. Translated by Catherine Cullen and Philip Cullen. New York: International Universities Press, 1981.

Rabinbach, Anson. "Critique and Commentary / Alchemy and Chemistry." *New German Critique* 17 (spring 1979): 3–14.

Radden, Jennifer, ed. *The Nature of Melancholy: From Aristotle to Kristeva*. Oxford: Oxford University Press, 2000.

Rescher, Nicholas. *Leibniz: An Introduction to His Philosophy*. Totowa, NJ: Rowan and Littlefield, 1979.

Richter, Gerhard, ed. *Benjamin's Ghosts: Interventions in Contemporary Literary and Cultural Theory*. Stanford: Stanford University Press, 2002.

———. "Introduction." In Richter, *Benjamin's Ghosts*, 1–19. Stanford: Stanford University Press, 2002.
Rickels, Laurence A. "Suicitation: Benjamin and Freud." In Richter, *Benjamin's Ghosts*, 142–53.
Rubin, Nissan. *The End of Life: Rites of Burial and Mourning in the Talmud and Midrash*. Tel Aviv: Ha'Kibutz Ha'meuchad, 1997.
Scholem, Gershom. *Tagebücher*. Vol. 2, *1917–1923*. Frankfurt am Main: Jüdischer, 2000.
Shakespeare, William. *The Tragedy of Hamlet, Prince of Denmark*. In *The Oxford Shakespeare: The Complete Works*. Edited by Stanley Wells and Gary Taylor, 653–90. Oxford: Clarendon, 1988.
Smith, Quentin. "On Heidegger's Theory of Moods." *Modern Schoolman* 58 (1981): 211–35.
Sontag, Susan. "The Last Intellectual." *New York Review of Books*, Oct. 12, 1978.
Steiner, George. "Introduction." In Benjamin's *The Origin of German Tragic Drama*. Translated by John Osborne, 7–24. London: Verso, 1998.
Szondi, Peter. *An Essay on the Tragic*. Translated by Paul Fleming. Stanford: Stanford University Press, 2002.
Tiedemann, Rolf. *Studien zur Philosophie Walter Benjamins*. Frankfurt am Main: Suhrkamp, 1973.
Tukazinski, Yehi'el Mikhal ben Aharon. *The Bridge of Life*. Jerusalem: N. A. Tukazinski, 1960.
Weber, Samuel. *Benjamin's -abilities*. Cambridge, MA: Harvard University Press, 2008.
———. "Genealogy of Modernity: History, Myth and Allegory in Benjamin's Origin of the German Mourning Play." *MLN* 106, no. 3 (1991): 465–500.
Weigel, Sigrid. *Body- and Image-Space: Re-reading Walter Benjamin*. Translated by Georgia Paul. London: Routledge, 1996.
Weisee, Rabbi Abner. *Death and Bereavement: A Halakhic Guide*. Hoboken, NJ: Ktav, 1991.
Wellbery, David E. "Stimmung." In *Ästhetische Grundbegriffe: Historische Wörterbuch in sieben Bänden*. Vol. 5. Edited by Karlheinz Barck. Stuttgart: Metzler, 2003.
Witte, Bernd. *Walter Benjamin: An Intellectual Biography*. Translated by James Rolleston. Detroit: Wayne State University Press, 1997.
Wysocki, Louis G. "Andreas Gryphius et la tragédie allemande au XVIIe siècle." Thèse de doctorat. Paris, 1892.

Index

Abraham, Nicolas, 33–34, 102–3, 105
Adorno, Theodor W., 8, 51, 66, 163, 200–201n31, 204n3
Agamben, Giorgio, 43–44, 95, 122–24, 190, 212n9, 222n32
allegory: Benjamin's approach and, 51, 86–87, 206–7n27; martyr's pain and work of, 100–101; meaning of mask for, 31–32; monad linked to, 219n4; playful seriousness of, 61–62; relationship to objects and, 202n45; unstable, fluctuating meanings of, 86–87, 147
Aristotle, 12, 71, 93, 123
artworks: categorization of, 12, 69–72; comedy genre and, 77–78, 81, 205n14; loss and legibility of, 25–27, 102; maturation of, 158–59. *See also* tragedy; translation; *Trauerspiel* (sorrow-plays)

Babel, Tower of, 138–40, 213n26, 214n28
baroque: Benjamin's approach to, 67–74; empiricism/idealism split in, 164–65; Hamlet as exemplar of, 68, 105, 204n3; as hyperbolic, 85, 96–97, 104–5; loss of eschatology and, 28–32; monad as specimen of thought in, 167–68; mourning and ostentation in, 82–96, 206n21; repetition in, 104–6, 150–51, 208n52; upswelling of lyricism in, 50. *See also* theatricality; *Trauerspiel* (sorrow-plays)
Baudelaire, Charles, 9, 60

Benjamin, Walter: as ghost, 210n65; melancholic disposition of, 8–9; melancholy as philosophical cornerstone of, 9–15, 60–61; other philosophers and Freud in relation to, 7–8, 14, 197–98n6, 198n8, 219n5. *See also* boundaries; expression; ghosts; history; intention and intentionality; language; melancholy; philosophy; translation; *Trauerspiel* (sorrow-plays); truth and meaning
—works: *Arcades Project*, 112, 163, 167; "Berlin Childhood Around 1900," 114, 209n56; "German Men and Women," 220–21n20; "Goethe's *Elective Affinities*," 27, 72, 201n32, 217n56, 221–22n28; "Language and Logic," 161–62, 178, 188; "The Life of Students," 52; *One-Way Street*, 203n64; "On the Concept of Criticism in German Romanticism," 26–27, 196n17, 200n24, 211n1; "On the Concept of History," 167, 210n69; "On the Program of the Coming Philosophy," 46–47, 118–19; "Outline of the Psychophysical Problem," 79–82, 174–75; "The Role of Language in *Trauerspiel* and Tragedy" (RL), 10, 72, 120, 132, 141–43, 147–51, 153–54, 216n44; "The Task of the Translator" (TT), 154–62, 176, 181, 218n57; "*Trauerspiel* and Tragedy," 10, 20, 72; "Truth and Truths . . . ," 221n26. *See*

also "On Language as Such . . . ";
Trauerspiel (book)
Birken, Sigmund von, 114
boundaries
—internal/external: concept of, 13;
  Descartes on body/soul interaction,
  101–2; health vs. pathology in, 17;
  instability of, for melancholic, 73–
  74; melancholic state as redefining,
  221n23; mourning and ostentation
  linked to baroque, 82–96, 206n21;
  pain and melancholy situated at, 75–
  80. *See also* lost object; subjectivity
—life and death: concept of, 13, 102–4;
  contingent, blurred, indeterminate
  nature of, 73–74, 101–12; hair and
  nails as hybrid entities in, 109–
  11, 209–10n62, 214n28; loss and
  legibility of, 26–27, 31; rest and
  stillness in, 116–17; Socrates's death
  and, 209n53; spaces of afterlife in,
  156–58; thresholds and transitory
  spaces of, 107–9, 209n60; work
  of mourning and, 57–58. *See also*
  ghosts; lost object
Brentano, Franz, 45
Buci-Glucksmann, Christine, 67, 85
Burdach, Konrad, 12, 70
Burton, Robert, 3
Butler, Judith, 27–28, 205n14, 213n19

Calderon de la Barca, Pedro, 54, 62,
  203n66
Catholicism, 29, 94
Christianity. *See* Luther, Martin;
  martyr figure
Comay, Rebecca, 21, 35
comedy, 77–78, 205n14
commitment and loyalty: childhood
  in context of, 202n45; ghost figure
  in relation to commitment, 112–16;
  melancholic betrayal vs., 36–41;
  persistence of melancholic, 33–36;
  presentation of object key to, 61
constellation figure (in prologue), 65,
166, 178–83, 185, 188–89, 220n17, 220–
21n20
content: mental, 121–22, 124–27, 131, 161;
  relationship between material and
  truth, 27, 72, 109, 164–68, 217n56; use
  of term, 205n10
Creation story (Genesis): Adam and
  Adamic language, 130–35, 141, 212–
  13n17; Benjamin's interpretation
  of, 120, 127–41, 159; expressive vs.
  fallen meaning in, 133–35; fallen or
  "bourgeois" language and, 134–36,
  140, 148–49, 152–53, 159; language
  and loss in, 120–21, 147; man,
  nature, and melancholy linked
  in, 136–41, 147, 214–15n29; naming
  and power relations in, 128–33,
  212n15; threefold structure of, 129–
  30, 132–33. *See also* God; naming;
  nature
Croce, Benedetto, 12

Darstellung (presentation): of audience's
  reality in *Trauerspiel*, 88–89; of ideas
  in harmony, 185–89; immersion
  and absorption as conditions
  for, 48, 51–55; loss as condition of
  possibility for, 25–32, 66, 181; of
  object, 61–65; philosophy's task as,
  1–5, 10, 63, 91, 154, 164–68, 172–73;
  representation distinguished from,
  1, 195n1; *Trauerspiel* in relation to
  presentation of death, 104–7; truth
  and, 55, 63–66, 165–66, 179–81. *See
  also* content; language; monad; truth
  and meaning
death. *See* boundaries; ghosts
Deleuze, Gilles, 183–84, 219n4, 220n13,
  221n25, 222n30, 223n38
De Man, Paul, 218n57
Derrida, Jacques, 103, 112–13, 161, 210–
  11n72, 212n9, 213n26
Descartes, René, 5, 68, 101, 168, 208n48
Duns Scotus, John, 45, 202n49
Dürer, Albrecht, *Melancholia I*, 3

Egginton, William, 67
Erdmannsdörffer, Bernhard, 84
eschatology, 28–32, 200n27
experience, 45–46, 56, 118–19
expression: *Aus-druck* (wringing, pressing), 84–85, 149, 151; bombastic, exaggerated type of, 82–96, 206n21; comfort in relation to, 148–49; concept of, 118–20; Creation as chain of, 131–33; expressibility and, 122–27, 148, 151, 155; expressionless and (*Ausdruckslose*), 216n40; failure of, 76, 78; fallen language vs., 133–35; language as, 120–27, 161–62; Leibniz's models of, 168–77; of mental essence, 153; by monad, 170–76, 220n13; obstruction of, producing lament, 147–49, 216n40; of pain, 74–76, 80–83, 174–75. *See also* feelings; language; loss

feelings: functioning in baroque plays, 49–51; grief/joy relationship in, 205n13; intention distinguished from, 48–56; relationship to language, 141–52. *See also* expression
—specific: desire, 6–7, 50; empathy, 52, 70, 202n56; fear and anxiety, 56; love, 21–23, 33–34, 51; pain vs. pleasure, 79–80. *See also* pain; sadness
Fenves, Peter, 122, 146, 200n27, 210n64, 212–13n17, 219n5
Ficino, Marsilio, 60
Freud, Sigmund: Benjamin's relationship with, 17–18, 197–98n6, 199n14; economic lexicon of, 198n13; on "fort-da game," 200n22; health/pathology boundary of, 17–19, 23, 73, 201n33; on hysteria, 76, 206n23; on libidinal desire, 20, 51; on pain (mental and physical), 76–77, 79; reality principle of, 35, 57–58. *See also* boundaries; loss; lost object; melancholia; mourning
—works: *Constructions in Analysis*, 18; *The Ego and the Id*, 24–25; "Inhibitions, Symptom, Anxiety," 79; "Mourning and Melancholia," 4, 19–23, 32–36, 41–42, 57–59, 61, 63, 66, 71, 116, 174, 198n12, 206n21; "Some Points for a Comparative Study of Organic and Hysterical Motor Paralyses," 206n23; *Studies on Hysteria*, 76
Fried, Michael, 83, 206n22
Friedlander, Eli, 72, 86, 96, 107, 119, 149, 157, 189

Gasché, Rodolphe, 217n51, 218n62
gender, 132, 213n19
genius, 2, 4, 9, 195n3
ghosts: Benjamin as, 210n65; Benjamin's childhood and, 209n56; call and recognizability of, 112–16, 210–11n72, 211n76; Freud's haunted melancholic and, 102–3; historical dimension and translation in relation to, 154–62, 208n51; indeterminacy of death and, 104–7, 111–12; loss appearing as, 23; rest and stillness of, 116–17; sound and echo model of, 151, 189, 211n73; as structure of meaning, 111–16; temporal structures of, 108–9; thresholds and transitory spaces of, 107–9, 209n60. *See also* boundaries; lost object
God, 129–36, 140, 176–78, 184, 186–87, 213n21. *See also* Creation story
Gryphius, Andreas, 68, 75, 99, 107–8, 207–8n40

Hallmann, Johann Christian, 68, 75, 106, 117, 208n44
Hamacher, Werner, 58, 203n62, 204n67, 210n69
Hamlet (character): as exemplar of baroque, 68, 105, 204n3; ghost's appearance and speaking to, 107–8, 113–14; melancholy and emptiness of, 29–31, 199n15; play staged and interpreted by, 89, 207n33

harmony. See *Stimmung*
Harsdörffer, Georg Philipp, 68, 199n15
Hebbel, Friedrich, 54
Hegel, G. W. F., 164, 169
Heidegger, Martin: *Befindlichkeit* (affectedness), 191, 192, 222n35; Being-in-the-world, 6–7, 29, 56, 190–92; *Dasein*, 6, 25, 190–92, 194, 196n11; on moods, 5–8, 14, 29, 55–56, 190–94, 197n20
history: "angel" of, 9; ghost figure and, 111–17; historian's task in, 114–15; historical index idea and, 112; spatialization of, 28; whirlpool image of, 2–3, 166
Hume, David, 4
Husserl, Edmund, 40, 45–47, 50, 51, 55, 56, 202n49

intention and intentionality: Benjamin's response to Husserl's concept, 45–47, 50–51; concept of (Husserl), 40, 45; as defense against sadness, 54–55; feelings distinguished from, 49–52; knowledge and truth distinguished in, 47–48, 55; tenacity of, 38, 49, 51–55; truth as death of, 47–56, 186; what is meant vs. the way of meaning, 159–62. *See also* feelings; nonintentionality
internalization: empathy compared with, 51; intention and externalization vs., 54; of loss, 21–25, 34, 39, 48, 53, 58–59, 201n33; work of mourning resisted in, 58–60

Jennings, Michael W., 69, 86
Jewish traditions, 110–11, 209–10n62, 213n20, 215n35
Johnson, Barbara, 135

Kant, Immanuel, 5, 46, 47, 56, 118–19, 122, 127, 157, 164
knowledge: concept and, 179–81; of good and evil, 133–35; Kant's concept of, 46, 118; power relations in, 145–46; truth distinguished from, 47–48, 55. *See also* language
Koepnick, Lutz L., 96

Lacan, Jacques, 24, 200n19
lament: of chorus, 92–93; feelings and language in relation to, 142–51; Gershom Scholem on, 151, 216nn44–45; in Jewish tradition, 215n35; music and, 148–52; of nature, 136–37, 142–49; production of, 147–48; spatialization of, 151–52; in *Trauerspiel*, 75, 84–85, 92–93
language: condition of possibility in, 157–58; expression and expressionless contained in, 147–49, 216n40; as expressive configuration, 120–27; fallen or "bourgeois," 134–35, 140, 143, 148, 152–53, 159; feelings' relationship to, 141–52; as key to philosophical truth, 118–20, 211n1; melancholy's relationship to, 13–14, 120, 141–52; "pain" and "pleasure" in (German), 80; potentiality and, 122–26, 128–29, 133, 134, 137, 141–42, 144, 153, 155, 158, 214–15n29; "pure," 152, 157, 159–62; purification or perfection of, 153–54; struggle to transform words into ideas, 1–5, 10, 63, 78, 91, 119, 154, 164–68, 172–73; two modes of linguistic relation in, 160–62; two stages in, 135–36; "worn-out words" in, 3. *See also* Creation story; expression; naming; "On Language as Such . . ."; translation
Laplanche, Jean, 33, 57, 198n12
Lehre (doctrine), 119
Leibniz, G. W.: Benjamin's relationship to, 14, 167–68, 219n5; on expression, 173–74, 176; on grief/joy relationship, 205n13; on harmony, 221n27, 222n30; *plenum* principle of, 175; preestablished harmony concept of, 183–89, 192, 221n27, 222n30. *See also* monad

Ley Roff, Sarah, 18, 198n8
Lohenstein, Daniel Casper von, 68, 108, 202n54
loss: absent/unlocatable nature of loss in melancholia, 21–25, 30, 42–44; as condition of possibility, 25–32, 181; creation, language, and, 127–41; idea of missing loss in Freud, 41–44; identification and, 24–25, 33; images of emptiness and, 28–32; internalization of, 21–25, 33–36, 48, 53, 58–59; language, expression, and, 118–27, 211n1; philosophical work at core of, 117; symbol formation and, 24. *See also* lament; melancholia; melancholy; mourning
lost object: borders and, 221n23; bringing to rest, 116–17; "killing" of or detachment from, 33, 34–35, 38–39, 201n39; as locatable or not, 41–44, 51–52, 57–58; love of and identification with, 21–25; melancholia vs. mourning of, 19–21, 32–33, 71; mourning fixed on, 41–42, 51–52, 57–58; as not yet dead but no longer alive, 102–3; persistence of melancholic commitment to, 32–36, 40–41; *Trauerspiel* courtier's loyalty and, 37–41; truth found in immersion in, 39–40. *See also* ghosts; melancholia; melancholy; mourning; object; *Trauerspiel* (sorrow-plays)
Lukács, Georg, 29, 200–201n31
Luther, Martin, and Lutheranism, 28–31, 203n65

martyr figure: female, 99, 208n44; pain, spectacle, and, 96–102; questions about depictions of, 74–75; as structure of meaning, 13, 101–2
materiality: childhood and, 202n45; hair and nails as hybrid entities in, 109–11, 209–10n62, 214n28; ideas in relation to, 27, 72, 109, 164–68, 217n56; martyr's pain and, 99–102; of

mosaic, 65–66, 166, 178–80, 182, 189, 204n70. *See also* content; objects
melancholia: borders and, 221n23; definition of, 102, 206n21; incorporation and, 33–34; intention in, 52; loss internalized in, 21–25, 33–36, 48; lost object unlocatable in, 42–44; melancholy transfigured into, 16–17; mourning distinguished from, 19–21, 32–33, 203n63; narcissism and, 23, 35, 197n5; passivity in, 2, 13, 60, 66, 195n3, 203n63; pathology of, 2, 4–5, 12–13, 16–17, 23, 73–74, 102–3, 116, 201n33, 206n21; persistence of commitment in, 32–36, 39–40; *Trauerspiel* model compared with, 20, 29–30, 34–35, 42–49, 57–64; work of mourning resisted in, 58–62. *See also* Freud, Sigmund; loss; lost object; melancholy; mourning
melancholy: approach to, 9–15, 44–45; baroque state of mind as, 67–68; commitment to lost object and, 32–41; conceptual scheme of, 1–5, 10–15, 17; correspondence of *Trauerspeil* to, 72–73; in failure of expression, 76, 78; gendered aspect of, 213n19; genius and, 2, 4, 195n3; history of, 2–5, 16–17; injunction to work and, 60–61; intentionality and nonintentionality in, 45–50; intentionless nature of truth and, 41–56; language's relationship to, 13–14, 120; loss and, 21–32, 181; man and nature linked in, 136–41, 214–15n29; meanings throughout history, 2–5, 16, 60, 199n16; monad's importance to, 192–94; as nonpathological and related to philosophical work, 60–61; of philosophers, 4–5; philosophical work and, 61–66; productivity and, 57–66; stone as emblem of, 117; subjective nature of, 3–6, 8–9; theatricality in relation to, 73; truth's relationship to, 48–49, 53–54, 193–

94; work of mourning compared with, 35, 58–61. *See also* boundaries; lost object; melancholia; moods; mourning; *Stimmung*

Meyer, R. M., 91, 202n56

monad: allegory linked to, 219n4; characteristics and definition of, 168, 170–71; clock metaphor of, 184–85; context of Benjamin's use of, 169–70, 219n5; expression by, 174–75, 186–87, 220n13, 221n23; harmonic foundation of, 183–87, 223n38; hierarchical configuration of, 176–83, 220n16; as idea, 14, 167–68, 172, 175–76, 193–94; individuality of, 173–74; as model for ideas, 172–73; perception and, 171–72; translation and meanings of *Stimmung* and, 191–93; windmill metaphor of, 171. *See also* Leibniz, G. W.

moods: of consciousness, 223n40; Heidegger's approach to, 5–8, 14, 55–56, 193–94, 197n20; meanings of *Stimmung* and, 189–94; objective possibilities of, 197n21. *See also* feelings; *Stimmung*

mortification, 26–27, 102, 109

mosaic figure (in prologue), 65–66, 166, 178–80, 182, 189, 204n70

mourning: acceptance of reality in, 20–22, 32–33, 41, 57–58; as antithetical to intention, 54–55; comedy as inner lining of, 77–78, 205n14; definition of, 77; emptiness in, 22–23, 31–32; forgiveness and reconciliation in, 115–16, 211n77; Freud's use of term, 77; hair and nails as hybrid entities in, 109–11, 209–10n62, 214n28; as intentional, 51–52; located at internal/external boundary, 83; lost object locatable in, 41–42, 51–52, 57–58; melancholia distinguished from, 19–21, 32–33, 71, 194, 203n63; mourning and ostentation linked to baroque, 82–96, 206n21; muteness and, 146–47;

Nature's speechlessness and, 136–37, 142–47; play of, 61–66; structure of, 49–50; two models of, 78–80. *See also* boundaries; lament; loss; lost object; melancholia; melancholy; *Trauerarbeit* (work of mourning)

music: harmony in, 14, 182, 185, 187–89, 190–92, 222n30; lament as, 148–49, 150–52; meaning and language of, 107, 121

Nägele, Rainer, 17–18, 52–53, 197–98n6, 202n55, 203n61, 215–16n37, 219n5

naming: chain of expression and, 131–33, 148, 153, 212n15; creativity in, 129, 212–13n17; criticism as replacing, 214n27; as expression of man's linguistic essence, 130–32, 137–38, 141; as first linguistic expression, 128; knowledge and Fall in, 130–31, 133–36; melancholy and loss of man as namer, 136–41, 214–15n29; Nature's lament and, 143–45; overnaming and, 136–37, 146–47; threefold structure of creation and, 129–30, 132–33

nature: language and naming of, 128–35; loss of language and lament of, 143–49, 150–52; loss of man as namer of, 136–41, 214–15n29

Nebuchadnezzar, 214n28

Neoplatonism, 38–39

Nietzsche, Friedrich, 1, 55

nonintentionality: in melancholia, 41–44; melancholic mood and, 45–50; monad and, 186; neutrality and, 46, 56; on "truth is the death of intention," 44–56, 186; truth reinforced by, 47–56. *See also* intention and intentionality; truth and meaning

objects: ego defined by choices of, 23–24; faithfulness to, 37–38, 40–41; fear of specific, 56; feelings' connection to, 49–51; ideas in relation to (material), 27, 72, 109, 164–68, 217n56; language and, 124–27; presentation and redemption of, 61, 63–65, 180–82; subject's immersion within, 46, 47–48, 52–54, 55; tenacity of intention in relation to, 38, 49, 51–55; *Trauerspiel*'s preoccupation with, 90–91; types of attachment to, 51. See also intention and intentionality; lost object

"On Language as Such and on the Language of Man" (LAN, Benjamin): on creation and loss, 127–41; on expression, 120, 121–22, 124–27; on language and feelings, 142–45, 148; models of linguistic structure in, 152–54, 175, 177–78; writing of, 10. See also Creation story

The Origin of German Tragic Drama (*TS*, Benjamin). See *Trauerspiel* (book)

Osborne, John, 71, 195n1, 196n16

pain: approach to studying, 13–14; bombastic, exaggerated expression of, 82–96, 206n21; expression of, 74–76, 80–83, 174–75; in failure of expression, 76, 78; in Freud, 76–77, 79; internal/external boundaries and, 76–80; passivity in, 98; spectacle's connection to, 96–102. See also martyr figure; melancholia; mourning

pantomime, 88–89, 207n30

Pensky, Max, 50, 197n12, 199n16, 202n45, 206–7n27, 213n20, 214n27, 220n17

phenomena, presentation of, 64–65, 164–66, 173, 179–83

philosophy: Adam as father of, 119; key influences on Benjamin's, 169–70; melancholy as cornerstone of, 9–15, 60–61; mood in relation to, 5–8; neutral sphere for knowledge in, 46–47, 56; play of mourning as work of, 61–66; as struggle for

the presentation of ideas, 1–5, 10, 63, 76, 78, 91, 154, 164–68, 172–73; translation and meanings of *Stimmung* and, 189–94. See also content; *Darstellung*; language; monad; *Stimmung*; truth and meaning; *and specific philosophers*

Plato, 119, 164, 169, 205n13

Pontalis, J.-B., 76–77

power relations: devotion in, 39–40; gendered, 213n19; of God, man, and nature, 132, 143, 145, 153, 177; in Leibniz's monadology, 176–83. See also *Stimmung*

preestablished harmony (Leibniz), 183–89, 192, 221n27, 222n30

presentation. See *Darstellung*

Radden, Jennifer, 16–17, 213n19

Rickels, Laurence A., 18

Romanticism, Benjamin's treatment of, 26–27, 62, 156, 196n17, 200n24, 211n1

sadness: expressed as bodily affliction, 83; intention as defense against, 54–55; as internal and/or external, 77, 78; in language-feeling relationship, 141–52; theatrical expression as only means to convey, 91–92. See also lament; melancholy

Schmitt, Carl, 94–95, 207n36

Scholem, Gershom, 8, 11, 151–52, 216nn44–45

Seligkeit (bliss), 129, 131, 135–36, 143–44, 213n20, 214–15n29

Shakespeare, William, 68. See also Hamlet

Sontag, Susan, 8, 38, 41, 60, 203n64

sovereign (ruler, tyrant) figure, 20, 93–96, 214n28. See also Schmitt, Carl

spectacle, 83–84, 96–102. See also martyr figure; theatricality

Stimmung: concept of, 14–15, 189–91, 221n27, 222n30; model for, 182–83; monad's foundation of, 183–85, 186–

87, 191–92, 223n38; in music, 14, 185, 187–89, 190–92, 222n30; *Stimme* compared with, 222n32; translation and meanings of, 189–94; truth as, 183, 185–89. *See also* Heidegger, Martin; melancholy; moods
Strachey, James, 77
subjectivity: absence of, in Benjamin's work, 63–64, 197n21; break from dichotomy of objective and, 14, 46–48, 197n20; immersion within object and, 52–54, 55; in melancholy, 3–6, 8–9, 50; scroll image as problematizing, 91; separation and symbol formation in, 24, 201n39
suffering. *See* martyr figure; pain; *Trauerspiel* (sorrow-plays)

theater, 31–32, 61–62. See also *Trauerspiel* (sorrow-plays)
theatricality: in baroque, 67–75, 88–90; bombastic, exaggerated nature of, 82–96, 206n21; expressions of pain in, 74–82; fundamental connection of suffering to, 96–102. See also *Trauerspiel* (sorrow-plays)
Thirty Years' War (1618–48), 68, 75, 208n51
Torok, Maria, 33–34
tragedy: chorus of, 92; conditions of possibility in, 87; death as presented in, 104, 105, 106; echo in, 152; martyr-drama distinguished from, 98; temporal dimension of, 108, 217n54; traditional criteria of, 12, 71, 90; tragic hero in, 85, 90, 102, 106; *Trauerspiel* distinguished from, 11–12, 20–21, 69–72, 85–86, 98, 102, 104–6
translation: afterlife and, 156–58, 217n53; of Benjamin's book title, 71–72, 196n16; independence of, 159–60, 218n58; instability and indeterminacy in, 157–58; meaning revealed in, 160–62; *modus significandi* and, 218n62; as original's natural continuation and essence in Benjamin's account, 155–59; of *Stimmung*, 189–90; translatability and, 155–59, 212n12, 217n51
Trauerarbeit (work of mourning): active nature of, 203n61, 203n63; definition of, 57–59; locatable object necessary to, 41–42, 51–52, 57–58; Lutheran view of, 29; melancholic stance compared, 33–35, 58–60, 63; transformed into philosophical work, 61–66
Trauerspiel (book, *The Origin of German Tragic Drama* [*TS*], Benjamin): approach to studying, 13; Benjamin's analysis of critics' response to, 198n11; conception and writing of, 10–11, 197n3; disturbances of expression in, 78; "heaviness" in, 60, 203n65; melancholy and mourning interchangeable in, 20–21, 199n15, 202n52; as philosophical-historical study of baroque, 67–73; philosophical truth concept in, 119–20; philosophical work concept in, 61–66; prologue of, 63–66, 91, 163–70, 172, 173, 175–76, 178–83, 187–89, 204n70, 221–22n28; translation of title, 71–72, 196n16. See also *Trauerspiel* (sorrow-plays)
Trauerspiel (sorrow-plays): afterlife of, 217n53; Benjamin's methodological approach to, 163–68; bombastic, exaggerated nature of, 82–96, 206n21; chorus of, 92–93; comedy's role in, 77–78, 205n14; courtier (intriguer or plotter) figure of, 36–41; death as presented in, 104–7; echo in, 149–52, 189; empty mask of, 31–32; expressions of pain in, 74–82; function of feelings in, 49–51; as genre, 11–12, 69–70; ghost figures and roles in, 103–17, 208n51; intended for those in mourning, 87–88; loss

of narrative expressed in, 27–29; martyr-drama subgenre of, 96–102; melancholia model compared with, 78–80; periodization of, 68; play of mourning in, 61–66; psychoanalytic approach to, 73–74; quick dissipation of pleasure in, 81; repetition in, 104–6, 150–51, 208n52; role and structure of language in, 141–42, 147–50, 188–89; silence's role in, 89, 207n32; sovereign (ruler, tyrant) figure in, 20, 93–96, 214–15nn28–29; structure of, 25–27, 72–73, 207n35; tragedy distinguished from, 11–12, 20–21, 69–72, 85–86, 98, 102. *See also* baroque; theater

truth and meaning: beauty and, 169; as death of intention, 44–56, 186; exploration of extremes in, 63–64; as formative power, 181; ghost figure and, 116–17; as harmony, 183–89; historical structure of, 158; knowledge distinguished from, 47–48, 55; linguistic structure key to meaning of, 118–27, 211n1; materiality of mosaic and, 65–66, 166, 178–80, 182, 189, 204n70; melancholy's relationship to, 48–49, 53–54, 193–94; missing loss and, 41–44; monad as model of, 168; in relation to immersion in object, 39–40; romantics' view of, 26–27. *See also Darstellung*; philosophy

tyrant. *See* sovereign

Überleben (afterlife), 156–59, 217n53. *See also* boundaries; ghosts; translation

Ursprung (origin), 166

Weber, Samuel, 36, 48–49, 72, 87, 94–95, 212n12, 220n18

whirlpool figure, 2–3, 166

Wilken, Ernst, 91

work: best conditions for, 203n64; concept of, 203n62; melancholic's devotion to, 60–61; philosophical type of, 61–66. *See also* melancholy: productivity and; *Trauerarbeit* (work of mourning)

Wysocki, Louis G., 75

Cultural Memory in the Present

Alexandre Lefebvre, *Human Rights as a Way of Life: On Bergson's Political Philosophy*
Theodore W. Jennings, Jr., *Outlaw Justice: The Messianic Politics of Paul*
Alexander Etkind, *Warped Mourning: Stories of the Undead in the Land of the Unburied*
Denis Guénoun, *About Europe: Philosophical Hypotheses*
Maria Boletsi, *Barbarism and its Discontents*
Sigrid Weigel, *Walter Benjamin: Images, the Creaturely, and the Holy*
Roberto Esposito, *Living Thought: The Origins and Actuality of Italian Philosophy*
Henri Atlan, *The Sparks of Randomness, Volume 2: The Atheism of Scripture*
Rüdiger Campe, *The Game of Probability: Literature and Calculation from Pascal to Kleist*
Niklas Luhmann, *A Systems Theory of Religion*
Jean-Luc Marion, *In the Self's Place: The Approach of Saint Augustine*
Rodolphe Gasché, *Georges Bataille: Phenomenology and Phantasmatology*
Niklas Luhmann, *Theory of Society, Volume 1*
Alessia Ricciardi, *After* La Dolce Vita*: A Cultural Prehistory of Berlusconi's Italy*
Daniel Innerarity, *The Future and Its Enemies: In Defense of Political Hope*
Patricia Pisters, *The Neuro-Image: A Deleuzian Film-Philosophy of Digital Screen Culture*
François-David Sebbah, *Testing the Limit: Derrida, Henry, Levinas, and the Phenomenological Tradition*
Erik Peterson, *Theological Tractates*, edited by Michael J. Hollerich
Feisal G. Mohamed, *Milton and the Post-Secular Present: Ethics, Politics, Terrorism*
Pierre Hadot, *The Present Alone Is Our Happiness, Second Edition: Conversations with Jeannie Carlier and Arnold I. Davidson*
Yasco Horsman, *Theaters of Justice: Judging, Staging, and Working Through in Arendt, Brecht, and Delbo*
Jacques Derrida, *Parages*, edited by John P. Leavey
Henri Atlan, *The Sparks of Randomness, Volume 1: Spermatic Knowledge*

Rebecca Comay, *Mourning Sickness: Hegel and the French Revolution*
Djelal Kadir, *Memos from the Besieged City: Lifelines for Cultural Sustainability*
Stanley Cavell, *Little Did I Know: Excerpts from Memory*
Jeffrey Mehlman, *Adventures in the French Trade: Fragments Toward a Life*
Jacob Rogozinski, *The Ego and the Flesh: An Introduction to Egoanalysis*
Marcel Hénaff, *The Price of Truth: Gift, Money, and Philosophy*
Paul Patton, *Deleuzian Concepts: Philosophy, Colonialization, Politics*
Michael Fagenblat, *A Covenant of Creatures: Levinas's Philosophy of Judaism*
Stefanos Geroulanos, *An Atheism That Is Not Humanist Emerges in French Thought*
Andrew Herscher, *Violence Taking Place: The Architecture of the Kosovo Conflict*
Hans-Jörg Rheinberger, *On Historicizing Epistemology: An Essay*
Jacob Taubes, *From Cult to Culture*, edited by Charlotte Fonrobert and Amir Engel
Peter Hitchcock, *The Long Space: Transnationalism and Postcolonial Form*
Lambert Wiesing, *Artificial Presence: Philosophical Studies in Image Theory*
Jacob Taubes, *Occidental Eschatology*
Freddie Rokem, *Philosophers and Thespians: Thinking Performance*
Roberto Esposito, *Communitas: The Origin and Destiny of Community*
Vilashini Cooppan, *Worlds Within: National Narratives and Global Connections in Postcolonial Writing*
Josef Früchtl, *The Impertinent Self: A Heroic History of Modernity*
Frank Ankersmit, Ewa Domanska, and Hans Kellner, eds., *Re-Figuring Hayden White*
Michael Rothberg, *Multidirectional Memory: Remembering the Holocaust in the Age of Decolonization*
Jean-François Lyotard, *Enthusiasm: The Kantian Critique of History*
Ernst van Alphen, Mieke Bal, and Carel Smith, eds., *The Rhetoric of Sincerity*
Stéphane Mosès, *The Angel of History: Rosenzweig, Benjamin, Scholem*
Pierre Hadot, *The Present Alone Is Our Happiness: Conversations with Jeannie Carlier and Arnold I. Davidson*
Alexandre Lefebvre, *The Image of the Law: Deleuze, Bergson, Spinoza*
Samira Haj, *Reconfiguring Islamic Tradition: Reform, Rationality, and Modernity*
Diane Perpich, *The Ethics of Emmanuel Levinas*
Marcel Detienne, *Comparing the Incomparable*
François Delaporte, *Anatomy of the Passions*
René Girard, *Mimesis and Theory: Essays on Literature and Criticism, 1959–2005*
Richard Baxstrom, *Houses in Motion: The Experience of Place and the Problem of Belief in Urban Malaysia*
Jennifer L. Culbert, *Dead Certainty: The Death Penalty and the Problem of Judgment*
Samantha Frost, *Lessons from a Materialist Thinker: Hobbesian Reflections on Ethics and Politics*

Regina Mara Schwartz, *Sacramental Poetics at the Dawn of Secularism: When God Left the World*
Gil Anidjar, *Semites: Race, Religion, Literature*
Ranjana Khanna, *Algeria Cuts: Women and Representation, 1830 to the Present*
Esther Peeren, *Intersubjectivities and Popular Culture: Bakhtin and Beyond*
Eyal Peretz, *Becoming Visionary: Brian De Palma's Cinematic Education of the Senses*
Diana Sorensen, *A Turbulent Decade Remembered: Scenes from the Latin American Sixties*
Hubert Damisch, *A Childhood Memory by Piero della Francesca*
José van Dijck, *Mediated Memories in the Digital Age*
Dana Hollander, *Exemplarity and Chosenness: Rosenzweig and Derrida on the Nation of Philosophy*
Asja Szafraniec, *Beckett, Derrida, and the Event of Literature*
Sara Guyer, *Romanticism After Auschwitz*
Alison Ross, *The Aesthetic Paths of Philosophy: Presentation in Kant, Heidegger, Lacoue-Labarthe, and Nancy*
Gerhard Richter, *Thought-Images: Frankfurt School Writers' Reflections from Damaged Life*
Bella Brodzki, *Can These Bones Live? Translation, Survival, and Cultural Memory*
Rodolphe Gasché, *The Honor of Thinking: Critique, Theory, Philosophy*
Brigitte Peucker, *The Material Image: Art and the Real in Film*
Natalie Melas, *All the Difference in the World: Postcoloniality and the Ends of Comparison*
Jonathan Culler, *The Literary in Theory*
Michael G. Levine, *The Belated Witness: Literature, Testimony, and the Question of Holocaust Survival*
Jennifer A. Jordan, *Structures of Memory: Understanding German Change in Berlin and Beyond*
Christoph Menke, *Reflections of Equality*
Marlène Zarader, *The Unthought Debt: Heidegger and the Hebraic Heritage*
Jan Assmann, *Religion and Cultural Memory: Ten Studies*
David Scott and Charles Hirschkind, *Powers of the Secular Modern: Talal Asad and His Interlocutors*
Gyanendra Pandey, *Routine Violence: Nations, Fragments, Histories*
James Siegel, *Naming the Witch*
J. M. Bernstein, *Against Voluptuous Bodies: Late Modernism and the Meaning of Painting*
Theodore W. Jennings Jr., *Reading Derrida / Thinking Paul: On Justice*
Richard Rorty and Eduardo Mendieta, *Take Care of Freedom and Truth Will Take Care of Itself: Interviews with Richard Rorty*
Jacques Derrida, *Paper Machine*

Renaud Barbaras, *Desire and Distance: Introduction to a Phenomenology of Perception*

Jill Bennett, *Empathic Vision: Affect, Trauma, and Contemporary Art*

Ban Wang, *Illuminations from the Past: Trauma, Memory, and History in Modern China*

James Phillips, *Heidegger's Volk: Between National Socialism and Poetry*

Frank Ankersmit, *Sublime Historical Experience*

István Rév, *Retroactive Justice: Prehistory of Post-Communism*

Paola Marrati, *Genesis and Trace: Derrida Reading Husserl and Heidegger*

Krzysztof Ziarek, *The Force of Art*

Marie-José Mondzain, *Image, Icon, Economy: The Byzantine Origins of the Contemporary Imaginary*

Cecilia Sjöholm, *The Antigone Complex: Ethics and the Invention of Feminine Desire*

Jacques Derrida and Elisabeth Roudinesco, *For What Tomorrow . . . : A Dialogue*

Elisabeth Weber, *Questioning Judaism: Interviews by Elisabeth Weber*

Jacques Derrida and Catherine Malabou, *Counterpath: Traveling with Jacques Derrida*

Martin Seel, *Aesthetics of Appearing*

Nanette Salomon, *Shifting Priorities: Gender and Genre in Seventeenth-Century Dutch Painting*

Jacob Taubes, *The Political Theology of Paul*

Jean-Luc Marion, *The Crossing of the Visible*

Eric Michaud, *The Cult of Art in Nazi Germany*

Anne Freadman, *The Machinery of Talk: Charles Peirce and the Sign Hypothesis*

Stanley Cavell, *Emerson's Transcendental Etudes*

Stuart McLean, *The Event and Its Terrors: Ireland, Famine, Modernity*

Beate Rössler, ed., *Privacies: Philosophical Evaluations*

Bernard Faure, *Double Exposure: Cutting Across Buddhist and Western Discourses*

Alessia Ricciardi, *The Ends of Mourning: Psychoanalysis, Literature, Film*

Alain Badiou, *Saint Paul: The Foundation of Universalism*

Gil Anidjar, *The Jew, the Arab: A History of the Enemy*

Jonathan Culler and Kevin Lamb, eds., *Just Being Difficult? Academic Writing in the Public Arena*

Jean-Luc Nancy, *A Finite Thinking*, edited by Simon Sparks

Theodor W. Adorno, *Can One Live after Auschwitz? A Philosophical Reader*, edited by Rolf Tiedemann

Patricia Pisters, *The Matrix of Visual Culture: Working with Deleuze in Film Theory*

Andreas Huyssen, *Present Pasts: Urban Palimpsests and the Politics of Memory*

Talal Asad, *Formations of the Secular: Christianity, Islam, Modernity*

Dorothea von Mücke, *The Rise of the Fantastic Tale*

Marc Redfield, *The Politics of Aesthetics: Nationalism, Gender, Romanticism*
Emmanuel Levinas, *On Escape*
Dan Zahavi, *Husserl's Phenomenology*
Rodolphe Gasché, *The Idea of Form: Rethinking Kant's Aesthetics*
Michael Naas, *Taking on the Tradition: Jacques Derrida and the Legacies of Deconstruction*
Herlinde Pauer-Studer, ed., *Constructions of Practical Reason: Interviews on Moral and Political Philosophy*
Jean-Luc Marion, *Being Given That: Toward a Phenomenology of Givenness*
Theodor W. Adorno and Max Horkheimer, *Dialectic of Enlightenment*
Ian Balfour, *The Rhetoric of Romantic Prophecy*
Martin Stokhof, *World and Life as One: Ethics and Ontology in Wittgenstein's Early Thought*
Gianni Vattimo, *Nietzsche: An Introduction*
Jacques Derrida, *Negotiations: Interventions and Interviews, 1971–1998*, edited by Elizabeth Rottenberg
Brett Levinson, *The Ends of Literature: The Latin American "Boom" in the Neoliberal Marketplace*
Timothy J. Reiss, *Against Autonomy: Cultural Instruments, Mutualities, and the Fictive Imagination*
Hent de Vries and Samuel Weber, eds., *Religion and Media*
Niklas Luhmann, *Theories of Distinction: Re-Describing the Descriptions of Modernity*, edited and introduced by William Rasch
Johannes Fabian, *Anthropology with an Attitude: Critical Essays*
Michel Henry, *I Am the Truth: Toward a Philosophy of Christianity*
Gil Anidjar, *"Our Place in Al-Andalus": Kabbalah, Philosophy, Literature in Arab-Jewish Letters*
Hélène Cixous and Jacques Derrida, *Veils*
F. R. Ankersmit, *Historical Representation*
F. R. Ankersmit, *Political Representation*
Elissa Marder, *Dead Time: Temporal Disorders in the Wake of Modernity (Baudelaire and Flaubert)*
Reinhart Koselleck, *The Practice of Conceptual History: Timing History, Spacing Concepts*
Niklas Luhmann, *The Reality of the Mass Media*
Hubert Damisch, *A Theory of /Cloud/: Toward a History of Painting*
Jean-Luc Nancy, *The Speculative Remark: (One of Hegel's bon mots)*
Jean-François Lyotard, *Soundproof Room: Malraux's Anti-Aesthetics*
Jan Patočka, *Plato and Europe*
Hubert Damisch, *Skyline: The Narcissistic City*
Isabel Hoving, *In Praise of New Travelers: Reading Caribbean Migrant Women Writers*
Richard Rand, ed., *Futures: Of Jacques Derrida*

William Rasch, *Niklas Luhmann's Modernity: The Paradoxes of Differentiation*
Jacques Derrida and Anne Dufourmantelle, *Of Hospitality*
Jean-François Lyotard, *The Confession of Augustine*
Kaja Silverman, *World Spectators*
Samuel Weber, *Institution and Interpretation: Expanded Edition*
Jeffrey S. Librett, *The Rhetoric of Cultural Dialogue: Jews and Germans in the Epoch of Emancipation*
Ulrich Baer, *Remnants of Song: Trauma and the Experience of Modernity in Charles Baudelaire and Paul Celan*
Samuel C. Wheeler III, *Deconstruction as Analytic Philosophy*
David S. Ferris, *Silent Urns: Romanticism, Hellenism, Modernity*
Rodolphe Gasché, *Of Minimal Things: Studies on the Notion of Relation*
Sarah Winter, *Freud and the Institution of Psychoanalytic Knowledge*
Samuel Weber, *The Legend of Freud: Expanded Edition*
Aris Fioretos, ed., *The Solid Letter: Readings of Friedrich Hölderlin*
J. Hillis Miller / Manuel Asensi, *Black Holes / J. Hillis Miller; or, Boustrophedonic Reading*
Miryam Sas, *Fault Lines: Cultural Memory and Japanese Surrealism*
Peter Schwenger, *Fantasm and Fiction: On Textual Envisioning*
Didier Maleuvre, *Museum Memories: History, Technology, Art*
Jacques Derrida, *Monolingualism of the Other; or, The Prosthesis of Origin*
Andrew Baruch Wachtel, *Making a Nation, Breaking a Nation: Literature and Cultural Politics in Yugoslavia*
Niklas Luhmann, *Love as Passion: The Codification of Intimacy*
Mieke Bal, ed., *The Practice of Cultural Analysis: Exposing Interdisciplinary Interpretation*
Jacques Derrida and Gianni Vattimo, eds., *Religion*

The authorized representative in the EU for product safety and compliance is:
Mare Nostrum Group
B.V Doelen 72
4831 GR Breda
The Netherlands

www.ingramcontent.com/pod-product-compliance
Lightning Source LLC
Chambersburg PA
CBHW021806220426
43662CB00006B/204